Amy Levy

critical essays

Amy Levy

critical essays

edited by
Naomi Hetherington
and Nadia Valman

Ohio University Press

Athens

Ohio University Press, Athens, Ohio 45701
www.ohioswallow.com
© 2010 by Ohio University Press

To obtain permission to quote, reprint, or otherwise reproduce or distribute
material from Ohio University Press publications, please contact our rights
and permissions department at (740) 593-1154 or (740) 593-4536 (fax).

Printed in the United States of America
Ohio University Press books are printed on acid-free paper ∞ ™

16 15 14 13 12 11 10   5 4 3 2 1

Library of Congress Cataloging-in-Publication Data
Amy Levy : critical essays / edited by Naomi Hetherington and Nadia Valman.
   p. cm.
 Includes bibliographical references and index.
 ISBN 978-0-8214-1330-2 (pbk. : alk. paper) — ISBN 978-0-8214-1329-6 (alk.
paper)
 1. Levy, Amy, 1861–1889—Criticism and interpretation. 2. Levy, Amy, 1861–1889
—Religion. 3. English literature—19th century—History and criticism.
4. Women—England—London—Intellectual life. I. Hetherington, Naomi, 1973–
II. Valman, Nadia.
 PR4886.L25A8 2010
 828'.809—dc22

2009047877

contents

contents

acknowledgments

Many of the chapters in this volume were first discussed at a colloquium on the work of Amy Levy held in 2002 at the University of Southampton. The editors gratefully acknowledge the assistance of the Arts and Humanities Research Board and the AHRB Parkes Centre for the Study of Jewish/Non-Jewish Relations, which funded the colloquium. We would also like to thank Dr. Jo Reilly for help organizing the colloquium; Professor Linda Hunt Beckman, who gave the plenary lecture on writing Levy's biography; Professors Cora Kaplan and Joseph Bristow for their intellectual support; and all the speakers for their contributions. Finally, our gratitude to David Sanders and Nancy Basmajian at Ohio University Press, and Eileen Quam, the indexer, with whom it has been a pleasure to work on the production of this book.

contributors

Susan David Bernstein, a professor of English, Jewish studies, and gender and women's studies at the University of Wisconsin–Madison, is the author of *Confessional Subjects: Revelations of Gender and Power in Victorian Literature and Culture* (1997) and the editor of two novels by Amy Levy: *The Romance of a Shop* (2006) and *Reuben Sachs* (2006). She has coedited (with Elsie B. Michie) *Victorian Vulgarity: Taste in Verbal and Visual Culture* (2009). Currently she is working on a book about the Reading Room of the British Museum, gender, and space, from George Eliot to Virginia Woolf.

Gail Cunningham is a professor of English and former dean of the faculty of arts and social sciences at Kingston University. She has published widely on nineteenth- and twentieth-century literature, particularly in the areas of women's writing and the New Woman. Her current interest is in representations of suburbia in Victorian and Edwardian writing.

Elizabeth F. Evans is an assistant professor of English at Pennsylvania State University–DuBois. She has published essays on George Gissing and Virginia Woolf and is now completing a book, provisionally titled "Liminal London: Gender and Threshold Spaces in Narratives of Urban Modernity," which investigates the roles of urban sites in the formation of new identities, power relations, and stories in London narratives, 1880–1940.

Emma Francis is an associate professor in the Department of English and Comparative Literary Studies at the University of Warwick. Her research focuses on nineteenth-century British women's writing and the intellectual history of feminism.

Alex Goody is a senior lecturer in English studies at Oxford Brookes University. She is the author of *Modernist Articulations: A Cultural Study of Djuna Barnes, Mina Loy and Gertrude Stein* (2007) and of a forthcoming book with the working title *Literature, Technology and Culture*, as well as of a range of articles and chapters on women's writing and poetry in the late nineteenth and early twentieth centuries.

Naomi Hetherington teaches nineteenth- and twentieth-century literature at Birkbeck College, University of London. She has previously published on Amy Levy's juvenilia in *The Child Writer from Austen to Woolf*, edited by Christine Alexander and Juliet McMaster (Cambridge University Press, 2005) and is currently completing a monograph on the religious structures of New Woman fiction.

T. D. Olverson is a researcher in nineteenth-century literature and culture and has recently completed her first monograph, *Women Writers and the Dark Side of Late Victorian Hellenism*. She is currently at work on the use of Hellenism in children's literature of the nineteenth century, and the issue of children and violence as represented in literature and culture.

Lyssa Randolph holds a doctorate on New Woman writing. *New Women Writers of the Late Nineteenth Century*, a study of New Woman fiction and drama, is coauthored with Professor Marion Shaw, and published by Northcote Books. Lyssa is a visiting lecturer on Victorian fiction at the University of Wales, Newport.

Meri-Jane Rochelson is a professor of English at Florida International University. The author of numerous articles on Victorian and Anglo-Jewish literature, she is coeditor with Nikki Lee Manos of *Transforming Genres: New Approaches to British Fiction of the 1890s* (1994) and editor of Israel Zangwill's 1892 novel *Children of the Ghetto* (1998). Her book *A Jew in the Public Arena: The Career of Israel Zangwill* was published in 2008.

Nadia Valman is a senior lecturer in English at Queen Mary, University of London. She is the author of *The Jewess in Nineteenth-Century British Literary Culture* (2007) and several articles on Jews and Victorian literature. She is the coeditor with Bryan Cheyette of *The Image of the Jew in European Liberal Culture, 1789–1914*. She is currently researching the literature of the East End of London.

critical essays

Introduction

Naomi Hetherington and Nadia Valman

Precocious, gifted girl, my nineteenth-century
voice of Xanthippe, I dreamed of you last night,
walking by the willows behind the Wren,
and singing to me of Cambridge and unhappiness.

"Listen, I am the first of my kind, and
not without friends or recognition,
but my name belongs with my family
in Bayswater, where the ghosts

of wealthy Sephardim line the walls,
and there I am alien because I sing.
Here, it is my name that makes me strange.
A hundred years on, is it still the same?"

Elaine Feinstein, "Amy Levy"

In "Amy Levy," Elaine Feinstein finds a nineteenth-century precursor for what the poem takes to be her own anomalous position as an educated Jewish woman poet. Feinstein, like Levy, studied at Newnham College, Cambridge, and the Cambridge setting of the poem as well as its melancholy evokes several of Levy's verses.[1] "Xantippe" (1880), to which Feinstein alludes, dramatizes women's marginal position in the intellectual life of the university.[2] It is a passionate plea for women's education in the voice of Socrates' wife, Xantippe, who was excluded from his circle of male philosophers on account of her sex. Levy's poem was performed at Newnham in 1881, the year in which women were formally permitted to sit university examinations, and recited again at the college's 125th anniversary celebrations in 1996 for which Feinstein's poem "Amy Levy" was written. For Feinstein, however, Levy's Jewish "name," more than her gender, is what marks her out in Cambridge's predominantly Christian environment. Levy was the first Jewish woman to go up to Newnham, and her Jewishness, associated (erroneously) here with a heritage of commerce, is at odds with the upper-class, pastoral English culture Cambridge represents. Conversely, while a college education fosters Levy's literary talent, her poetry is "alien" to Jewish Bayswater. It is Levy's inability to fit either Jewish or English tradition that makes her, for Feinstein, the first modern Jewish women poet. Her presence in late-nineteenth-century Cambridge is particularly poignant on account of the university's subsequent role in the establishment of an elite canon of English literature. Levy was one of many women writers and writers of hyphenated English identity who were retrieved through the advent of feminist and postcolonial theory in the 1970s and '80s. Identified in Feinstein's poem by her Jewish origins, urban upbringing, and college education, Levy was also a queer writer who had passionate attachments to other women. It is her multiplicity of identities as an intellectual Jewish woman, a feminist, and a lesbian that makes Levy so compelling.

Feinstein's interest in Levy follows her recuperation by feminist scholars and critics of postemancipation Jewish literature and culture in the 1980s and early '90s. In the decade since Feinstein was writing, scholarship on Levy has burgeoned, and she features regularly in doctoral dissertations and undergraduate and postgraduate courses on Jewish and lesbian literature, nineteenth-century feminisms, women's poetry, and the New Woman. This resurgence of interest is in some measure due to the accessibility of her writing. Her complete novels and selected writings (edited by Melvyn New) were republished by the University Press of Florida in 1993, and her poetry is available online as part of the Victorian Women Writers Project at Indiana University.[3] Selections appear in anthologies of Victorian poetry, nineteenth-century women poets, and lesbian writing.[4] Levy's Jewish novel *Reuben Sachs* (1888) was reissued by Persephone Books in 2000 and in a Broadview critical edition by Susan David Bernstein in 2006.[5] Appearing in 2000, Linda Hunt Beckman's biography has added enormously to our knowledge of the contexts in which Levy wrote.[6] Beckman's introduction sets out to challenge a number of misconceptions that have taken hold in critical writing on Levy. Not least of these is the negative set of associations between Judaism, female self-expression, and artistic representation which Feinstein's poem freely exploits. In fact, as Beckman demonstrates, Levy's family were highly supportive of both her writing and her feminist politics. Yet it is as a symbol of cultural marginality that Levy has achieved iconic status.

This is all the more poignant on account of her suicide at the age of twenty-seven, which has almost invariably been read as the tragic outcome of identity conflict, either between her Jewishness and her feminism and/or lesbianism or as the result of her dissident position in a predominantly male, heterosexual, and Christian culture. To interpret Levy's death in this way is, as Holly Laird warns, to construct a consistent account of Levy's life and death, whose assumptions necessarily influence critical reception of her work.[7] This collection resists such a monochromatic reading, bringing together a multiplicity of perspectives on Levy in a single volume for the first time. These are introduced through the following outline of her life and work and critical scholarship on Levy to date.

Amy Levy was born on 10 November 1861 in the Lambeth district of London, the second daughter of Lewis Levy and Isobel (née Levin). Her parents were English Jews who, like the majority of native Jews by the mid-nineteenth century, strongly identified with English culture and values. Like many other middle-class Jews, they were not religiously observant at home. Levy's parents held seats at the West London Synagogue of British Jews, Britain's first Reform congregation, but the family did not regularly attend services. They maintained close social ties with other members of London's Jewish community. Moving across London as they rose in economic and social status, they lived in areas increasingly occupied by middle-class Jews. For a time, Lewis Levy ran an export business in Brighton, where there was a significant Jewish population. At fifteen, Levy was sent to Brighton High School, a member of the Girls' Public Day School Company and an unusual choice for a middle-class Jewish girl; but Levy's father appears to have particularly valued his daughters' education. Levy learned Latin, Greek, and mathematics; in 1879, she was one of a small cohort of girls from Brighton to go up to Newnham together with her friend Constance Black (later Garnett, the Russian translator). Newnham at that time was one of two newly opened women's colleges at Cambridge. Female students had classes in college and could sit university examinations and attend lectures at the discretion of individual dons. Levy studied languages, and on leaving Cambridge in 1881, she spent the next four years intermittently traveling the Continent either alone or with friends. When back home, she threw herself into London life, forging a network of intellectual and literary connections through the British Museum Reading Room and her friends from Brighton and Cambridge: Ernest and Dollie Radford and Constance Black and her sister Clementina. Nearly all of Levy's friends were socialists or social reformers and writers, including the Radfords and Clementina Black, a journalist and active trade unionist. In London, Levy met Olive Schreiner, Eleanor Marx, East End investigator Beatrice Potter (later Webb) and her cousin Margaret Harkness, and Karl Pearson, evolutionary biologist and professor of mathematics at University College London. In 1883, Levy joined Pearson's discussion club, one of many such clubs in London of this time providing a space for intellectuals of both sexes to meet. In 1885, Levy's family moved to Bloomsbury, placing them in the heart of intellectual and artistic London. She gained introductions to literary luminaries such as Thomas Hardy, W. B. Yeats, Arthur Symons, and the American playwright and suffragist Elizabeth Robins Pennell. In the last year of her life, Levy attended the first Ladies' Literary Dinner, founded to celebrate the achievements of women writers and provide a discrete space for them to socialize and network. In the Chair was Mona Caird, whose article on marriage had provoked a debate in the *Daily Telegraph* the previous year with some 27,000 responses.[8] Levy returned the thanks for fiction. Three months later, she killed herself. She had suffered from episodes of depression throughout her adult life, and she died of charcoal gas inhalation on 10 September 1889, two months before her twenty-eighth birthday.

By the time of her death, Levy had written three novels and three collections of verse as well as translations of German and Hebrew poetry, social satire, literary criticism, and a substantial collection of short stories. Levy's first published poem, "The Ballad of Ida Grey," appeared in a feminist campaign journal, the *Pelican*, when she was just thirteen.[9] By the age of fifteen, Levy had begun to experiment with the dramatic monologue, a form she used increasingly to interrogate the relationships between race, gender, and class. "Run to Death" is spoken by a gypsy woman hunted down with her child by nobles in prerevolutionary France. It was published in the *Victoria Magazine*, issued by Emily Faithfull's women-run Victoria Press, the summer Levy left Brighton.[10] Whilst at Newnham, Levy became a regular contributor of poems and translations to the *Cambridge Review*. Her first volume of poetry, *Xantippe and Other Verse*, was published in 1881, the year she left Cambridge to travel the Continent. Back in London, she published a second collection of verse, *A Minor Poet and Other Verse* (1884). The suicide of the title character, isolated and excluded by the literary establishment, reflects the volume's concern with marginal and dispossessed voices. At this time, Levy appears to have been setting herself up as a professional writer, earning an independent income by penning short stories for women's and society magazines. Some follow romantic formulae; the finest reflect Levy's feminist politics, satirizing middle-class sexual morality and the limited opportunities for women to gain meaningful employment and financial security outside of marriage. These stories found a ready market with the establishment of *Woman's World* in 1888 under the editorship of Oscar Wilde as a new and progressive forum for women writers. Two essays by Levy appear in the first volume: "The Poetry of Christina Rossetti" and "Women and Club Life," which extols the importance of women's clubs as a newly available space for women in London to meet and work undisturbed by the demands of domestic life.[11] The same year, Levy published her first novel, *The Romance of a Shop,* about four sisters who set up a photographic studio in London to maintain financial independence on the death of their father.[12]

As an established woman of letters, Levy began to exploit a Jewish publishing market. Her translations of Heinrich Heine and Jehudah Halevi were included in a collection titled *Jewish Portraits* (1888), edited by Lady Katie Magnus, a Jewish benefactor who had founded the first club for Jewish immigrant girls in the East End.[13] Levy is also widely credited with a series of anonymous articles on Jewish topics appearing in the *Jewish Chronicle* from March to November 1886.[14] These comment on and satirize different aspects of contemporary Jewish identity and culture. In "Middle-Class Jewish Women of To-Day," Levy brings her feminist politics to bear on her co-religionists. As Emma Francis has commented, contemporary Anglo-Jewry is represented here as an "overdetermined version of Victorian patriarchy," its preoccupation with wealth and social status leading to the moral degradation of many of its women.[15] Levy's second novel, *Reuben Sachs* (1888), places her critique of Bayswater Jewry before an English reading public. Published by Macmillan, it was widely praised in the mainstream press for its realistic portrait of Jewish life. Levy's third novel, *Miss Meredith,* was serialized the following year in the *British Weekly.*[16] A lighthearted romance about an English girl appointed governess to an aristocratic Italian family, it is a pastiche of an established tradition in English fiction of the genteel governess who succeeds in marrying into the upper classes. When Levy killed herself, she left the corrected proofs for her third volume of poetry on her desk. *A London Plane-Tree and Other Verse* (1889) attempts to construct a new urban aesthetic, exchanging Levy's characteristic form of the dramatic monologue for short compact lyrics that imitate the fast pace of city life. The volume was dedicated to Clementina Black, Levy's closest friend in adult life, who arranged for its posthumous publication. Finally, in 1915, the editor Clement Shorter privately published twelve copies of Levy's poem "A Ballad of Religion and Marriage,"[17] in which the collapse of a Judeo-Christian epistemology signals the end of the present system of marriage.

Amy Levy as a Jewish Novelist

Although Levy did not begin publishing work on Jewish themes until the last three years of her life, it is as a Jewish writer that she was first reclaimed by literary scholars. The recovery of Levy's work, however, has been marked by a persistent ambivalence about the force of her critique of late-Victorian Anglo-Jewry. In her address to the Jewish Historical Society of England in 1927, Beth-Zion Lask noted how completely Levy had been forgotten just a generation after her death and declared that she was "our greatest contributor to English literature."[18] For Lask, the desire to see Levy as an unsung hero of Anglo-Jewry could be reconciled with her harsh portrait of that community by viewing her work within a specifically Jewish literary tradition: "It was not a malicious representation. . . . She knew the Jewry of her day; she was aware, inherently, subconsciously if you will, of the qualities that had gone to make up the glorious traditions of the Jewish people. She saw the void that stretched between the real and the ideal; and her soul, like those of the Prophets before her, burned in anguished indignation."[19] Echoing, in rather more elevated terms, the verdict of the fin-de-siècle Anglo-Jewish intellectual Israel Zangwill that "she was accused, of course, of fouling her own nest; whereas what she had really done was to point out that the nest was fouled and must be cleaned out," Lask here initiated the critical tradition of casting Levy as a misunderstood visionary.[20]

Yet Lask's demand that the posthumous "neglect" of Levy's literary legacy be redressed was not taken up until the 1980s.[21] Even then, attempts to celebrate Levy's achievement were uncertain. In his 1983 study of six prominent Jewish women, Edward Wagenknecht, like many subsequent scholars, moves quickly from an account of the praise bestowed on Levy by her contemporaries to an attempt to explain her "disillusionment and unhappiness" by reading her writing as autobiography. He considers whether "unhappy love" played a part and, on the basis of her "hostile'" portrait of Jews, concludes that "religion did."[22] Levy's negative generalizations about Jews in *Reuben Sachs,* coyly described by Wagenknecht as "curious," are more troubling to Linda Gertner Zatlin. In her remarkable rediscovery of a host of unknown writers in *The Nineteenth-Century Anglo-Jewish Novel* (1981), Zatlin views her subjects as responding to a series of challenges, initially from "Without" (antisemitism, conversion) and, in the latter part of the century, from "Within" (assimilation and intermarriage, immigration). Zatlin reads Levy as one of the writers engaging with the questions of assimilation and intermarriage, who "view severely the Jew who modifies his or her religion in order to worship the Golden Calf." Here, Levy appears in the literary context of others, such as Julia Frankau, whose *Dr Phillips: A Maida Vale Idyll* (1887) similarly satirized the rampant materialism of the upwardly mobile Jews of west London. "In *Reuben Sachs*," Zatlin writes, "Levy maliciously depicts the Anglo-Jewish community. In addition to portraying late nineteenth-century accultured middle-class Jews as gradually yielding to the pressures of assimilation and intermarriage, as grappling unsuccessfully with the issues of conversion and the philosophy by which one should live, Levy shows them to be snobbish materialists. Conjointly, she negatively links her depictions of these Jews to all."[23] For Zatlin, Levy's view of Jews suggests a "bigotry" analogous to that of English novelists such as Trollope, and her writing "foreshadows the quality of self-hatred which informs a portion of twentieth-century Jewish literature."[24]

If early scholars of Levy evinced discomfort with her critique of Anglo-Jewry, a second wave of interest in her work viewed this critique as cause for veneration. Reconstructing a history of nineteenth-century Anglo-Jewish writing in which Jewish writers felt obliged to produce a moralized account of Jewish life in order to justify emancipation, Bryan Cheyette placed Levy in the vanguard of a movement of "revolt." Audaciously refusing "to engage in literary apologetics on behalf of Anglo-Jewry's version of morality," Levy "modernized the Anglo-Jewish novel."[25] *Reuben Sachs*, her realist account of the Jewish transition to modernity—an account woven from conflicts of class, gender, and generation—constituted a challenge to Anglo-Jewry's established public narrative of progressive integration into British social and political life. This emphasis characterized the account of Levy produced by a generation of scholars similarly concerned with debunking the "Judaized version of 'Whig History'" that dominated Anglo-Jewish historiography in the nineteenth and twentieth centuries.[26] Implicitly linking Levy's modernity with his own critique of the "hysterical quest for conformity" that limited the aesthetic and intellectual scope of much Victorian Anglo-Jewish writing, Cheyette figured Levy as a forerunner of the late twentieth-century reaction against the tradition of Anglo-Jewish apologia.[27] By the time that Geoffrey Alderman's history of modern British Jewry appeared in 1992, therefore, Levy's story could be exaggerated to constitute her as a fully fledged hero of antiestablishment Judaism. Viewing *Reuben Sachs* uncomplicatedly as documentary, Alderman describes it as "the best and most realistic account we have of the undisguised nepotism and the deep, irreverent materialism of the Jewish middle classes in London in the third quarter of the nineteenth century." Yet this account relies on the (erroneous) assumption that Levy was representing "the [Maida Vale and Bayswater] Jewish milieu in which she had grown to adulthood" and that her target was the "corruption" of "Jewish values." Alderman's pithy but inaccurate summary— "*Reuben Sachs* was a literary success. Its authoress became a communal outcast" —figures Levy (much as Lask had done) as a brave martyr, isolated by her moral integrity and Jewish authenticity.[28]

Reuben Sachs continues to attract attention, but interest since the mid-1990s has shifted on the one hand toward increasingly historicized readings of its approach to Jews, and on the other to a more nuanced examination of its narrative technique. In the light of new scholarly interest in the ways that the "Jew's body" was imagined across a range of disciplines and texts in fin-de-siècle Europe, including medicine, psychiatry and sociology, Levy's use of the language of race and racial degeneration in relation to Jews has come into clearer focus. Both the ailing, ugly, and degenerate Ashkenazim and the refined, healthy Sephardim in Levy's novel are expressions of contemporary race-thinking that, as both Emma Francis and Nadia Valman argue, Levy unthinkingly replicates.[29] Rather than seeing her commentary on Anglo-Jewry as a personal jeremiad, they read it as part of a more widespread semitic discourse produced by Jews as well as non-Jews.

In contrast, other critics have turned to a close reading of Levy's texts to tease out the distinctiveness of her literary interventions. In "Amy Levy and the 'Jewish Novel': Representing Jewish Life in the Victorian Period" (1994), Linda Hunt (later Beckman) defends *Reuben Sachs* on both aesthetic and political grounds by arguing that its intertextual allusions to *Daniel Deronda* signal Levy's innovative departure from "classic realism." Levy was led to reject realism as a literary technique for representing Jews, Hunt claims, in response to George Eliot's inability to resist the antisemitic assumptions harbored in British culture: "Aware that a writer's ability, including her own, to imagine the world and produce meaning is limited and defined by the belief-system which she receives from the systems of representation that the society makes available, Levy writes her Jewish novel in such a way that 'truth' is hard to pin down. *Reuben Sachs* is a text whose stance toward the sector of Jewish society it seeks to represent is far from resolved." Thus, the uncertainty of the novel's narratorial point of view—shifting from an insider's sympathy with the characters to an outsider's critique—is interpreted as a deliberate literary strategy, producing a modernistic "polyphonic" text. Negative comments about Jews are thus read in relation to the narrative voice by which they are uttered, which "functions inconsistently, sometimes calling attention to its omniscience and at other times undercutting its own authority."[30] For Hunt, in contrast to Cheyette and Alderman, Levy's representation of Anglo-Jewry critiques the limitations not of the minority community but of the broader, dominant culture. Contesting the view of earlier critics of Levy, Hunt argues that, far from expressing Jewish self-hatred, *Reuben Sachs* makes hatred of Jews its very subject.

A similar interest in the relationship between narrative technique and the question of representing Jews features in Susan David Bernstein's fine introduction to the recent reissue of *Reuben Sachs* (2006). Bernstein offers a close analysis of Levy's prose, focusing on the ways the novel "models how the defining gazes of gentile society infiltrate the narration and characters' representations of their Jewishness." Bernstein regards Levy's position as an acculturated Jewish woman, living in a world in which Jewishness was already interpreted by discourses of nationalism and racism, as the key to reading the "double-consciousness" that the novel performs.[31] The narrator's shifts from the perspective of an affectionate insider to that of a critical outsider suggest the intermittent but inevitable intrusion of dominant Christian discourses into portraits of Jews. In further "diluting borders between narrator and character" through her use of free indirect discourse, Levy "fractures any unified perspective on Jewish identity." Moving on from the debate over whether *Reuben Sachs* endorses or deplores antisemitism, Bernstein presents Levy's text as an explosion of postmodern irony that questions the very possibility of "authentic" Jewishness.[32]

Bernstein also draws attention to the relationship between stylistic innovation and the feminist theme of *Reuben Sachs*. The importance of reading Levy's representations of Jews in relation to her feminism has become increasingly evident in scholarly work, initiated by Meri-Jane Rochelson's 1996 article, "Jews, Gender, and Genre in Late-Victorian England: Amy Levy's *Reuben Sachs.*" As Rochelson argues, *Reuben Sachs* was predominantly seen by scholars as a "Jewish novel," a categorization that led to the neglect of its place in a feminist tradition and a misapprehension of "the rage embodied in the book . . . as antisemitism, or Jewish self-hatred." But as a feminist novel, *Reuben Sachs* "examines the options available for female rebellion within a segment of Jewish society, and makes part of its critique the fact that those options are so limited and so rarely exploited."[33] In Levy's story of a woman entrapped in materialistic values, led to reject her potential for passion by a conservative fear of social exclusion, and ignorant of her own sexuality, can be seen echoes of many other late-nineteenth-century feminist texts. "[I]t is the intensity of Judith's disappointment," Rochelson writes, "and the reader's engagement with it throughout the novel, that make her fate a more striking symbol of the effects of the spiritually bereft Jewish life that Levy represents."[34] In thematizing female disillusion, Levy anticipates many of the New Woman writers of the 1890s. This claim has been reinforced more recently by Iveta Jusová in *The New Woman and the Empire* (2005), which argues for the particular and important contribution made by Levy's Anglo-Jewish novel to the New Woman literary tradition.[35]

Amy Levy as New Woman Poet

It was Levy's poetry rather than her fiction, however, that initially led to her categorization as a New Woman.[36] Independent of Jewish interest in *Reuben Sachs*, Levy's poetry was appropriated by feminist literary critics with the rediscovery of a host of Victorian women poets in the 1980s and '90s. Early accounts of nineteenth-century women's poetics by Isobel Armstrong, Kathleen Hickok, and Angela Leighton all seize on Levy's dramatic monologues for their radical repudiation of civic and sexual institutions oppressive to women.[37] Leighton's study of women poets and the Victorian "fallen woman" praises Levy's "Magdalen" (1884) for its condemnation of a social morality founded on the sexual propriety of women.[38] Both Leighton and Armstrong evaluate Levy's use of the dramatic monologue against the affective register conventionally ascribed to women's poetry. Downgraded in the construction of the Victorian poetic canon, affect is a mode of expression that Leighton associates with melodrama and sentimentality and which, when detected, lessens Levy's poetic achievement. Armstrong points up the respect accorded to women poets in the nineteenth century by "an account of women's writing as occupying a distinct sphere of influence, and working inside defined religious and moral conventions."[39] She argues for "the dissonances women's poetry created by making problematical the affective conventions . . . associated with a feminine modality of experience even when, and perhaps particularly when, poets worked within these conventions."[40] Nevertheless, Armstrong praises Levy together with Augusta Webster for the extent to which their dramatic monologues depart from rather than extend this expressive tradition.

The ways in which individual nineteenth-century women poets continue to be read and analyzed have been shaped by two anthologies coedited by Armstrong (with Joseph Bristow and Cath Sharrock) and Leighton (with Margaret Reynolds) in the mid-1990s. Selections of Levy's poems highlight her radical repudiation of marital heterosexuality, her pessimism, and her love poems to other women. Indeed, it was through unrequited love that the pessimism of her verse was first read. In *Religious Trends in English Poetry* (1962), Hoaxie Neil Fairchild claims that "Miss Levy's almost complete religious negativism is not the fruit of any systematic philosophising, but simply a deduction from her misery."[41] He diagnoses sexual frustration, asserting that "Amy Levy desired to be loved by a man."[42] Fairchild's patronizing dismissal of Levy is clearly indicative of the sexism and homophobia that dominated critical readings of women's poetry until its successful challenge by feminist and lesbian critics in the 1980s and 1990s. In Levy's case, this has brought into view not only her lesbianism but also her place in a pessimistic tradition of British poetry. As Angela Leighton identifies, in her introduction to Levy in the coedited anthology *Victorian Women Poets* (1995), Levy's "pessimism, far from being personal and lovelorn, is an almost cool, philosophical attitude in the face of a morally senseless world."[43] Levy was familiar with Schopenhauer's pessimistic philosophy and a European tradition of *Weltschmerz* exemplified by Heine and Lenau, whose poetry she translated. This avenue, though frequently noted in studies of her poetry, has not been explored thoroughly, perhaps because Levy's critics lack her fluency in German.[44]

Widely studied, Levy's love poetry to other women is fraught with a different set of critical difficulties. In "Sexual Politics of the (Victorian) Closet; or, No Sex Please—We're Poets" (1999), Virginia Blain raises the difficulty of establishing a hermeneutics for reading lesbian poetry in "a 'so-called' pre-lesbian era."[45] Blain's refusal to fix an essentialized lesbian identity onto particular Victorian poets is a necessary caveat in the case of Levy, whose love poems are about rejection and disappointment and about whose sexual relationships with men or women nothing certain is known. Nevertheless, associating Levy's poems with what Blain terms a "lesbian position," "aslant to the usual heterosexual position," proves productive.[46] While some of Levy's love poems are dedicated to individual women she knew well, others invoke an unnamed and unresponsive, usually female, beloved. The sexuality of these poems, Emma Francis argues, is not stable or consistent. They use the passage between waking and dreaming, life and death to explore the dynamics of desire and frustration, imagining the beloved on a deathbed scene or, already dead, haunting the poet's dreams and the city streets. Francis claims that these poems "might be regarded as amongst the most significant 'lesbian poetry' of the late-nineteenth century" for their interrogation of sexuality and conventional accounts of sexual identification.[47] Moving beyond the explicit polemic of Levy's early dramatic monologues, they offer "a highly complex exploration of femininity, of sexuality and of women's relation to power."[48]

Francis was the first to raise the "apparent contradiction" between the sophistication of Levy's sexual politics in breaking down identifications and boundaries, and her writing on Anglo-Jewry, which "[r]ather than breaking down identifications, reinforces and overdetermines them; it translates identity into stereotype."[49] Further work on Levy attempts both to explain and to complicate this verdict. In a later study of Levy and Eleanor Marx, Francis rephrases the relationship between Levy's feminism and Jewish discourse in a cogent discussion of feminism's engagement with a range of Darwinian arguments. Here, Francis compares *Reuben Sachs* with *The Woman Question* (1886), which Marx co-authored with her future husband, Edward Aveling, to point up both their common intellectual structure and the pessimism of Levy's particular strand of Darwinism. *The Woman Question* negotiates questions of sexuality and sexual identity through a Darwinian concept of "instinct" as a force for development and progress. Sexual instinct is seen as having "a direction and integrity . . . compromised by capitalism."[50] In *Reuben Sachs*, this is inflected by Levy's preoccupation with race. Reuben's failure to choose romantic love over commercial ambition is the thwarting of both racial instinct and sexual desire. Rejected by Reuben, Judith exacts "the price not just of her individual suffering but also that of the degeneration of her people."[51] Francis's arguments are taken further by Nadia Valman, who considers *Reuben Sachs*'s critique of Jewish "orientalism" in the context of the widespread use of ethnographic language in contemporary feminist debate about the discontents of marriage.[52]

These two strands of scholarship have been brought together by Cynthia Scheinberg in her work on the significance of Jewishness in Levy's poetry. Scheinberg argues that for Levy, Judaism "was one of a variety of characteristics that could position a writer as 'other'" and sees her work as a bold challenge to poetic conventions grounded in both Christian theology and heterosexual love.[53] Scheinberg uses Levy's poetry to contest influential readings of the Victorian dramatic monologue, which emphasize its capacity to produce sympathy in the reader. Levy's dramatic monologues, addressed to uncomprehending listeners, thematize the contingency of poetic identification and thus "destabilize any notion of universal poetic utterance."[54] Inferring a poetic theory from Levy's essays on James Thomson and Heine, in which she seeks to valorize these poets' particularity rather than their capacity to speak universal truths, Scheinberg suggests that Levy's "commitment to Jewish identity" leads her overtly to challenge the universalizing assumptions of Christian poetry.[55] While *Reuben Sachs* and Levy's short story "Cohen of Trinity" (1889) demonstrate the impossibility of representing Jewish identity in English literature, "Magdalen" offers a more successful intervention.[56] Scheinberg reads the poem as the dying speech addressed not to the seducer of a Victorian fallen woman but to Jesus Christ by the biblical Mary Magdalen, whose story Levy revises "from a Jewish perspective" and whom she recasts as a defiantly unconverted and unrepentant Jewish woman.[57] Once again, in Scheinberg's work, Levy emerges as a herald: by "[i]nterrogating the ways dominant assumptions of Christianity and heterosexuality have structured the identity of the English poet and English literary conventions," Levy "explored the concept of 'minority' writers long before such a category had any real cultural or critical meaning."[58]

Levy's essay on Thomson identifies what Joseph Bristow calls the "double bind" of "minor" poets, kept out of the canon in which they should have their rightful place, even while their work gains in value precisely because it has been sidelined.[59] In this way, Bristow explains the distinction of Levy's position in a decade when the privileged value accorded to Englishness and the Anglican Church, heterosexual desire and the male sex was "to some degree in doubt."[60] That Levy used the suicidal male poet as an analogue for her own "minor" status is a view Bristow shares with Karen Weisman, who examines the relationship between poetic form and self-identification in "A Minor Poet" and "Xantippe." She reads the opening of "Xantippe"—"What, have I waked again?" —as a failed suicide attempt and argues that by taking suicidal speakers as their subjects, both poems qualify the conventions of the elegy and the dramatic monologue. This playing with figures "really did become a struggle between life and death," Weisman asserts, reading the "precariousness" of Levy's aesthetic dynamics through her subsequent suicide.[61] This slippage between death and art is precisely what Holly Laird faults in her analysis of the critical reception of poetry by three fin-de-siècle woman suicides. Levy, Laurence Hope (Adela Cory Nicholson), and Charlotte Mew all killed themselves in a deliberate act of suicide, and the resurgence of interest in their work has sparked extensive speculation about their deaths. Even the most sophisticated critics,

Laird argues, generally find themselves explaining the poet's suicide in terms provided by what appears to them most significant about her identity—the lesbianism of Mew and Levy, Levy's marginality as an intellectual Jewish woman, Nicholson's expat identity as an English writer living most of her adult life in India and publishing her poetry in the guise of translations of Indian love lyrics. An examination of the different ways in which each poet directly engages with the discourse of suicide, Laird hopes, will rescue her from "reductive applications of the suicide as identity tag."[62]

Amy Levy as Urban Writer

Such a rescue can be achieved in Levy's case through her engagement with pessimism. Bristow connects her "minor poet" with the pessimism of Thomson and argues that, for Levy, London marks out "the location where poets like Thomson would suffer."[63] Levy particularly praised Thomson's epic poem *The City of Dreadful Night* (1874), narrating the poet's despair through his pilgrimage through the dark, friendless streets of the modern metropolis. The correspondence Levy drew between modern selfhood and urban navigation is explored more fully by Ana Parejo Vadillo in her chapter on Levy in *Women Poets and Urban Aestheticism: Passengers of Modernity* (2005).[64] Vadillo's study is a new historicist account of the relationship between the new material and technological conditions of urban life in the late Victorian period and women poets' construction of the lyric self. Vadillo uses London's new and expanding public transportation system to identify women's physical presence in the city and its suburbs. She includes a series of fascinating area maps of London neighborhoods at the fin de siècle, plotting the proximity of each woman poet to other literary and cultural figures of note. Each space gives rise, in Vadillo's reading, to a different urban aesthetic. Levy, in Bloomsbury, exemplifies the lyric work of women poets to attain mobility and transience. The neighborhood's nomadic nature, with the influx of middle-class Jews and intellectuals in the late nineteenth century and daily visitors to the British Museum Reading Room, is expressed, for Vadillo, in Levy's motif of the poet as passenger.

Vadillo's is the finest in a series of studies of Levy's urban aesthetics. Where she focuses on mass transportation and the increasing mechanization of urban mobility, it is the streetscape of Levy's London poetry that has been most thoroughly explored. Historical studies of women's public presence in London life at the end of the nineteenth century have tended to focus on the streets of the metropolis.[65] Shopping, reporting, campaigning, visiting clubs, museums or music halls, engaging in philanthropic and other work, women's active presence on the city streets challenges the centrality of the urban male stroller in discourses of modernity. Applying the figure of the "streetwalker" to the middle-class woman, however, yields a different and highly suggestive set of meanings. In Levy's case, these are inflected not only by gender and class but also by sexual orientation and race. In an early discussion of Levy's urban lyric, Deborah Epstein Nord notes what she terms Levy's remarkable ability to achieve "impersonality" in the anonymous space of the city using "another's voice—a man's voice" to address an "unresponsive, usually female beloved."[66] Considering Levy's urban writing alongside the investigative journalism and fiction of her friends Harkness and Potter, Nord constructs a community of independent women particular to 1880s London. Eschewing traditional definitions of women's work, these women did not have the freedom of their early-twentieth-century counterparts to choose "spinsterhood, celibacy, and female companionship outside marriage as a self-conscious political gesture."[67] For Nord, the male persona of Levy's urban lyrics reflects the difficulty of reconciling her professional identity with the dictates of femininity, whereby, for Linda Hunt Beckman, Levy's invention of an urban identity provides her with a "usable self."[68] In Beckman's reading, Levy employs both the city and the figure of a missing woman for whom she searches as symbols of the effect that life has on her. Examining the extent to which these poems rely on an analogy between the mind and the external world, Beckman argues that they imitate French symbolist techniques advocated and modeled by Baudelaire and Mallarmé.

Beckman draws attention to a further constituent of Levy's urban identity —the strong historical connection between England's expanding Jewish population in the late nineteenth century and increased urbanization. In this respect, Levy's urban lyrics can be read not only as one of the first British responses to symbolism but also as a precursor to modernism. In *Streetwalking the Metropolis: Women, the City and Modernity* (2000), Deborah Parsons compares Levy to Dorothy Richardson for the ways in which her attempts to represent the female streetwalker are inflected by the figures of both the acculturated and the immigrant Jew. Richardson considered converting to Judaism, and, for Parsons, both she and Levy find in the Jew "a spiritual identity and a restriction on the free expression of that identity."[69] Alex Goody's more recent article "Murder in Mile End: Amy Levy, Jewishness and the City" examines the conjunction of sexual and racial rather than religious identifications in Levy's cartography of the city; but she, too, finds in Levy's urban lyrics "the ambiguity of the city and its subjectivities that comes to dominate in the literature of a later generation of modernist women writers; . . . what Levy's work specifically serves to highlight are the dangers of this ambiguity."[70] Goody looks at narratives of sexual danger in a series of poems from *A London Plane-Tree* set in the East End of London. Within the discursive context of the Whitechapel murders of 1888, and speculation that Jack the Ripper might be a Jew, these poems point up the uncertainty of transgressive gender, racial, and sexual identities "co-opted in a hegemonic act of representational violence."[71] In this way, Goody draws together different critical perspectives on Levy as a Jew, feminist, and queer writer in a composite reading.

Amy Levy: Public and Private

A new departure in scholarship on Levy is an increasing interest on the part of both literary and feminist historians in tracing the social, cultural, and professional networks in which women writers moved. This kind of neobiographical approach has been particularly successful in Levy's case on account of the availability of her unpublished papers auctioned in 1990 to a private company. Levy's engagement diary for 1889 pinpoints her attendance at the radical salon of Rosamund Marriott Watson (the poet "Graham R. Tomson"), a freethinker who divorced her first husband. It is used by Ana Parejo Vadillo to construct the existence of a female salon culture during the fin de siècle, based on shared ideas about religion and sexual politics.[72] The Levy collection contains a range of material from letters, juvenilia, sketchbooks, and unpublished short stories. Thus, it provides new opportunities for enhancing and challenging existing readings of Levy's published works. Emma Francis gains support for her reading of Levy's lesbian poetics from letters that Levy wrote from Brighton and Cambridge describing her passionate attachments to her teachers. The way in which she teases her sister Katie about her relinquishment of these "'divinities' in favour of attachment to men shows her understanding being 'in love with' women as conflictual with attraction to men."[73] Here, Francis uses material evidence to challenge historical models of sexuality that dismiss "an identification separate from and in opposition to that produced by heterosexuality . . . as a possibility in this period."[74] Naomi Hetherington's study of Levy's unpublished juvenilia similarly challenges existing models of Levy's Jewish upbringing as being in conflict with her literary aspirations and feminist politics.[75] Hetherington traces Levy's development from precocious child scribbler to professional writer through a series of amateur journals on which she collaborated with her siblings, Jewish cousins, and friends. If Hetherington's study extends the family context of the Victorian child writer to the acculturated Jewish home, Beckman mines the Levy collection for Levy's problematic representations of her Jewish roots. In "Leaving 'The Tribal Duck-pond': Amy Levy, Jewish Self-Hatred and Jewish Identity" (1999), Beckman reproduces sketches by Levy that depict "Jewish looks, culture and religion . . . as comic and vulgar."[76] In an appendix to her biography, Beckman makes public for the first time a body of correspondence in which Levy's voice emerges as charming, confident, and witty.

The contradiction between the tenor of Levy's private and published writing is just one of the enigmas that Beckman attempts to explain in the biography—a project severely hampered from the outset by the destruction of most of Levy's personal papers by her family after her death. The remaining fragmentary evidence at times breaks down entirely; most tantalizingly, Levy's calendar for 1889 (the year of her death) records in minute detail the domestic tasks and frequent social and professional appointments she conducted in these months while giving no indication of her state of mind. Levy's paradoxes are given symbolic form in Beckman's book by her use of three of the author's fictional figures—the "Hungry Poet" (the writer tormented by unfulfilled passion), "Miss Creak" (Levy's idolized New Woman schoolteacher), and "Leopold Leuniger" (the self-hating Jew)—as "fictive selves." Beckman produces a psychoanalytic reading of Levy's life and work structured by these contending elements of Levy's personal identity. Ultimately, however, Beckman, like many other critics, seeks a redemptive narrative in Levy' writing, asserting that *Reuben Sachs* evidences that Levy "worked . . . hard to defeat the 'Leopold Leuniger' voice within" and that by 1888 she was "recovering a positive sense of Jewish identity" and "was able to take advantage of what had once been felt as discord but now felt like healthy cultural hybridity." For Beckman, the narrator who coldly and unsympathetically relates the tragic story of "Cohen of Trinity" expresses Levy's own "anxiety and guilt" at representing Jews from the position of an outsider.[77]

Perhaps the most interesting approaches to Levy, however, are those that move beyond trying to establish straightforwardly positive identifications in her work. In the chapter on Levy in her book on women poets and religion, Cynthia Scheinberg begins this shift. Although she regards Levy as lamenting the "loss of a spiritual center for Anglo-Jewry" in *Reuben Sachs* and, in her verse, refusing the authority of Christian discourse as well as drawing on the heritage of Hebrew poetry, Scheinberg also contends that Levy's poetry poses the challenge of "finding a spiritual/religious identity outside of a common binary understanding of Jewish/Christian identity"; in her use of both Christian and Jewish scriptural allusion, Levy destabilizes this binary.[78] Scheinberg's perspective resonates with that of Susan Bernstein, who notes that "[t]he lines between inside and outside depictions of Jews were not so firmly drawn for an acculturated, middle-class woman who received a progressive education beyond the London Jewish community." Levy's writing can thus come into focus for modern readers as an exceptionally striking expression of the ambiguities of modern, urban, postreligious (Jewish) identity—an identity now widely viewed as "hybrid, complex and vacillating."[79] The same approach might usefully be applied to Levy's writing on women, which, after all, encompasses the formulaic heterosexual romance as well as the more radical attempts to deconstruct the gendered lyric voice. In the excited attempt to reclaim Levy as an uncompromising critic of the social organization of gender and religious difference, scholars have erred on the side of understating the difficulties of constructing a confident voice of critique in this period. For Levy, on the cusp of radical changes in the ways gender, sexuality, and ethnicity were imagined, literary articulation could not but be uncertain, ambiguous, and contradictory.

Amy Levy: Critical Essays

Encompassing her entire oeuvre, including novels, short fiction, essays, poetry, and letters, contributions to this volume take scholarship on Levy in exciting new directions. Firstly, Levy's work is considered in relation to several crucial cultural contexts, illuminating the especially fraught intellectual and political debates and literary conversations in which she participated. Two chapters consider Levy's feminist politics as articulated in her lesser-known first novel *The Romance of a Shop* (1888). Elizabeth Evans draws attention to the gendered culture of consumerism in which Levy sets her story of a female-run photography business. The increased presence of women in London retail establishments, Evans argues, involved a threatening erosion of boundaries of class and gender, and while Levy's novel suggests the difficulties encountered and self-doubt provoked by the entry into the public sphere of professional women, her narrative strategies also work to insist on their respectability. A less celebratory account of the novel is offered by Emma Francis, who compares its limited focus on economic self-determination for a middle-class elite with the more expansive analysis of women and labor—one that extended to the aims and aspirations of working women—in the fiction and prose writing of Levy's close friend Clementina Black.

Late-Victorian scientific thought was an equally significant influence both on Levy and on contemporary response to her work. Gail Cunningham's chapter turns to Levy's short stories and letters for evidence that Levy incorporated her own experience of social exclusion and anxiety about biological unfitness into her writing. By contrast Lyssa Randolph focuses on contemporary responses to Levy to argue that she was deliberately and instrumentally misread as an overeducated neurotic. Levy's pessimism, Randolph argues, in fact had a more universalist philosophical basis, but both her fiction and her suicide were interpreted instead through fin-de-siècle socio-medical discourses of degeneration. Levy's case could be invoked to demonstrate the cherished belief that the limited energies of the female body could not endure the demands of higher education without threat to women's sexual and mental health.

Restoring a sense of the literary contexts in which Levy wrote is also an important aim of this volume. Nadia Valman's chapter situates Levy's writing on the plight of the middle-class Jewish woman, both in *Reuben Sachs* and in her essay on the subject, within a much longer representational tradition. The figure of the suffering but elevated Jewess, as Valman shows, has a specific cultural provenance in nineteenth-century Christian conversion fiction and thus lent itself well to Levy's updated critique of Judaism and Jews. T. D. Olverson, in contrast, points to Levy's originality in appropriating the increasingly dominant elite male discourse of Victorian Hellenism in her accomplished early dramatic monologues. Reworked for its feminist potential, the story of Socrates' shrewish wife Xantippe becomes an articulation of Victorian women's aspirations for classical learning, while "Medea," written at a time of widespread moral panic over infanticide, boldly expresses the rage of the racial "Other."

A second theme of this collection is Levy's much-vaunted complex identity, which is examined in detail here as a series of innovative textual strategies. Gail Cunningham argues that Levy's use of an ironic but often brittle narratorial persona in her short stories plays a provocative game with the reader. Incorporating confessional elements into her texts and semifictionalizing her own experience, Levy challenges the boundary between autobiography and fiction. Susan David Bernstein also concentrates on Levy's fiction as a site of experimentation with boundaries, analyzing Levy's "double vision" as both insider and outsider to Anglo-Jewish society through her deployment of "vulgarity" as subject and as literary style. Levy's Anglo-Jewry, Bernstein argues, is "a mixed representation for a mixed audience by a writer who herself was fraught by the in-between condition of middle-class Victorian Jews." Alex Goody, meanwhile, explores further dimensions of this theme in relation to Levy's late poetry. For Goody, the locus of so many of these poems in the city street is especially significant; Levy's poetry of fleeting encounter in the anonymous urban space produces a mobile and ambiguous subjectivity rather than a firm sexual or racial identification.

Finally, we turn attention to the figure of Levy herself, as the subject of both political and literary appropriations. *Reuben Sachs*, as Nadia Valman's chapter notes, became a formative text for novelists advancing a critique of contemporary Anglo-Jewry, including those who continued, even at the end of the century, to seek the conversion of Jews. However, as Naomi Hetherington explores in detail, the novel and its author's biography also proved an extraordinarily rich resource for imagining the regeneration of Judaism in England. It provided the reference point for Israel Zangwill's recuperation of Judaism as a vital spiritual force in his novel *Children of the Ghetto* (1892). In a move that was frequent among Levy's contemporaries, Zangwill intermeshed the figure of Levy and her experience as a writer with the characters and arguments of *Reuben Sachs*, thereby creating Esther Ansell, the Jewish woman writer who embodies a synthesis of intellectuality and spirituality and leads Anglo-Jewry into the future. But, as Lyssa Randolph shows in her chapter, as the backlash against women's education gathered pace in the years following her suicide, Levy's work, life, and death could be just as powerfully invoked to argue for her frailty and misery as a woman who aspired to intellectual achievement. Extending in many unexpected directions, then, Levy's literary influence, these essays remind us, made her as iconic a figure in the years immediately following her death as, rescued from obscurity, she has become to a new generation of critics.

Notes

The chapter epigraph is Elaine Feinstein's "Amy Levy," from *Collected Poems and Translations* (Manchester, UK: Carcanet, 2002), 156. Used by permission of the publisher.

1. Amy Levy, "Imitation of Heine," *Cambridge Review* (1881), republished as "A Farewell" in *A Minor Poet and Other Verse* (London: T. Fisher Unwin, 1884), 92–93; "To E," *London Society* 49 (1886), reprinted in *A London Plane-Tree and Other Verse* (London: T. Fisher Unwin, 1889), 92–94; "Alma Mater," *Cambridge Review* (1887), reprinted in *London Plane-Tree*, 59–60; "Cambridge in the Long" in *London Plane-Tree*, 72–73.

2. Amy Levy, "Xantippe," *Dublin University Magazine* (1880), reprinted in *Xantippe and Other Verse* (Cambridge: E. Johnson and Co., 1881), 1–13.

3. Melvyn New, ed., *The Complete Novels and Selected Writings of Amy Levy, 1861–1889* (Gainesville: University Press of Florida, 1993); http://www.indiana.edu/~letrs/vwwp (home page for the Victorian Women Writers Project).

4. For example, Daniel Karlin, ed., *The Penguin Book of Victorian Verse* (London: Penguin, 1998), 737; Vivienne Rundle and Thomas J. Collins, eds., *The Broadview Anthology of Victorian Poetry and Poetic Theory* (Peterborough, ON: Broadview, 1999), 1131–48; Christopher Ricks, ed., *The New Oxford Book of Victorian Verse* (Oxford: Oxford University Press, 2002), 529–30; Francis O'Gorman, ed., *Victorian Poetry: An Annotated Anthology* (Oxford: Blackwell, 2004), 630–42; Angela Leighton and Margaret Reynolds, eds., *Victorian Women Poets: An Anthology* (Oxford: Blackwell, 1995), 589–610; Isobel Armstrong and Joseph Bristow, eds., with Cath Sharrock, *Nineteenth-Century Women Poets: An Oxford Anthology* (Oxford: Clarendon Press, 1996), 767–80; Emma Donoghue, ed., *What Sappho Would Have Said: Four Centuries of Love Poems between Women* (London: Hamish Hamilton, 1997), 99–102; Alison Hennegan, ed., *The Lesbian Pillow Book* (London: Fourth Estate, 2000), 241–43, 269, 325–26; Margaret Reynolds, ed., *The Sappho Companion* (London: Chatto and Windus, 2000), 269–70.

5. Amy Levy, *Reuben Sachs*, ed. Susan David Bernstein (Peterborough, ON: Broadview, 2006).

6. Linda Hunt Beckman, *Amy Levy: Her Life and Letters* (Athens: Ohio University Press, 2000).

7. Holly Laird, "The Death of the Author by Suicide: Fin-de-Siècle Poets and the Construction of Identity," in *The Fin-de-Siècle Poem: English Literary Culture and the 1890s*, ed. Joseph Bristow (Athens: Ohio University Press, 2005), 69–100.

8. Mona Caird, "Marriage," *Westminster Review* 130 (August 1888): 186–201, reprinted in Caird, *The Morality of Marriage and Other Essays on the Status and Destiny of Woman* (London: George Redway, 1897), 63–111. For an account of the responses, see Harry Quilter, ed., *Is Marriage a Failure?* (London: Swan Sonnenschein, 1888), 2.

9. Amy Levy, "Ida Grey: A Story of Woman's Sacrifice," part 1, *Pelican* 2 (1875): 20. The journal folded before the second part of Levy's poem could be published.

10. Amy Levy, "Run to Death," *Victoria Magazine* 33 (1988): 248–50.

11. Amy Levy, "The Poetry of Christina Rossetti," *Woman's World* 1 (1888): 178–80; "Women and Club Life," *Woman's World* 1 (1888): 364–67.

12. Amy Levy, *The Romance of a Shop* (London: T. Fisher Unwin, 1888).

13. Amy Levy, translations of Halevi and Heine in Lady Katie Magnus, ed., *Jewish Portraits* (London: Routledge, 1888), 10–11, 16–17, 46.

14. "The Ghetto at Florence," *Jewish Chronicle*, 26 March 1886, 9; "The Jew in Fiction," *Jewish Chronicle*, 4 June 1886, 13; "Jewish Children," *Jewish Chronicle*, 5 November 1886, 8; "Jewish Humour," *Jewish Chronicle*, 20 August 1886, 9–10; "Middle-Class Jewish Women of To-Day," *Jewish Chronicle*, 17 September 1886, 7.

15. Emma Francis, "Amy Levy: Contradictions?—Feminism and Semitic Discourse," in *Women's Poetry, Late Romantic to Late Victorian: Gender and Genre, 1830–1900*, ed. Isobel Armstrong and Virginia Blain (London: Macmillan, 1999), 183–204, quotation on 184.

16. Amy Levy, *Miss Meredith*, serialized in *British Weekly*, April–June 1889; published in one volume as *Miss Meredith* (London: Hodder and Stoughton, 1889).

17. Amy Levy, "A Ballad of Religion and Marriage" (privately printed and circulated by Clement Shorter, [1915]), n.p.

18. Beth-Zion Lask, "Amy Levy," *Transactions of the Jewish Historical Society of England* 11 (1928): 168–89, quotation on 179.

19. Ibid., 180.

20. Israel Zangwill, "A Ghetto Night at the Maccabaeans: Dinner to Mr. Samuel Gordon," *Jewish Chronicle*, 25 January 1901, 19.

21. Lask, "Amy Levy," 168.

22. Edward Wagenknecht, *Daughters of the Covenant: Portraits of Six Jewish Women* (Amherst: University of Massachusetts Press, 1983), 56–93, quotations on 85.

23. Linda Gertner Zatlin, *The Nineteenth-Century Anglo-Jewish Novel*, Twayne's English Authors Series (Boston: Twayne, 1981), 88, 90–91.

24. Ibid., 97, 105.

25. Bryan Cheyette, "From Apology to Revolt: Benjamin Farjeon, Amy Levy and the Post-Emancipation Anglo-Jewish novel, 1880–1900," *Transactions of the Jewish Historical Society of England* 24 (1982–86): 253–65, quotations on 260.

26. David S. Katz, *The Jews in the History of England* (Oxford: Clarendon Press, 1994), vii. For an extended discussion, see Nadia Valman, "Semitism and Criticism: Victorian Anglo-Jewish Literary History," *Victorian Literature and Culture* 27, no. 1 (1999): 235–48.

27. Cheyette, "From Apology to Revolt," 264.

28. Geoffrey Alderman, *Modern British Jewry*, new ed. (Oxford: Clarendon Press, 1998), 72, 73.

29. Emma Francis, "Socialist Feminism and Sexual Instinct: Amy Levy and Eleanor Marx," in *Eleanor Marx (1855–1898): Life, Work, Contacts*, ed. John Stokes, 113–27 (Aldershot, UK: Ashgate, 2000); Francis, "Amy Levy: Contradictions?" 183–88; Nadia Valman, "The Shadow of the Harem: Fin-de-siècle Racial Romance," chapter 6 in Valman, *The Jewess in Nineteenth-Century British Literary Culture* (Cambridge: Cambridge University Press, 2007). On racial discourse in relation to Jews, see, for example, Sander Gilman, *The Jew's Body* (London: Routledge, 1991).

30. Linda Hunt, "Amy Levy and the 'Jewish Novel': Representing Jewish Life in the Victorian Period," *Studies in the Novel* 26, no. 3 (1994): 235–53, quotations on 248.

31. Susan David Bernstein, introduction to Levy, *Reuben Sachs*, 30, 31.

32. Ibid., 34, 35.

33. Meri-Jane Rochelson, "Jews, Gender, and Genre in Late-Victorian England: Amy Levy's *Reuben Sachs*," *Women's Studies* 25 (1996): 311–28, quotations on 312.

34. Ibid., 323.

35. Iveta Jusová, "Amy Levy: The Anglo-Jewish New Woman," chapter 4 in *The New Woman and the Empire* (Columbus: Ohio State University Press, 2005).

36. Elaine Showalter, *Sexual Anarchy: Gender and Culture at the Fin de Siècle* (London: Bloomsbury, 1991), 26.

37. Kathleen Hickok, *Representations of Women: Nineteenth Century British Women's Poetry* (Westport, CT: Greenwood Press, 1984), 10, 69–70, 109–10; Angela Leighton, "'Because men made the laws': The Fallen Woman and the Woman Poet," *Victorian Poetry* 27 (1989): 109–27; Isobel Armstrong, *Victorian Poetry: Poetry, Poetics and Politics* (London: Routledge, 1993), chap. 12.

38. Amy Levy, "Magdalen," in *Minor Poet and Other Verse*, 65–68.

39. Armstrong, *Victorian Poetry*, 321.

40. Ibid., 323.

41. Hoaxie Neil Fairchild, *Religious Trends in English Poetry*, vol. 5, *1880–1920: Gods of a Changing Poetry* (New York: Columbia University Press, 1962), 53.

42. Ibid., 55.

43. Angela Leighton, "Amy Levy," in Leighton and Reynolds, *Victorian Women's Poetry*, 591.

44. An exception to this is Sharona A. Levy's excellent doctoral dissertation, "Amy Levy: The Woman and Her Writings," University of Oxford, 1989, chap. 2. This work remains unpublished, and the space accorded within it to European discourses of pessimism on Levy's writing has only recently been acknowledged in Beckman's biography of Levy and in Ana Parejo Vadillo's chapter on Levy in her monograph on women poets and urban aestheticism (see below).

45. Virginia Blain, "Sexual Politics of the (Victorian) Closet; or, No Sex Please—We're Poets," in Armstrong and Blain, *Women's Poetry*, 135–63, quotation on 137.

46. Blain, "Sexual Politics," 138.

47. Francis, "Socialist Feminism," 127.

48. Francis, "Amy Levy: Contradictions?" 201.

49. Ibid., 201.

50. Francis, "Socialist Feminism," 121.

51. Ibid., 122.

52. Nadia Valman, "'Barbarous and Medieval': Jewish Marriage in Fin de Siècle English Fiction," in *The Image of the Jew in European Liberal Culture, 1789–1914*, ed. Bryan Cheyette and Nadia Valman (London: Vallentine Mitchell, 2004), 111–29. See also Valman, *Jewess*, chap. 6.

53. Cynthia Scheinberg, *Women's Poetry and Religion in Victorian England: Jewish Identity and Christian Culture* (Cambridge: Cambridge University Press, 2002), 192.

54. Cynthia Scheinberg, "Recasting 'Sympathy and Judgment': Amy Levy, Women Poets, and the Victorian Dramatic Monologue," *Victorian Poetry* 35, no. 2 (1997): 173–91, quotation on 184.

55. Cynthia Scheinberg, "Canonizing the Jew: Amy Levy's Challenge to Victorian Poetic Identity," *Victorian Studies* 39, no. 2 (1996): 173–200, quotation on 177. Scheinberg refers to Levy's "James Thomson: A Minor Poet," *Cambridge Review* (21 and 28 February 1883): 240–41, 257–58; and "Jewish Humour," *Jewish Chronicle*, 20 August 1886, 9–10 (reprinted in New, *Complete Novels*, 501–9, 521–24).

56. Amy Levy, "Cohen of Trinity," *Gentleman's Magazine* 266 (May 1889): 417–24; reprinted in New, *Complete Novels*, 478–85.

57. Cynthia Scheinberg, "Amy Levy and the Accents of Minor(ity) Poetry," chap. 6 in Scheinberg, *Women's Poetry*, 192.

58. Ibid., 191.

59. Joseph Bristow, "'All Out of Tune in This World's Instrument': The 'Minor' Poetry of Amy Levy," *Journal of Victorian Culture* 4 (1999): 76–103, quotation on 94.

60. Ibid., 80.

61. Karen Weisman, "Playing with Figures: Amy Levy and the Forms of Cancellation," *Criticism* 43 (2001): 59–79, quotations on 59.

62. Laird, "Death of the Author," 94.

63. Bristow, "All Out of Tune," 97.

64. Ana Parejo Vadillo, *Women Poets and Urban Aestheticism: Passengers of Modernity* (Basingstoke, UK: Palgrave Macmillan, 2005).

65. Erika Diane Rappaport, *Shopping for Pleasure: Women in the Making of London's West End* (Princeton: Princeton University Press, 2000); Judith R. Walkowitz, *City of Dreadful Delight: Narratives of Sexual Danger in Late-Victorian London* (London: Virago, 1992); Elizabeth Wilson, *The Sphinx in the City: Urban Life, the Control of Disorder, and Women* (London: Virago, 1991).

66. Deborah Epstein Nord, "'Neither Pairs Nor Odd': Female Community in Late Nineteenth-Century London," *Signs: Journal of Women in Culture and Society* 15 (1990): 733–53, quotations on 748; reprinted in *Walking the Victorian Streets: Women, Representation and the City* (Ithaca, NY: Cornell University Press, 1995), chap. 6.

67. Nord, "Neither Pairs Nor Odd," 735.

68. Linda Hunt Beckman, "Amy Levy: Urban Poetry, Poetic Innovation, and the Fin-de-Siècle Woman Poet," in *The Fin-de-Siècle Poem: English Literary Culture and the 1890s*, ed. Joseph Bristow, 207–30 (Athens: Ohio University Press, 2005), quotation on 210.

69. Deborah L. Parsons, *Streetwalking the Metropolis: Women, the City and Modernity* (Oxford: Oxford University Press, 2000), 101.

70. Alex Goody, "Murder in Mile End: Amy Levy, Jewishness and the City," *Victorian Literature and Culture* 34, no. 2 (2006): 461–79, quotation on 475.

71. Ibid.

72. Ana I. Parejo Vadillo, "New Woman Poets and the Culture of the Salon at the Fin de Siècle," *Women: A Cultural Review* 10, no. 1 (1999): 22–34. Coming out of her research for her recent biography of Graham R. Tomson, Linda K. Hughes's study of the Literary Ladies also positions Levy as a precursor to the New Woman through her presence at the club's inaugural dinner in 1889. See Hughes, "A Club of Their Own: The 'Literary Ladies,' New Women Writers, and Fin-de-Siècle Authorship," *Victorian Literature and Culture* 35, no. 1 (2007): 233–60.

73. Francis, "Amy Levy: Contradictions?" 196.

74. Ibid.

75. Naomi Hetherington, "New Woman, 'New Boots': Amy Levy as Child Journalist," in *The Child Writer from Austen to Woolf*, ed. Christine Alexander and Juliet McMaster (Cambridge: Cambridge University Press, 2005), 254–68.

76. Linda Hunt Beckman, "Leaving 'The Tribal Duckpond': Amy Levy, Jewish Self-Hatred and Jewish Identity," *Victorian Literature and Culture* 27, no. 1 (1999): 185–201, quotation on 190.

77. Beckman, *Amy Levy*, 204, 206.

78. Scheinberg, *Women's Poetry*, 202, 195.

79. Bernstein, introduction to Levy, *Reuben Sachs*, 12, 24.

1

"We Are Photographers, Not Mountebanks!"

spectacle, commercial space, and the new public woman

Elizabeth F. Evans

In its portrayal of new opportunities for women's work and mobility, Amy Levy's first novel, *The Romance of a Shop* (1888), provides a lens through which to examine the gendered culture of consumerism and spectacle in fin-de-siècle London. In this novel, the Lorimer sisters not only produce images for the marketplace by running a photography studio but also become spectacles as women in business and participants in urban life. Disavowing the status of "mountebanks" but needing the business that publicity brings, the sisters seek a precarious balance in their self-presentation. The narrator, too, must balance contemporary assumptions about the lives of working women to depict both the difficulties facing women attempting to make their own living and to argue that their respectability is the greater for their independence. The figure of the shopgirl, known for her ambiguous class status and respectability, compromised by her associations with commercialism and spectacle, epitomized for many late Victorians the breakdown of traditional gender and class divisions and boundaries between public and private spaces. Though Levy's characters are not strictly "shopgirls" in that their economic and educational resources enable them to manage their own shop, *The Romance of a Shop* is crucially engaged with discourses about the female shop worker that were prevalent in contemporary social criticism, literature, and popular culture. Levy appropriates these discourses to negotiate the interconnected issues of gender, self-representation, and the nature of spectatorship, as well as to imagine a place for professional women in the urban landscape.

In spite of the renaissance of interest in Levy's life and work, critical attention to this novel has been decidedly limited, partly because of its supposedly conventional characterization, narrative development, and resolution. For Deborah Epstein Nord, the last part of the novel resembles a bad imitation of *Pride and Prejudice* with "all four sisters searching for the appropriate mate." Even Linda Hunt Beckman, who recognizes the novel's "parodic" relationship to Victorian realism, finds that it "neither strives for profundity nor reaches for originality." More recently, Susan David Bernstein has reappraised the novel by situating it amid contemporary debates about photography, representation, and modern independent women in London.[1] As Bernstein's work suggests, the novel's historical and literary contexts merit closer attention. Levy's negotiated use of representations of the shopgirl involves greater complexity and ambivalence toward middle-class women's increasing public presence in the city than scholars have acknowledged. Whereas writers as diverse as George Gissing, Cicely Hamilton, and Henry James portray the sometimes pleasant, often trying life of the shopgirl, Levy's novel is unusual in that the characters are shop proprietors, not paid assistants. Rather than commodities on display, modeling clothes for the purchasing public, Levy's "women in business" are the producers of spectacles, not the subject of them. And amid literature on working women, Levy provides a rare portrait of a woman who chooses to continue her work after marriage and children. Through her characters' position as women in business and in their excursions in London, Levy employs discourses about the shopgirl to expose the difficulty women have in escaping the spectacle of their gender even as they articulate a space for themselves in the public spaces of the city.

When the four middle-class Lorimer sisters are suddenly orphaned and thrown upon their own resources, they reject the expected recourse of becoming governesses or teachers and determine to use their knowledge of photography, which had been their family hobby, to open a photographic studio. The news is received with horror by their friends and family worried about the girls' "loss of caste" and "damage to [their] prospects."[2] The novel follows the sisters as they find the appropriate place in London for their enterprise, attempt to make the studio "pay," and use their independence to explore relationships of business and pleasure.

The decision, which is made by the independently minded middle sisters, Gertrude and Lucy, to enter the marketplace appalls the conventional eldest sister, Fanny. Her exclamation "[N]eed it come to that—to open a shop?" encompasses all the ways in which such a "fall" to commerce involved a loss of status, marital eligibility, and respectability. While Lucy "hastily" responds, "Fanny, you are behind the age," and Gertrude defends the decision in terms of its practicality and progressiveness (the sisters would be able to stay together, and it is an enterprise "capable of growth," a quality "in which women's work is dreadfully lacking"), the novel continually threatens to validate Fanny's response (54–55). Though Levy frequently portrays Fanny as an out-of-date relic of simpering Victorian femininity—"a superannuated baby"—she also reveals Fanny's opposition to women's public involvement in a commercial enterprise to be not behind the age, but very much *of* the age (52).

In the last decades of the century, women were entering many occupations that involved their presence in public spaces, including as postal clerks, office workers, and telegraphers, but their full-scale entry into retail establishments elicited the most popular attention. Partly, this was due to the large numbers of women who were employed there. Contemporary estimates numbered female shop assistants in England between half a million and one million and found shop employment the most numerically significant source of new employment for women.[3] Although the term encompassed a wide range of positions in a wide variety of businesses, *shopgirls* referred most specifically to female workers in department stores who were responsible for restocking goods, helping customers with their purchases, and receiving payments over the counter. As a new phenomenon resulting from changes in production and the distributive trades, the department store prompted strong feelings. It was both criticized and celebrated for its mingling of every sort of product from all over the world and for its targeting of the female consumer, including through the provision of refreshments and toilet facilities that made the city a more hospitable place for women.[4] Department stores were marketed as a bridge between public and private spheres, and female shop assistants were among the most visible of the new social actors that historian Judith Walkowitz identifies. These were women whose presence "challenged the spatial boundaries—of East and West, of public and private—that Victorian writers on the metropolis had imaginatively constructed to fix gender and class difference in the city."[5]

The shop itself is a threshold space that inherently blurs the boundary between public and private by offering for sale in the marketplace products that enter private homes. This ambiguity became of heightened concern in the late nineteenth century, when prevalent conceptions of gender and class distinctions were challenged on many fronts. As though to mitigate or refute the public nature of the shop, promoters of department stores called them not shops but "houses." The shopgirl, too, was an ambiguous figure, particularly when she displayed on her person the clothes for sale. She was a model for the middle-class lady at the same time that she was herself an object for public consumption. The problems and contradictions that shopgirls were seen to embody were expressive of widespread anxiety about the dissolution of traditional social distinctions and boundaries between domestic and commercial space. As commentators struggled to make the shopgirl legible, her apparent coherence as a category, which often obscured dramatic differences in relative economic prosperity and work conditions, helped her to function metonymically for women's changing relationship to the public sphere.

The shopgirl was also one of the most visible examples of the fin-de-siècle's *new public woman*—a term I use to evoke the New Woman's claim to independent thought and action and to mark a different emphasis in a woman's relationship to public spaces, one that regards her public presence as a key constituent of her identity. Encompassing a broad range of female "types," including Odd Women, "professional women," and shopgirls, as well as New Women, the category of "new public women" highlights anxieties about the increasing visibility of women in the turn-of-the-century city that these types all elicited and expressed, though in diverse ways.[6] As Sally Ledger has convincingly argued in her essay on Gissing's *The Odd Women,* the shopgirl rather than the New Woman was the more problematic figure of modern urban life.[7] The shopgirl's knowledge of public transportation and self-confident navigations of the city seemed to claim ownership of the city and social, sexual, and economic independence. The figure of the shopgirl was used by contemporary observers of the modern metropolis to explore relationships between physical mobility and mental freedom, women and work, gender and the city. While Levy distinguishes the Lorimer sisters' position in several important respects from that of the prototypical shopgirl, she draws upon the concerns and prejudices surrounding them to explore the circumstances and opportunities for new public women.

Fiction and nonfiction of the period depict the conditions under which the shopgirl labored and the problematic character of her profession, attempting to make sense of her ambiguous class and social status. Some writers countered cultural attitudes that tended to reduce "the shopgirl" to a uniform archetype by exposing the heterogeneity of the class and social origins of these working "girls." One observer finds that "every kind of girl, drawn from every class and strata of society, is found behind the counters of the modern emporium . . . —the daughters of artisans, of agricultural labourers, of skilled mechanics, of struggling and of prosperous shopkeepers, of clerks and of professional men."[8] For some, including George Gissing, this close proximity of the daughters of laborers with the daughters of professional men could be dangerous to the latter's respectability.[9] Others evoked their diverse social backgrounds to call for better treatment by the public, as well as by employers. A former shopgirl enjoins shopping ladies to treat girls behind the counter with more kindness, writing in 1888, "Many young ladies at home have little or no sympathy with the 'common shop-girls,' as they often term them. . . . In many cases they are girls suited to a higher sphere, but, through force of circumstances, have been obliged to go early into the world."[10] Levy evokes this descent from the expected social sphere and plays with the social confusion elicited by her characters' new position. Phyllis, for instance, recalls in *The Romance of a Shop* how one former friend "dodged round the corner at Baker Street the other day because he didn't care to be seen bowing to two shabby young women with heavy parcels" and how another former acquaintance ignored Lucy on the train because she was traveling third class and wearing an old gown (125–26). As the passage makes clear, the sisters' lack of new clothes, signifiers of a certain class position, also removes them from their former social circle by limiting their attendance at social functions.

While commentators on the shopgirl's trials were motivated by diverse ideological views and goals—including labor rights, equitable treatment of women, and social morality—they largely agreed that the conditions of shop labor were physically and morally dangerous. The chief concerns were the lengthy workday, low wages, an exorbitant system of fines, the payment for work in truck (goods), and the living-in system.[11] The system of living-in, which required employees to live in housing provided by their employer, was frequently criticized for the liberty allowed young female employees, including the provision of latchkeys enabling them to let themselves in late at night, and for encouraging illicit relations among shop assistants by making marriage nearly impossible.[12] According to social observers, the moral dangers resulting from the absence of parental surveillance and the freedom to wander the streets alone were compounded by the low salaries shopgirls received, for if they were to enjoy commercial entertainment, most shopgirls had to depend on being "treated" by male acquaintances, with the consequences that that might entail.[13]

Levy certainly knew of the popular concern about the circumstances of female shop assistants. Her close friend Clementina Black—who, along with Black's sisters, likely provided a model for the Lorimer sisters' independent London lives—wrote publicly about the hardships of service workers, including shopgirls. Appearing just two years after the publication of *The Romance of a Shop*, Black's 1890 article "The Grievances of Barmaids" compares the hardships of barmaids to those of shopgirls.[14] Black would describe the lives of shopgirls in greater detail in a chapter of her book *Sweated Industry and the Minimum Wage*.[15] Levy's placement of the Lorimers' shop at 20B Upper Baker Street may also be significant in that it is just a few houses up from 12 York Place, Baker Street, the location of Lincoln House, which in 1886 was one of seven homes for working-class working women.[16] As her novel quickly makes clear, Levy is concerned with how the respectability of any woman working with the public is called into question.

Levy removes much of the morally dangerous elements of the shopgirl's work conditions when she has the sisters live together above their own business, rather than as boarders with other girls of diverse backgrounds. But her treatment of the sisters' new position, and its incompatibility with traditional societal views of feminine respectability, is indebted to contemporary debates about female shop assistants. Although the sisters are not subject to the system of living-in, they do live on their own and make their own decisions. And, perhaps more dangerously, they have entered the public realm of commercial exchange. Fanny's objections to opening a shop thus are not only about the fall in social position but also are indicative of a constellation of class and gender codes. At the very least, to enter the marketplace as young, unmarried women made for an ambiguous social position with consequences for their perceived respectability.

Concern about the shopgirl's moral status was largely due to the sexual availability her employment implied. Her involvement in commerce was itself a problem: as Walkowitz puts it, "if she sold things, did she not sell herself?" For women who sold the clothes they modeled, their own bodies were in a sense involved in the commercial exchange. Like the prostitute in being subject to the desires of the marketplace, the successful shopgirl marketed herself as well as her wares in a threatened merging of economic and sexual exchange. As Walkowitz argues, "the shopgirl . . . and other service workers occupied the 'middle' ground of sexuality," as neither "ladies" nor "prostitutes."[17] Female service workers appeared as managers of a "carefully channeled rather than fully discharged," "open yet licit sexuality" that Peter Bailey terms "parasexuality."[18]

One of the few contemporary fictional representations of a woman owning her own shop indicates that self-employment was no preserver of respectability. Mabel E. Wotton's story "The Hour of Her Life" (1896) portrays the dubious morality conferred by a woman's involvement in the public arena of commerce. The events of the story take place entirely within a flower shop in London's club land; its proprietress (and the story's protagonist), Annette Browning, sells men's buttonholes, "whose perfection and cost put a certain *cachet* upon the customers." The shop's exclusively male customers, Annette's two maids, and the "inner sanctum" to which a "favoured few were occasionally admitted" all undermine demarcations between sexual and economic exchange and even suggest a brothel, though we are told that the only object was "flirtation."[19] Born in France and the daughter of an English officer and an orange seller in Drury Lane, Annette straddles multiple identities. Cast off by her father's family and wanting nothing to do with her mother's, Annette says of her class origins, "I am a sort of Mahomet's coffin . . . and hang between the two worlds without belonging to either."[20] Though Annette models her social engagements on what the society papers suggest is acceptable ("[L]adies —real ladies—went out in the evening with men who were not their husbands" [104]), the one man she cares for cannot see her as an appropriate match for a man of his class: "A woman in her position, who had been fêted by a vast number of the fastest men in town; whose beauty had enabled her to sell flowers at fancy prices, and whose life generally since the opening of the shop had proved she was answerable to no one for her actions, was assuredly not the sort of woman to become the future Lady Sydthorpe" (106). That his comments are made without a will to hurt adds piquancy to her situation. She is, as he tells her, "too young and too beautiful to be here by [her]self" (105). In depicting the challenge to social propriety and notions of feminine respectability represented by an independent woman in business who is responsible to none but herself, Wotton also shows such a woman's consequential marginalization. Annette's position in-between two classes, her borderline respectability, is represented by her shop, itself like Mahomet's coffin, hovering between its identity as an exclusive business in club land and its association with transgressive heterosocial environs. Annette's placelessness is graphically represented at the story's end with the narrator's depiction of the shop closed and with a placard affixed to its shutters reading "gone away." Annette presumably disappears from London as she does from the story, as though her incoherent social position makes her presence untenable.

Levy's portrayal of women in business is remarkable in that the Lorimer sisters' precarious balance between domesticity and professionalism maintains their respectability and insists on the respectability of their profession, even while it defines them as pushing the boundaries of what is appropriately "feminine." This balance between domesticity and professionalism is represented both by the spatial composition of their shop and lodgings on Baker Street and by the sisters' manipulation of that space. The promise and excitement of the Lorimer sisters' new independent life in London is immediately figured geographically with an opposition between the "large, dun-coloured house" on Campden Hill, west of central London, and the rooms they find on Baker Street. Whereas the first is "enclosed by a walled-in garden" and seems quiet enough to be in the country, the latter are above a chemist's shop on Upper Baker Street, a busy thoroughfare (51). The narrator takes the reader, along with the sisters, on a tour of the house, describing the layout at length: the sisters will live in the top two stories; a dressmaker has her business on the next floor down; a chemist and his wife, the owners of the building, have their shop and home on the ground and basement floors, respectively.[21] The reader is also provided with descriptions of the renovations the sisters undertake as they make their bedrooms on the second of the two floors, at the top of the house, and their sitting room and kitchen on the floor below. This preoccupation with the spatial components of their new home—the rooms that "bounded the little domain" (77)—serves to highlight their essential domesticity with their eagerness to make their rented rooms homelike. At the same time, it emphasizes their embrace of a new active role in the home, for such labor was performed by servants in the home on Campden Hill.

The emphasis on the ways in which the sisters domesticate their rented rooms is extended to the photographic studio and its adjoining waiting room. Situated at the back of the house, the studio is reached from the street by going up a short flight of stairs and down a "little, sloping passage." The distance from the street seems to make their business more private and less in the public domain. However, the sisters recognize the truth of their friend's advice that "[y]ou will have to make this place as pretty as possible," as "you will be nothing if not aesthetic" (76). As testified by the increasingly elaborate displays in department stores, to beautify the market space had come to be seen as a commercial necessity. Their friend's use of the personal pronoun "you" to refer to the business ("you will be nothing if not aesthetic") is indicative of how the sisters' identities are tied up with that of their shop—and how both shop and sisters must please the public eye. Accordingly, the sisters decorate their shop with "various aesthetic devices," such as lanterns and reproductions of celebrated paintings, "artfully" mingled with examples of their own work (78). Narrated hand-in-hand with their domestic arrangements, the sisters' decorating of the studio is positioned in between a feminine role of beautifying the home and a market-driven need to appeal to the consumer.

The part-public, part-private Baker Street building is a liminal space, open to passing strangers yet a domestic haven. While the sisters' private rooms are spatially separate from the studio and its waiting room, they are revealed to be vulnerable to intrusion. Levy emphasizes the sisters' vulnerability when, one evening, they are alarmed at a commotion from the floor below their living rooms, where the dressmaker has her business. They (and we) learn later that she has attempted to kill herself and was only stopped by the landlord's vigorous opposition. Because the dressmaker scarcely appears in the text aside from this scene (and even here she is heard about, not seen by the sisters), she seems to serve solely as a cautionary figure, or so Gertrude interprets her. After the woman's attempted suicide, Gertrude lay awake, feeling that there was "[o]nly a plank—a plank between them [her and her sisters] and the pitiless, fathomless ocean . . . into whose boiling depths hundreds sank daily and disappeared, never to rise again." True to Gertrude's musings, the dressmaker does disappear —"A day or two later" she "vanished for ever"—and her fate emphasizes the precariousness of the sisters' lives (95). The dressmaker's placement on the floor between the photography studio and the girls' living space suggests that danger lies in the space between their professional work and their domestic lives. They inhabit a porous space in which the "boiling depths" might rise from the streets below.

The sisters' association with, but difference from, discursive constructions of the shopgirl places them on the threshold between vulnerable and protected, an ambivalence that Levy explores through the multiple possibilities of the windows in their living quarters that reveal as much as they shield. As Victor Burgin has said in reference to Walter Benjamin, the porosity of the window, which allows actions of the street to be seen from inside, and vice versa, competes with a dialectic of interior and exterior.[22] Levy gives Phyllis, the youngest sister, a delicate and beautiful girl, "a frequent custom" of amusing herself "by looking into the street"—a practice to which Lucy objects, saying that "any one can see right into the room" (105). Because in the course of the novel Phyllis will succumb to temptation and "fall" from respectability, one might infer that her love of watching from the window, no matter who watches her in turn, signals a susceptibility to transgression. This kind of viewing might also be contrasted with the sisters' work with the camera lens, a professional, respectable window. Yet Gertrude, a character read by most critics as the sister with whom Levy most closely identifies, "had herself a secret, childish love for the gas-lit street, for the sight of the hurrying people, the lamps, the hansom cabs, flickering in and out of the yellow haze," a love that is later represented as a source of creative inspiration for Gertrude (105). Levy thus indicates the importance of urban spectatorship to her aesthetic aims and evokes the problems this poses for the female artist. If taking up the role of spectator endangers a woman's respectability because she is a priori a spectacle, then how is the woman artist to represent modern life? Taking this tension as its subject, Levy's poem "A London Plane-Tree" features a speaker who looks at the plane-tree in the square through a window—"Here from my garret-pane" (5)— imagining that the tree loves the town of which it, unlike the speaker, is a part.[23] As Ana Parejo Vadillo observes in her wonderfully nuanced reading of the poem, the speaker behind the windowpane is both prisoner and spectator, confined outside urban life and posited as an observer of that life.[24]

The trope of a woman watching urban life from behind a windowpane recurs in Levy's oeuvre, providing her with a fecund image through which to illustrate and protest limits to women's participation in urban life, limits that are particularly restrictive for women of the lower middle class. With middle-class definitions of respectability that prevented interactions with strangers but without the financial resources that enabled middle- and upper-middle-class women to travel about the city shopping and visiting, lower-middle-class women had few social opportunities, particularly for meeting men of their age. Levy uses the trope of viewing urban life through a window in her short story "Eldorado at Islington," published in a magazine edited by Oscar Wilde, to probe the difference that class makes for women's social opportunities.[25] In the lower-middle-class London borough of Islington,

> Eleanor Lloyd, from her window in the roof, could see not only the wall
> and the plane-trees, but, by dint of craning her neck, the High Street itself,
> with its ceaseless stream of trams and omnibuses. There was a public-
> house at the corner, and, as the door swung backwards and forwards,
> Eleanor caught glimpses of the lively barmaid behind her tall white tap-
> handles. A group of flower-girls . . . stood outside on the pavement, jesting
> with the 'busmen and passers-by. Eleanor, who was a "lady," (Heaven help
> her!) used sometimes to envy the barmaid and the flower-girls their social
> opportunity. (488)

Eleanor recognizes that female service workers—who, as a matter of course,
interact with diverse people—enjoy some advantages over a woman of her station, who must carefully maintain her middle-class respectability; barmaids and
flower girls, like shopgirls (who were otherwise a rung higher on the social lad-
der), had many more opportunities for a range of social interactions, much to
the disapproval of social moralists. Positioning Eleanor as a prisoner of social
expectations and a limited urban spectator who must "cran[e] her neck" to see
the activity of High Street, Levy evokes sympathy for the lower-middle-class
woman who is herself a kind of "Mahomet's coffin," without the liberty of
either the working classes or the better off. As Phyllis neatly observes in *The
Romance of a Shop*, "It is a little dull, ain't it, Gerty, to look at life from a top-floor
window?" (106). Levy illustrates how a natural desire to enjoy greater participation in urban life is incompatible with restrictions on what respectable women
with limited financial resources might do without damage to their reputations.
Through the Lorimer sisters' attempt to negotiate these opposing needs, *The
Romance of a Shop* reformulates definitions of female respectability to posit a new
relationship between women and public urban spaces.

Levy challenges limits imposed on respectable women's urban travel by
evoking stigmas against public transport and quickly dismissing them as both
pretentious and outdated. In one memorable scene, Gertrude returns home
from the British Museum, "careering up the street on the summit of a tall, green
omnibus, her hair blowing gaily in the breeze." The sisters' friend and neighbor,
"Frank, passing by in painting-coat and sombrero, plucked the latter from his
head and waved it in exaggerated salute, an action which evoked a responsive
smile from Gertrude but scandalized Aunt Caroline Pratt who was dashing
past in an open carriage" (99). Although Aunt Pratt's reaction to the vision of
her niece smiling at a man on the street from atop an omnibus is sharply critical and overbearing, it is not necessarily extreme. The open top of the omnibus
was traditionally the province of men; women were expected to sit in the first

level's interior. Gertrude's choice to mount "boldly to the top" of an omnibus marks her incisive claim to public urban space and to the free vistas that such a perch allowed (80).[26] Furthermore, with a spectrum of classes represented by the women using public transportation, fine distinctions in deportment were important markers. Mrs. Humphry's *Manners for Women*, an etiquette guide for young women, describes the difference between "well-bred" and "underbred" women through their occupations of public space:

> There is a quiet self-possession about the gentlewoman, whether young or old, that marks her out from the women of a lower class, whose manner is florid. This is perhaps the best word to describe the lively gestures, the notice-attracting glance and the self-conscious air of the underbred, who continually appear to wish to impress their personality upon all they meet. . . . The well-bred woman goes quietly along, intent on her own business and regardless of the rest of the world, except in so far as to keep from intruding upon their personal rights. . . . A delicate sense of self-respect keeps her from contact with her neighbour in train or tramcar or omnibus. . . . The woman of the lower classes may spread her arms, lean up against her neighbor, or in other ways behave with a disagreeable familiarity; the gentlewoman never.[27]

A women's social status could thus be read by her degree of engagement with strangers and by the amount of public space she claimed; the gentlewoman would remain detached and self-contained, while the woman of the lower classes would invade the consciousness and space of her neighbors—taking more than her share. While *Manners for Women* argues that a woman's class is rendered legible by her behavior, as an etiquette guide it inadvertently but inevitably suggests how class itself is a performance. Levy indicates the difficulty of this performance; not only is a respectable female body defined negatively by what it does not *do* (as Mrs. Humphry writes, it does not move so as to draw attention to itself), it also does not elicit actions from others. Should a lady be so unfortunate as to be recognized and saluted by a passer-by, Aunt Pratt implies, she should have the decency not to notice, to remain impervious to the gaze and gestures of others.

In raising this issue, however, Levy undercuts its importance. One of Gertrude's keenest pleasures is to go about London. Choosing to ride an omnibus rather than travel via the Underground, Gertrude "argues to herself": "Because one cannot afford a carriage or even a hansom cab . . . is one to be shut up away from the sunlight and the streets?" (80). Levy celebrates this form of transportation in her "Ballade of an Omnibus," published the following year in *A London Plane-Tree and Other Verse.* Gertrude's perspective on this point is also endorsed by the novel's plot and in the narrator's sympathy with Gertrude's identity as *flâneuse:* "[F]or Gertrude, the humours of the town had always possessed a curious fascination. She contemplated the familiar London pageant with an interest that had something of passion in it; and, for her part, was never inclined to quarrel with the fate which had transported her from the comparative tameness of Campden Hill to regions where the pulses of the great city could be felt distinctly as they beat and throbbed" (80). While contemporary commentators warned women about the dangers of urban travel, Levy evokes the specter of danger to firmly dismiss it.[28]

Levy also minimizes the scandal of Gertrude's being seen as at home on the streets by using the university-educated "Girton girl" as a foil who demonstrates by contrast the gentility of the sisters. She is given a peripheral place in the text, described only as an "ex-Girtonian without a waist, who taught at the High School for girls hard-by" and strode with "her arms swinging like a bell-rope" (160–61). The narrator cursorily sums her up in terms of her university education (her waistless gown suggests that she carries her academic background with her), her current vocation, and her unfeminine public presence. More unflattering observations are made through the sisters' consciousness: when the Girton girl moves into the lodgings vacated by Frank, they "chose to regard her as a usurper; and with the justice usually attributed to their sex, indulged in much sarcastic comment on her appearance; on her round shoulders and swinging gait; on the green gown with balloon sleeves, and the sulphur-coloured handkerchief which she habitually wore" (161). Because we never learn anything more about this graduate of Girton, it would seem that all we need to know is that academia is far more dangerous to a woman's grace than is dignified labor—a point that is likely tongue-in-cheek, because Levy herself was a student at Newnham, Cambridge's other college for women. As with Levy's detailed description of the sisters' work to decorate and make homelike their rented lodging rooms, the use of the Girton graduate as a foil insists on their preservation of a feminine domesticity in spite of their labor in the marketplace.

Contrary to widespread fears about the threats of independent urban life to young women, real danger to the Lorimer sisters does not come from traveling on public transport or from enjoying "the humours of the town." Rather, Levy has Phyllis, the youngest sister and the only victim of their enterprise, die the quintessential Victorian female death from consumption. Her moral fall, which precipitates her death, occurs with her seduction by a wealthy and married painter for whom she models.[29] In spite of—or to spite—representations of urban dangers, Levy has Phyllis's fall come through socially elevated circles, not through the city streets. That Phyllis's acquaintance with the painter begins through his patronage of the photography studio suggests the dangers to women in the public eye; her fall is symbolically represented in visual terms by her removal from the sisters' studio, where she helps to produce images, to the painter's studio, where she is an object for the artist's gaze. But Levy is ambiguous about the degree to which the sisters' relationship to commodity production and consumerism is to blame. Phyllis's susceptibilities—her boredom with a quiet life and her love of male attention—are as important as her circumstances to the story of her fall.[30] The other three sisters are happily, and virtuously, married at the novel's end.

Scholars have criticized the tidiness of the novel's closure, in which the beautiful fallen sister is "killed off" and the other three are "married off."[31] But such assessments do not simply neglect audience expectations for a resolution consistent with the generic mode suggested by the "Romance" of the novel's title; they have also failed to recognize Levy's playful use of a familiar narrative. I would suggest that the novel's closure, particularly in Gertrude's marriage to a lord, contains ironic reference to the mythology surrounding the shopgirl and the fantasy of an elevating marriage. It was widely accepted that most shopgirls were eager to escape the hardships of the trade through marriage, and shop work was typically imagined as a temporary stopgap between childhood and wifehood. Indeed, literature (both fiction and nonfiction) of the day suggests that the likelihood of marriage is what stimulates much of the discomfort with the shopgirl's ambiguous class origins and social status, the hardships of her employment, and their implications for her morality. After all, could a woman so associated with the marketplace and public by-ways really make a good wife and mother?[32] This question was all the more pressing given shopgirls' perceived aspiration for social advancement. Members of the working class termed them "counter-jumpers," aspirers to middle-class respectability, and periodical literature frequently makes reference to shopgirls' perceived ambition to marry above their station. Even while one writer argues that many shopgirls are, by birth, "suited to a higher sphere," she also claims, "Many of these shop-girls have attended private classes for self-improvement so that they may acquit themselves properly should fortune favour them with a step higher in life."[33]

Mass entertainment suggested that this ambition to marry "up" was often fulfilled. The freedom and independence of the shopgirl made her a popular subject for late-Victorian musicals, which propagated a mythology that a working girl could better her position in life by taking work in a department store, where she could meet a better class of men and, presumably, accept a proposal of marriage from a man who would then be able to "free her" from her shop labor. Erika Diane Rappaport discusses the genre of shopgirl musicals, enormously popular in the 1890s and 1910s, in which "the shop girl never remains a worker. . . . At some point in the play she usually changes places with an upper-class shopper" through marriage or unexpected inheritance.[34] In Cicely Hamilton's comic play *Diana of Dobson's*, for example, the shopgirl Diana, who "wasn't brought up to earn her own living," unexpectedly inherits three hundred pounds, travels to the Alps disguised as a rich widow because "[y]ou're ever so much freer when you're married," receives several proposals from gentlemen, and after several twists and turns of the plot, engages to marry one of them.[35] These stories of marital success were, of course, in tension with the supposed moral dangers of the shopgirl's work conditions, and some contemporary periodical articles are forthright in rejecting this fantasy of social ascension, presenting the fantasy itself as another danger of the trade. An essay of 1890 recounts the downfall of a shopgirl who is deceived by dishonorable attention from a gentleman's son, attributing her susceptibility to how "romance of this very kind was the typical legend of the order to which she belonged, the one wild hope shot across its grey reality: though . . . to what dismal swamps it may lead."[36] Levy includes both the romance of social ascension with Gertrude's marriage and the threat of a tragic fall with Phyllis's fate.

If the novel's closure contains ironic reference to popular formulations of shopgirls' marital ambitions, it is also more affirmative of women's public involvement in artistic and professional circles than is usually recognized. Rather than halting all nondomestic work with marriage, and especially with children, Levy imagines an alternative. After Lucy's marriage, we are told, she "is going to carry on the [photography] business" in a new location where there will be "studios for both" her and her artist husband (187). And in the novel's epilogue, we learn that though she has two children, "photography . . . has not been crowded out by domestic duties." In fact, she has "succumbed to the modern practice of specializing, and only the other day carried off a medal for photographs of young children from an industrial exhibition" (193). Though the modernity of Lucy's specialization is perhaps tempered by its maternal component, her technical and artistic abilities are confirmed by her success in competition with others in the industry, as well as by her equal stature with her husband.

The novel's epilogue also suggests that 20B Upper Baker Street continues to be a space of opportunity for women when the narrator reveals that "[t]he Photographic Studio is let to an enterprising young photographer, who has enlarged and beautified it beyond recognition." The gender of this young photographer is left ambiguous, but the studio's beautification implies a feminine occupant. This suggestion of continuity is both troubled by and amplified with the nostalgic last sentence: "As for the rooms . . . : the sitting-room facing the street; the three-cornered kitchen behind; the three little bed-rooms beyond;— when last I passed the house they were to let unfurnished, with great fly-blown bills in the blank casements" (194). The narrator's intrusion in the first person is rare in the novel, and its deliberate insertion here does more than enhance its reality effect, the belief that this is a true story of which the narrator has first-hand knowledge. In this concluding sentence, the reader is invited to participate in a nostalgic practice of looking back and also to continue the story. With a thriving studio below, the rooms' blank casements invite new tenants, suggesting that there is space available in London for enterprising young women.

Throughout the novel, Levy insists on the respectability of women's commercial pursuits. Unlike contemporary representations of the lives of shopgirls, in Levy's work the young women are given skills and financial resources that they can turn to professional use so that they are able to own their business and to live together in lodgings of their own. It is especially remarkable that Levy chose to make her characters practitioners of a skilled profession. While women did own their own businesses in 1880s London, including their own photography studios,[37] the few literary representations that allow the shopgirl to graduate to shop owner generally conclude the story with that transformation. And as with Wotton's "Hour of Her Life" and Shaw's *Pygmalion*, female shop owners are generally restricted to the more feminine commodity of flowers, which would also seem to require little professional training. In contrast, the Lorimer sisters increase their technical knowledge of photography through the study of books in the British Museum Reading Room and apprenticeship at an established studio. As we have seen, the sisters further demonstrate their status as artists as well as businesswomen by mingling the products of their work with the work of well-known painters in the halls of their business.

Levy has her protagonists insist on and earn respect, as women, artists, and professional workers. Gertrude, for example, refuses interviews with columnists interested in lady photographers because she wants herself and her sisters to be respected as photographers, not patronized as "mountebanks." Such a label, with its suggestions of public performance, self-degradation, and charlatanism, would be an affront to the sisters' careful shaping of their public image, as female professionals who have maintained a feminine domesticity and as producers of images, not spectacles themselves. But Levy also reveals how insistence on respect can be difficult in the face of social prejudices and the realities of the marketplace, so that the sisters can only be grateful for the extra business when "some unauthorised person wrote a little account of the Lorimers' studio in one of the society papers, of which, if the taste was questionable, the results were not to be questioned at all." The sisters' business thrives as "[p]eople who had theories about woman's work; people whose friends had theories; people who were curious and fond of novelty; individuals from each of these sections began to find their way to Upper Baker Street." Depicting the spectacle of women in business with a touch of mockery, Levy ironically adds that "it had got about in certain sets that all the sisters were extremely beautiful, and that Sidney Darrell was painting them in a group for next year's Academy, a *canard* certainly not to be deprecated from a business point of view" (135). Beneath the narrator's lighthearted tone, Levy depicts the serious tension between the sisters' self-representation as professional and respectable wielders of the camera lens and popular perceptions of them that would transform them into spectacles, to be seen either in person or in an artist's rendering.

In *The Romance of a Shop*, Levy draws on familiar discourses surrounding the figure of the shopgirl to assert that femininity, respectability, and business acumen can coexist and even facilitate each other. Making both a home and a business for themselves in the urban marketplace, the Lorimer sisters challenge popular and literary expectations for shopgirls and New Women. By manipulating the gaze of spectators and turning the lens outward, Levy's new public women negotiate their own representation to forge both independent and respectable London lives.

Notes

I would like to express my appreciation to the American Association of University Women, whose provision of a dissertation fellowship supported the research foundational to this chapter.

1. Deborah Epstein Nord, *Walking the Victorian Streets: Women, Representation and the City* (Ithaca, NY: Cornell University Press, 1995), 202; Linda Hunt Beckman, *Amy Levy: Her Life and Letters* (Athens: Ohio University Press, 2000), 158; Susan David Bernstein, introduction to *The Romance of a Shop*, by Amy Levy (Peterborough, ON: Broadview, 2006), 11–41.

2. Amy Levy, *The Romance of a Shop* (1888), ed. Susan David Bernstein (Peterborough, ON: Broadview, 2006), 72. Subsequent references to this edition appear parenthetically in the text.

3. Amy Bulley and Margaret Whitley judged that in England "the total number of both sexes in the retail trade is about one million, and about four-fifths of the assistants in the drapery trade are women. In other trades [such as the grocery trade] the proportion is not quite so high." Bulley and Whitley, *Women's Work* (London: Methuen, 1894), 49. M. Mostyn Bird estimated that "two million persons serve over the shop-counters of the UK, of which far more than half are women." Bird, *Woman at Work: A Study of the Different Ways of Earning a Living Open to Women* (London: Chapman and Hall, 1911), 62. Historian Lee Holcombe puts the number of female shop assistants in England in 1914 at nearly half a million (about half the total number of shop assistants) and "by far the largest group of middle-class women workers in the country." Holcombe, *Victorian Ladies at Work: Middle-Class Working Women in England and Wales, 1850–1914* (Hamden, CT: Archon Books, 1973), 103.

4. For a fascinating discussion of depictions of middle-class women shoppers and department stores' tactics of self-promotion, see Erika Diane Rappaport, *Shopping for Pleasure: Women in the Making of London's West End* (Princeton: Princeton University Press, 2000).

5. Judith R. Walkowitz, *City of Dreadful Delight: Narratives of Sexual Danger in Late-Victorian London* (London: Virago, 1992), 68.

6. While these metropolitan female types were related and had overlapping characteristics, they also differed in important ways. For example, unlike the discursive construction of the New Woman, new public women did not always proceed with what we might call a feminist agenda; they may even have been opposed to female suffrage. However, representations of women who took up new professional roles often invested them with the belief that they were entitled to keep the money they earned, thus indirectly endorsing changes in gender roles. And unlike prevalent constructions of the New Woman as educated and with a relatively privileged background, new public women could come from any class, though they often emerged from the upper-working, lower-middle, and middle classes. Their new occupation of public urban sites might have been motivated by necessity rather than, or as well as, by choice. Their public presence and the multiple

ways in which it might be experienced, both by themselves and by others, was the new public women's defining characteristic.

7. Sally Ledger, "Gissing, the Shopgirl and the New Woman," *Women: A Cultural Review* 6 (1995): 263–74.

8. Bird, *Woman at Work*, 65.

9. In *The Odd Women*, for example, the middle-class Monica Madden must share lodgings with other shop assistants. The libertine ways of some of the shopgirls, along with other pernicious influences of shop life, lead to Monica's deviation from the behavioral strictures she was raised with, as when she takes up with a man she meets in a park. For more on Gissing's ambivalent portrayal of the figure of the shopgirl, see my essay "'Counter-Jumpers' and 'Queens of the Street': The Shop Girl of Gissing and His Contemporaries," in *Gissing and the City: Cultural Crisis and the Making of Books in Late-Victorian England*, ed. John Spiers (London: Palgrave Macmillan, 2005), 109–17.

10. Anonymous, "Sympathy with Shop-Girls [By One of Them]," *Chambers's Journal of Popular Literature, Science and Arts* 65 (1888): 351–52, quotation on 351.

11. Inordinate time standing, insufficient time for inadequate meals, and unsanitary and crowded living environs were also concerns.

12. Holcombe, *Victorian Ladies at Work*, 117.

13. For more on the lives and work of female shop assistants in this period, see Holcombe, *Victorian Ladies at Work* and Lise Shapiro Sanders, *Consuming Fantasies: Labor, Leisure, and the London Shopgirl, 1880–1920* (Columbus: Ohio State University Press, 2006). Sanders also analyzes contemporary constructions of "the shopgirl," focusing especially on her importance as both subject and audience of a range of popular forms of entertainment. Sanders's study is impressive overall but inconsistent in its claims for the shopgirl, finding her at times a unique discursive construction and at other times a figure representative of all working women in public urban space, an inconsistency that itself illustrates the multifaceted and sometimes contradictory identity of "the shopgirl."

14. Clementina Black, "The Grievances of Barmaids," *Woman's World* 3 (May 1890): 383–85.

15. Clementina Black, *Sweated Industry and the Minimum Wage* (London: Duckworth, 1907). Black also worked politically for employment reform at the Women's Trade Union Provident League. Bernstein notes that a brief review of Levy's last novel, *Miss Meredith*, "relates that profits from Levy's posthumous publications were to be applied to the 'philanthropic work of Miss Clementina Black'" (26).

16. For a discussion and an accompanying map of important locations for women in the West End in the last half of the nineteenth century, see Lynne Walker, "Vistas of Pleasure: Women Consumers of Urban Space, 1850–1900," in *Women in the Victorian Art World*, ed. Clarissa Campbell Orr (Manchester: Manchester University Press, 1995), 70–85. The address of the sisters' shop and home also recalls 221B Baker Street, the residence of Arthur Conan Doyle's Sherlock Holmes and Dr. Watson, first named in *A Study in Scarlet* (1887).

17. Walkowitz, *City of Dreadful Delight*, 46.

18. Peter Bailey, "Parasexuality and Glamour: The Victorian Barmaid as Cultural Prototype," *Gender and History* 2 (1990): 148–72 (quotations on 148 and 167).

19. Mabel E. Wotton, "The Hour of Her Life," in *A New Woman Reader: Fiction, Articles, and Drama of the 1890s*, ed. Carolyn Christensen Nelson (Peterborough, ON: Broadview Press, 2001), 101. Subsequent references to this story appear parenthetically in the text.

20. Ibid., 106. Wotton seems to take for granted her reader's familiarity with "Mahomet's coffin" as an expression for the sensation of being pulled equally in two directions, so that one is suspended in midair without support. In Victor Hugo's *Notre-Dame de Paris* (1831), the beginning of part 2, chapter 4 (titled "The Inconveniences of Following a Pretty Woman Through the Streets at Night") finds Gringoire "fond of comparing himself to the tomb of Mahomet, attracted in opposite directions by two lodestones, and eternally hesitating between the high and the low, between the vault and the pavement, between fall and ascent, between zenith and nadir" (168). This passage as a whole suggests the imaginative possibilities of *flânerie* and, especially with the drama that follows, women's vulnerability in public urban space: "Gringoire, a practical philosopher of the streets of Paris, had noticed that nothing is more propitious to reverie than following a pretty woman without knowing where she is going. There was in this voluntary abdication of his freewill, in this fancy submitting itself to another fancy, which suspects it not, a mixture of fantastic independence and blind obedience, something indescribable, intermediate between slavery and liberty, which pleased Gringoire" (167–68) (my translation from Victor Hugo, *Notre-Dame de Paris* [Paris: Eugène Renduel, 1836]).

21. Levy's choice to describe 20B Upper Baker Street through a "tour" rather than a "map" (to use Michel de Certeau's terminology) includes the reader in the sisters' discovery. De Certeau, *The Practice of Everyday Life*, trans. Steven Rendall (Berkeley: University of California Press, 1984), 121.

22. This is an ambivalence that Burgin notes "marks the representational space of modernism in general." Victor Burgin, "The City in Pieces," *New Formations* 20 (1993): 37. Levy's use of the window provides further evidence for the view that literary modernism has its precursors in the late nineteenth century with New Women writers, as Ann Ardis persuasively argues in *New Women, New Novels: Feminism and Early Modernism* (New Brunswick, NJ: Rutgers University Press, 1990).

23. The poem opens *A London Plane-Tree and Other Verse*, published posthumously in 1889. It is reprinted in *The Complete Novels and Selected Writings of Amy Levy, 1861–1889*, ed. Melvyn New (Gainesville: University Press of Florida, 1993), 385.

24. Ana Parejo Vadillo, *Women Poets and Urban Aestheticism: Passengers of Modernity* (Basingstoke, UK: Palgrave Macmillan, 2005), 54.

25. Amy Levy, "Eldorado at Islington," *Woman's World* 2 (1889): 488–89. The next number of this magazine appeared after Levy's suicide on 10 September 1889 and includes a tribute to and obituary of Levy written by Oscar Wilde (*Woman's World* 3 [November 1889]: 51–52), reprinted in an appendix of the Broadview edition of *The Romance of a Shop* (ed. Bernstein).

26. For a concise history of the development of mass transport and its effects on late-Victorian women's participation in urban life, see Vadillo, *Women Poets*. Vadillo argues

that the new public transport system provided Levy and three other London-based women poets a means with which to develop a distinct urban aestheticism that uses the figure of the urban passenger as an emblem of the modern poet. With her focus on lyric, Vadillo does not examine *Romance* except to note its references to public transport.

27. Mrs. Humphry, *Manners for Women* (London: Ward, Lock and Co., 1897), 18–19.

28. Harassment was a real concern for women in the city, as evidenced by personal testimony and published advice about where and how to walk safely, but concerns about safety were also used to curtail women's movements. See Walkowitz, *City of Dreadful Delight* and "Going Public: Shopping, Street Harassment, and Streetwalking in Late Victorian London," *Representations* 62 (Spring 1998): 1–30.

29. Gertrude "saves" her in the nick of time and takes her home through a snow-storm. The text is ambiguous about Gertrude's decision to take her from the seducer's house, no matter the consequences to her sister's physical health. Contrary to other commentators on this novel, I do not believe that Levy's portrayal of Gertrude is purely affirmative. Gertrude's myopia, for instance, indicates that her perception or judgment is not always accurate.

30. From the novel's start, Phyllis is associated with aestheticism and decadence, in contrast to her sisters' more pragmatic sense of social forms and obligations, leading Gertrude to cry on one occasion, "Phyllis, will you never learn where to draw the line?" (*Romance*, 141). While Phyllis's seduction by an unscrupulous married gentleman draws on a Victorian stock plot, Phyllis is unlike other late-nineteenth-century fallen women, such as Thomas Hardy's title character Tess, in that she participates willingly and with full knowledge that her seducer is married. As Bernstein argues, "Levy challenges the typical fallen woman of Victorian fiction by refusing to frame her character as either innocent female victim or knowing temptress" (40).

31. For example, Nord claims that Levy "does not know what to do with her independent, idiosyncratic heroines . . . and resorts to killing off the beautiful, 'fallen' sister and marrying off the remaining ones" (*Walking the Victorian Streets*, 202). Melvyn New agrees, though he argues that this closure is not so much a novelistic weakness as a reasonable recognition of "proletarian" reality (*Complete Novels*, 26). To Nord's complaint that the last third of the novel resembles "a shoddy *Pride and Prejudice*" (202), Beckman counters with the faint praise that Levy was not attempting to be original, only amusing and appealing to a popular audience (154). Deborah L. Parsons similarly finds that "Levy backs down from the implied female radicalism by concluding the girls' stories with the conventional endings of marriage or fall and death." Parsons, *Streetwalking the Metropolis: Women, the City and Modernity* (Oxford: Oxford University Press, 2000), 93.

32. Periodical articles exhibit a preoccupation with this domestic suitability. One commentator worries, "What woman, after this environment, would know how to make a home pleasant?" O. M. E. Rowe, "London Shop-Girls," *Outlook* (February 1896): 397–98, quotation on 397. According to another, many shopgirls "make good marriages . . . and they must find the habits of patience, good temper, courtesy, and self-control learnt by them in business serve them in good stead in their after married life." M. A. Belloc, "The Shop-Girl," *The Idler* (August 1895): 12–17, quotation on 16.

33. Anonymous, "Sympathy with Shop-Girls," 351.

34. Rappaport, *Shopping for Pleasure*, 198. Rappaport clarifies that this was not a radical social inversion, because the denouement almost always revealed that the shopgirl was not actually born into the lower orders; her marriage "restored her to her rightful place among her class" (194). Rappaport's chapter 6, "Acts of Consumption: Musical Comedy and the Desire of Exchange," examines the history of these musical comedies, which were inspired by "the unstable and fluid quality of class and gender identity" and "commodified and, in a sense, enjoyed" the "anxieties associated with mass consumer culture" (178–80). For a focus on the shopgirl as consumer of these popular productions, see also chapter 5, "Distracted Pleasures: Gender, Leisure, and Consuming in Public" (esp. 178–82), in Sanders, *Consuming Fantasies.*

35. Cicely Hamilton, *Diana of Dobson's: A Romantic Comedy in Four Acts* (1908), ed. Diane F. Gillespie and Doryjane Birrer (Toronto: Broadview, 2003), 77, 89.

36. Anonymous, "The Case of Amy Parker," *Leisure Hour* (November 1890): 55–60, quotation on 57.

37. Michael Pritchard's *Directory of London Photographers, 1841–1908* (Bushey: ALLM Books, 1986) includes several studios owned by women, though most of these proprietors, titled "Mrs.," are either married or widowed or are perhaps claiming the relative social freedom of that title.

Why Wasn't Amy Levy
More of a Socialist?

levy, clementina black,
and liza of lambeth

Emma Francis

$\mathcal{T}$HE dramatic resurgence of interest in Amy Levy over recent years has been characterized by a strong, sometimes explicitly personalized, political identification. Given the context within which, for feminists, such celebratory investment has become increasingly difficult, as a Jewish intellectual, as a sexual dissident, as an archetypal "New Woman," as the possessor of a strong and culturally pivotal poetic identity, Levy seems to offer contemporary British and American feminist criticism an image of many of the things it would still like to find valuable in itself.[1] As Linda Hunt Beckman points out in the prologue to *Amy Levy: Her Life and Letters,* there has been something of a slippage from this into the assumption that Levy was also a socialist, or at least a social liberal who had direct engagement with reformist or radical social movements. Beckman's study disabuses us of the error promulgated by Edward Wagenknecht in 1983 (and reproduced in Levy's recovery by feminist scholars in the subsequent decade) that Levy was the secretary of the charitable foundation the Beaumont Trust, assisting the president, Lewis Levy (whom Wagenknecht assumes is Levy's father), in raising funds to build a People's Palace in East London. In fact, as Beckman demonstrates, they were quite different Lewis and A. Levys.[2]

If Wagenknecht enchanted himself with an image of Levy as a liberal philanthropist, then Warwick James Price earlier in the twentieth century went even further, to produce a fantasy of Levy as bona fide working class. A misunderstanding of the significance of Levy's urban poems, a lack of awareness of their stake in debates of the 1880s about the presence of middle-class women in the metropolis (and perhaps a lack of knowledge that Clapham, South London, where the Levys lived until 1876, was at that time, if not four decades later, a place where a middle-class family with some pretensions to respectability might have their principal residence) would seem to explain his insistence that Levy was a factory worker: "One wonders how this Clapham Factory girl, small, slight, weak, ever stood beneath London's endless sea of roofs [*sic*]. . . . [S]he lived in her thoughts, she read voraciously. . . . Her life had fallen to her amid vulgar surroundings and within her beat the heart of a super-sensitive woman and poetess."[3] Price gives no evidence for this thesis at any point during his sentimental meditation on Levy's supposed material and emotional deprivation in the "narrow streets and dirty alleys of Clapham," and there is nothing in the scholarship or manuscript materials that have emerged subsequently to support it. After her studies at Cambridge, Levy departed for a postcollege "finishing" trip to the Continent. Beckman reproduces a letter written to her mother from Dresden in November 1881 in which Levy expresses some anxiety about the financial support she is receiving from her family and reports her success in recruiting pupils, whose tuition fees she plans to use to fund her studies.

> I have some new pupils—two boys (15 & 16) for English, but don't begin with them till after next week. They will bring in 3/ a week, so I shall be earning 5/ a week. I am also reading Greek with a Cambridge man here, to whom Mr. Gilderdale (the English clergyman) recommended me. I don't know how much it will be—he wanted to do it for nothing, but of course I didn't want that, & he said we wd. settle it afterwards. I will ask him about it next time, & only hope it isn't too much: if it is, I won't go on long. . . . Please thank Papa for his letter wh. I will answer soon; I am

glad to see fr. the magnificent way in wh. he talks that he has at last struck oil! But, you know that I can't feel very happy about myself & the money I spend, in spite of all his kindness.[4]

It seems, then, that that the family may have experienced a measure of financial difficulty, but the situation was certainly not so severe as to compel Levy to fit in her writing between shifts at the factory. Indeed, concern for their daughter's reputation and respectability clearly predominated over any other parental worries. Levy's next letter to her mother, dated five days later, evidences that her parents have dissuaded her from taking on the two teenaged pupils: "You will see fr. my letter to Papa that I have given up the idea of teaching those boys, though I can't see the matter from your point of view. . . . I regret to say that I am as safe as Grandmama could be; there wouldn't be any impropriety (excepting from an outside point of view) in my teaching any number of young men."[5]

Not in factual error, but in creative license, this insertion of Levy into a fantasy of working-class life is, of course, also the move made by Israel Zangwill in *Children of the Ghetto* (1892). In book 2 of the novel, Zangwill's heroine, Esther Ansell—by then adopted by wealthy Kensington patrons, university educated, atheistical, and militant—is revealed as the author of *Mordecai Josephs,* a novel depicting the corruptions of middle-class Anglo-Jewry, which is scandalizing Zangwill's Kensington Jewish elites. This is very obviously modelled on Levy's *Reuben Sachs* and the controversy it created, a reference that would have been abundantly clear to Zangwill's readers at the end of the nineteenth century. But Zangwill imagines a beginning for Esther that is very different from Levy's. As a little girl, she also carries the burden of Zangwill's narrative at its start, as the original child of the ghetto. In the opening paragraphs of the novel, Esther runs the gauntlet of the full cast of outcast London, through the wintry streets of the East End, on her way to the soup kitchen, to collect her destitute family's "bread of affliction."

> A dead and gone wag called the street "Fashion Street," and most of the people who live in it do not even see the joke. If it could exchange names with "Rotten Row," both places would be more appropriately designated. It is a dull, squalid, narrow thoroughfare in the East End of London, connecting Spitalfields with Whitechapel, and branching off its blind alleys. In the days when little Esther Ansell trudged its unclean pavements, its extremities were within earshot of the blasphemies from some of the vilest quarters and filthiest rookeries in the capital of the civilized world. Some of these clotted spiders'-webs have since been swept away by

the besom of the social reformer, and the spiders have scurried off into darker crannies.

There were the conventional touches about the London street-picture, as Esther Ansell sped through the freezing mist of the December evening, with a pitcher in her hand, looking in her oriental coloring like a miniature of Rebecca going to the well. A female street-singer, with a trail of infants of dubious maternity, troubled the air with a piercing melody; a pair of slatterns with arms a-kimbo reviled each other's relatives; a drunkard lurched along, babbling amiably; an organ-grinder, blue-nosed as his monkey, set some ragged children jigging under the watery rays of a street-lamp. Esther drew her little plaid shawl tightly around her, and ran on without heeding these familiar details, her chilled feet absorbing the damp of the murky pavement through the worn soles of her cumbrous boots.[6]

Zangwill's depiction clearly had a role in producing some of the confusion about Levy's class status during the early parts of the twentieth century, but perhaps some of her commentators have fallen under the spell of these fantasies of a direct connection of Levy with working-class life because she was located geographically, socially, and in some respects intellectually at one of the most significant interfaces between socialism and feminism in British history. Carolyn Steedman has pointed to the crucial importance of the "fictional and real square mile of Bloomsbury," during the 1880s and 1890s. Intellectually and politically vibrant with "bright glittering ideas spoken in dim rooms,"[7] it included Endsleigh Gardens, where the Levy family lived during the later 1880s.[8]

> [W]e must lay a fictional grid of one square mile, south of Euston Station. It is the square mile in which, in historical and topographical time, Eleanor Marx and Margaret MacMillan lived and wrote, and from which they journeyed out: to the East End, to the dock gates during the Great Dock Strike of 1889, to a thousand provincial union and socialist meetings. . . . In these streets, in its meeting rooms and societies, the campaign for the Eight Hour Day was organized, and that extraordinary series of meetings in Hyde Park in May 1890, when Marx said that she heard "for the first time since 40 years, the unmistakable voice of the English proletariat."[9]

In the right place at the right time, Levy also knew a not-insignificant number of the right people—and knew them very well. The socialist feminist Eleanor Marx was a good friend. Marx translated *Reuben Sachs* into German and worked alongside Levy in the British Library, which also lay within the magic mile.[10]

Olive Schreiner was, by her own account, in the later 1880s, during the period of her intense friendship with Levy, completing a section of the first, lost, manuscript of *Woman and Labour*.[11] This complex, sometimes chaotic work is Schreiner's attempt to imagine a materialist feminism, to understand and to theorize the conditions for the transformation of women's relationship with work and for women's economic and political self-determination. In her introduction to the text, Schreiner identifies its germinal inspiration as a conversation she had at the age of eighteen, in South Africa, with a "Kafir woman still in her untouched primitive condition." Schreiner's encounter with the testimony of this "person of genius" revealed to her the sobering truth of women's relationship with revolutionary social change, that "the women of no race or class will ever rise in revolt or attempt to bring about a revolutionary adjustment of their relation to society, however intense their suffering and however clear their perception of it, while the welfare and persistence of their society requires submission."[12]

Deborah Epstein Nord's essay of 1990, "'Neither Pairs Nor Odd': Female Community in Late Nineteenth-Century London," which takes its title from one of Levy's poems, describes the work of two of Levy's other associates, Beatrice Webb (then Potter) and Webb's cousin and sometime flatmate Margaret Harkness. Both were involved with social housing projects in the East End of London, experiences that fed into their later writing about working-class life— Webb's works of social investigation and Harkness's novels. Nord argues that Levy, Webb, and Harkness should be understood together as a group of "single women in London . . . who resisted rigid notions of sexual difference and rejected the idea that women's public work need be an extension of domestic virtues and talents. . . . They understood their own marginality . . . as a product of their socialist politics."[13]

However, Webb, for one, would have been uncomfortable with this political grouping. In her autobiography, *My Apprenticeship*, Webb looks back at the diary notes she wrote during the strange and difficult months of August and September 1889. While beginning to mourn for her father, who was slipping slowly away to an undignified death, she became obsessed by reporting on the London dock strikes. Confused, but also inspired and excited by the release of revolutionary energy she sees, she feels the growth of her political conversion: "I watch myself falling back for encouragement on a growing faith in the possibility of reorganising society by the application of the scientific method directed by the religious spirit."[14] Webb draws a contrast between the route out of her personal grief made possible by identification with working-class struggle and what she sees as the political and moral bankruptcy of suicide, the solution Levy found to her emotional turmoil in September 1889. Webb repudiates Levy's lack of socialist vision as much as her atheism:

> We talk of courage to meet death; alas in these terrible days . . . it is the courage to *live* that we most lack, not courage to die. . . . Poor Amy Levy! If there be no other faith for humanity but to eat, drink and be merry for tomorrow we die, she has done well and wisely in choosing death. . . . But if this be only a passage to other things, a pilgrimage among other pilgrims whom we may help and cheer on the way then a brave and struggling life, a life in which suffering measures progress, has the deepest meaning—in truth embraces the whole and the sole reason for human existence.[15]

In this chapter, I too ponder Levy's relationship with this political moment and resist the tendency to elide Levy's social politics with those of the socialists who were her friends; instead, I wish to throw into relief the dimensions of her absence and difference from them.

To do this, I consider Levy's relationship with another of the "right people" —Clementina Black. Black is a much less well-known figure than the others I have mentioned, but she was closer to Levy than any of them, apparently being Levy's closest friend during her adult life and, as becomes evident from the correspondence reproduced in Beckman's study, a significant mentor. Black was reading Levy's work and actively promoting her career from at least the late 1870s. The older sister of Constance Black (afterward Garnett), with whom Levy went to school, she was the dedicatee of *A London Plane-Tree and Other Verse*, Levy's final collection of poetry of 1889, and the person to whom Levy bequeathed all her letters, manuscripts, and copyrights. It seems to me extraordinary that Black has so far largely escaped the kind of meticulous recuperative attention paid over the past decade or so to the socialist feminists and feminist social reformers of the late nineteenth and early twentieth centuries. The range of her extensive work, from the 1870s until her death in 1922—as a novelist, poet, biographer, social investigator, social reformer, art critic, suffrage campaigner, and trade union activist at the forefront of the campaign to unionize women workers—is far beyond the scope of this essay. However, after very sparse treatment during the twentieth century, at least one recent study has included discussion of Black's relation to aesthetic and political debates of the period.[16]

If for no other reason, Black deserves her place in the socialist feminist hall of fame for her pivotal role in the match girls' strike of 1888. It was her attendance at Black's lecture on female labor, given to the Fabian Society on 15 June of that year, which first alerted Annie Besant to the scandal of the exploitation of the women at the Bryant and May Factory. The following day, Besant visited the factory to see for herself what was going on. On 23 June, she wrote up the testimony of the women who had spoken to her about their hazardous working conditions and poor pay in an article in her radical newspaper the *Link*, under the headline "White Slavery in London." This, of course, led quickly to the attempts of the Bryant and May management to compel the workers to sign a repudiation of Besant's piece, the sacking of the alleged ringleader of those who refused, and, in retaliation, by July 1888, the mass strike of around fourteen hundred match workers.[17] Black became involved with the strike after it was under way, with the raising of funds to provide strike pay, with the creation of a consumer protest movement—encouraging people to boycott Bryant and May's matches until the factory cleaned up its act—and with the process of formal unionization of the strikers. She had been elected secretary of the Woman's Provident and Protective League (or WPPL, founded by Emma Ann Paterson in 1874 and subsequently renamed the Women's Trade Union League) in 1887, and in this capacity she advised on the legal and financial detail of the creation of the Match Workers' Union.[18]

Black lacks the glamour of some of the other socialist feminists of the period. The portrait of her that emerges from her writings and from the testimony of her commentators places her largely at the organizational and bureaucratic end of things, rather than, like Marx or Besant, in a more theatrical, romantic role, delivering inspirational speeches to massed rallies or leading delegations of workers to lobby Parliament. Although Black apparently knew Eleanor Marx and some of Marx's family well (and Liselotte Glage, Black's twentieth-century biographer, regards this association as crucial to Black's political awakening), this did not prevent Marx, in a somewhat overheated moment typecasting Black as a mere bourgeois philanthropist, from commenting disdainfully that Black had "never done a day's manual labour."[19] Black was a pragmatist rather than an ideologue, a utopian rather than a scientific socialist; the precise complexion of her politics is difficult to pin down. Although she did engage with the Fabians (and her sister Constance was on their executive committee), she never joined them: "family tradition has it that . . . Clementina not only abhorred the idea of State Socialism developed by the Webbs but also personally detested the Potter sisters."[20] Her private life has left few traces. She never married and apparently did not go in for the kind of dramatic, doomed affairs with charismatic and unsuitable men that enliven the biographies of Schreiner, Marx, and Besant. As yet, no records have emerged of romantic relationships with women, unsuitable or otherwise. The servantless flat she shared with her sister Grace in London during the 1880s gives off a conventual rather than Bohemian air.[21] Her most important domestic relationship as an adult seems to have been with her niece, Speedwell, whom Black adopted at the age of five, in 1891, following the suicides of her brother and sister-in-law.[22] There is also the problem that her fictional writings, with one exception (which I discuss below), are not about working-class struggle. They are romances, focusing on middle-class characters, mostly set in picturesque rural locations, which today read as sentimental and largely unremarkable. They form a curious contrast with the relentless schedule of her social reform and trade union work, as well as with the sharp analytic intelligence she displays within her social investigative writings. Glage argues that she wrote them as a form of escapism, to give herself a break from the squalor and misery she was confronted with daily as she visited the homes and workplaces of the impoverished East End.[23]

Despite the frustration that arises from Black's failure to write quite the kind of novels one might have wished her to, I would argue that she should be reconsidered as an important figure in late-nineteenth-century socialist feminism precisely in terms of her writing, as well as for her social and political achievements. She did something significant in the history of working-class fiction—the fiction of working-class life—particularly in relation to the depiction of working-class women. Not within her novels and stories but within her social investigative writings, there appears a brief but significant portrait of the woman worker, which does something highly unusual for the turn of the twentieth century. Such depictions are snapshots rather than extended studies, and perhaps it is significant that they are not situated within novels and so are not required to bear a narrative burden; but I suggest that Black goes further toward imagining a full, autonomous, and dignified subjectivity for the working-class woman, as both woman and worker, than many writers were able to do at this time, either inside or outside the novel. It is this portrait that shows up the contrast between her perspective and Levy's most sharply.

Levy's friendship with Black meant that she was in close contact with the unfolding of the events of the match girls' strike and with the broader movement for the unionization of women workers that drew energy from it. Levy by no means shut her eyes to Black's trade union and socialist activity; indeed, with the relentless schedule of meetings, travel, and investigative visiting with which Black packed her days, Levy would have been hard-pressed to ignore this aspect of her friend's work.[24] Beckman provides proof that Levy was proud of Black's appointment as secretary of the WPPL in 1887 and that by 1889 Levy was helping out, apparently with some regularity, in the office of the league, which was located in Bloomsbury, in convenient proximity to her home in Endsleigh Gardens.[25]

This proximity, however, had no impact on her writing. Nord is right to place Levy within debates about women's changing roles and experiences within the city, but, unlike Harkness and Webb, the preoccupation of Levy's prose of the later 1880s is solely with middle-class women. In an essay of 1888, "Women and Club Life," published in Oscar Wilde's magazine *The Woman's World*, Levy explores the new social and professional relationships that were developing between mostly university-educated middle-class women in London at that time. Invoking a language of socioeconomic inevitability, Levy argues that financial exigency was compelling middle-class women to refuse traditional dependent roles and instead seek entry into the workplace.

> I am considering things as they are, not as they might be. We are in England, not in Utopia; it is the nineteenth century, and not the Golden Age; the land is not flowing with milk and honey; those commodities can only be obtained by strenuous and competitive effort.
>
> It is not for me to rejoice over, or to deplore, the complete and rapid change of the female position which has taken place in this country during the last few years. It is a phenomenon for our observation rather than an accident for our intervention; the result of complex and manifold circumstances over which none of us can be thought to have much control. The tide has set in and there is no stemming it.
>
> It is not without regret that one sees the old order changing and giving place to new in this respect. The woman who owns no interests beyond the circle of home, who takes no thought for herself, who is content to follow where love and superior wisdom are leading—this ideal of feminine excellence is not, indeed, to be relinquished without a sigh.
>
> But she is, alas! Too expensive a luxury for our civilisation; we cannot afford her.[26]

Levy stresses that these changes were giving rise to the need for women to set up the kind of social networks conducive to the fostering of professional relationships that men had always used. She sees the mixed-gender and all-female clubs that had been opening in London beginning in the early 1880s as "the natural outcome of the spirit of an age which demands excellence in work from women no less than from men, and as one of the many steps toward the attainment of that excellence."[27]

This emphasis on the economy as the crucial motor of social change and of London as the location of middle-class women's entrepreneurial opportunity is explored further in Levy's first published novel, *The Romance of a Shop* (1888). The story opens just after the death of the father of the four Lorimer sisters. They discover that he has made no financial provision for them and are faced with the prospect of being separated, to live with different sets of relatives. Refusing these offers and realizing that their lack of qualifications makes the procurement of good situations as governesses unlikely, they decide instead to try to earn their livings by turning a hobby in which the three youngest sisters (Gertrude, Lucy, and Phyllis) have become skilled—photography—to financial account. Initially, the eldest, Fanny, is horrified at the prospect of an entry into "trade" and the abandonment of respectable bourgeois idleness (her response is ironic, since the novel makes clear that at thirty years old, with her last, failed, romantic entanglement a decade in the past, her thickening figure and "coarse red" complexion, she is the most definitively past her sell-by date within the marriage market).[28] But the others embrace the challenge enthusiastically.

> "O, Gertrude, need it come to that—to open a shop?" cried Fanny aghast.
> "Fanny, you are behind the age," said Lucy, hastily. "Don't you know that it is quite distinguished to keep a shop? That poets sell wall-papers, and first-class honour men sell lamps? That Girton students make bonnets, and are thought none the worse of for doing so?" (54–55)

Levy's novel represents the move away from the conventional life of the late-nineteenth-century middle-class woman not as a regrettable loss of status and as thrusting them into inevitable social and economic peril (as is the fate of the Madden sisters, who find themselves in a similar predicament in George Gissing's *The Odd Women*, published seven years after Levy's novel)[29] but as an exciting opportunity and, most of all—the word is repeated continually—"modern." Gertrude rhapsodizes: "Think of all the dull little ways by which women, ladies, are generally reduced to earning their living! But a business—that is so different. It is progressive; a creature capable of growth; the very qualities in which women's work is dreadfully lacking" (55).

To some extent, this optimism proves not to be misplaced. The Lorimers travel to London and open a photographic studio in Baker Street, with Fanny housekeeping and worrying over the unchaperoned meetings with male clients that her sisters' work involves, while the others work hard to build their business and its reputation. The novel explores the new kind of social life that the Lorimers' independence makes possible. The younger sisters come increasingly to regard themselves as fortunate to have been forced into this new life, as it means that they can choose their friends on the basis of "affinity" and are no longer forced into relationships merely because of "juxtaposition" (135). Gertrude argues that the ideal society is one "not of class, caste or family—but of picked individuals" (115). She defends their liberated social outlook to their aunt Caroline:

> We are poor people, and we are learning to find out the pleasures of the poor, to approach happiness from another side. We have none of the conventional social opportunities for instance, but are we therefore to sacrifice all social enjoyment? You say we "follow Mr. Jermyn to his studio"; we have our living to earn, no less than our lives to live, and in neither case can we afford to be the slaves of custom. . . . [A]re not judgment and self-respect what we most of us do rely on in our relations with people, under any circumstances whatever? (101)

Frank Jermyn, an artist living in the house opposite, has hired the Lorimers to produce a photographic record of his work. He falls in love with Lucy and bestirs himself to improve his financial situation so that he can marry her. To ram home her point that economic and social self-determination is the route to happiness for the middle-class woman, Levy provides the foil of the Lorimers' friend Conny, left at home, continuing her life of conspicuous leisure. Conny has been in love with Frank. She cries on Gertrude's shoulder when she realizes that she has lost him to Lucy: "We rich girls always end up with sneaks—no decent person comes near us" (132).

However, the dangers to which this liberty exposes women are explored through the study of the youngest sister, Phyllis. Always less focused on the business than Gertrude and Lucy, she becomes entangled with another artist, Sidney Darrell, whom she knows to be married. Significantly, they form a relationship not through his contracting of Phyllis's professional services but because they meet socially. He becomes aesthetically obsessed by her—she is the most beautiful of the sisters—and persuades her to model for him. In an oddly melodramatic episode that contrasts with the brisk, pared-down style of the rest of the novel, Gertrude, who has been suspicious of Darrell from the start, receives a letter from Phyllis telling her that she is eloping, and Gertrude rushes out to rescue her sister from Darrell's St. John's Wood house. The symbolism Levy invokes to describe what Gertrude finds there leaves no doubt that Phyllis has passed the Rubicon of virtue: "It was Phyllis who stood there by the little table, on which lay some fruit and some coffee, in rose-coloured cups. Phyllis, yet somebody new and strange; not the pretty child that her sisters had loved, but a beautiful wanton in a loose, trailing garment, shimmering, wonderful, white and lustrous as a pearl; Phyllis, with her brown hair turned to gold in the light of the lamp swung above her; Phyllis with diamonds on the slender fingers, that played with a cluster of bloom-covered grapes" (171). The incident proves to be such a shock to Phyllis's already fragile health—her glittering eyes and rasping chest have hinted throughout the novel at her developing consumption—that she dies shortly afterward. Levy is clear that Bohemianism on these proto-Pre-Raphaelite terms is catastrophic for women. The others make more successful endings, each marrying for love. Lucy continues her work as a photographer, joined by her husband, and Gertrude, marrying into the aristocracy, is able to return to her writing, which she had sacrificed in favor of the family business, gaining success in publication at last. Although Levy kills off Phyllis, she does not fully sustain the remorseless, bleak Darwinism that she goes on to develop in *Reuben Sachs* (likewise adopted by Gissing in *The Odd Women*) in the fate she gives to Fanny.[30] Fanny's erstwhile suitor returns, widowed, from the antipodes to plight his troth once more, and this time they make it down the aisle.

So Levy's vision is of economic self-determination for a cultural, middle-class female elite, which will allow for the formation of elective affinities and an escape from the coercions of the bourgeois marriage market, depicted most chillingly through the experience of Judith Quixano in *Reuben Sachs*. Clementina Black's vision, by contrast, extended to working-class experience and aspirations. She did take on, in some respects, the role that middle-class feminists such as Harkness and Webb developed for themselves among the urban poor during the late nineteenth century, focusing on the kinds of social housing and health projects pioneered by Octavia Hill. But Black is somewhat unusual in terms of her channelling of her activity through trade unionism to the extent that she did, and in her perhaps-consequent high level of awareness of the friction inherent in the encounter between working-class people seeking improvements in their lives and the middle-class socialists and philanthropists who sought to help the working class toward change on their own (middle-class) terms.

In Black's sole fictional treatment of working-class issues, *An Agitator,* published in 1894, this friction is evident. Its central study is of the resistance of the working-class hero, a trade union activist named Christopher Brand, to being bought off and politically compromised by middle-class pressure. Refusing offers of money and a powerful role within the Liberal party from the powerful local MP, Sir John Warwick (who, in a late twist of the plot, turns out to be his father), Brand travels to London to address the "Russell Square Socialist Society." Unflinchingly, the provincial activist castigates the "parlour socialists" of Bloomsbury:

> Think what it would mean to have your wife sitting up in her bed, finishing shirts and making match-boxes, before her baby was 24 hours old. . . . Think what it would mean to have *your* girls working in a laundry from six in the morning till nine at night for 3 farthings an hour. . . . Now you who sit here tonight, clean and well-dressed and with a good meal to go home to—are you doing the work that you profess to believe in? How many of you ladies are teaching the unorganised women workers to organise? And how many of you men are ready to denounce any and every politician or newspaper of whatever party, that systematically misrepresents or neglects these matters? On my conscience, as an honest man I believe and I am bound to say it, that you don't do these things. You talk, and you make neat epigrams, and you declaim against the capitalist. That's pretty easy and amusing, but it doesn't go far.[31]

Clearly, at least part of Black's target here are the Fabians (whom, as we have seen, rightly or wrongly, she considered to be overfond of esoteric theorizing). But this outburst is an interesting and curious moment within the structure of the novel for another reason. The focus of Brand's rhetoric here, on the plight of working women and girls, has not previously surfaced in the novel. Brand's agitational activities back at home have been wholly among male workers. The novel does not tell us how he came by this knowledge of the pay and working conditions of women workers—they are, in fact, as Lynne Hapgood points out, clearly drawn from Black's study "Women and Work," which appeared in the *New Review* in 1891.[32] Nor does Black provide any motivation in Brand's character to convince the reader that women workers were a burning concern for him before this point. It is an incongruous irruption of Black's agenda and rhetoric into a novel whose protagonist, despite the phonetic association of his name with that of his creator, follows a political trajectory quite different from the one she pursued.

Hapgood argues that this dislocation is an inevitable result of genre, that it was impossible within the conventions of the late-nineteenth-century novel to represent either a strong female protagonist as a working-class leader or substantial detail of working women's experience. Hapgood sees this as the result of the combination of women's general silencing and marginalization within socialist and Fabian circles and the co-option of realism as the favored genre of socialist reformist movements—the pressure on the writer being to reflect what were regarded as the "real" (that is, male-dominated) events. Hapgood argues that even women novelists such as Black found that "their political allegiances [did not] allow them as clear cut an option to investigate the public world by exploring its intersections with the private world of individual men and women, as, for instance, George Eliot does in mid-century in a novel like *Middlemarch*. Despite the fact that socialist groups were comprised of predominantly middle-class intellectuals, playing a significant part in the achievement of socialism meant being defined in the public arena as a worker or agitator and as male."[33] The research done on the important roles of women socialists of the later nineteenth century in the years since Hapgood published her essay (including that done by Hapgood herself) might be seen to place a question mark over the first part of this explanation.[34] But, certainly, a strong tradition within working-class fiction developed at the end of the nineteenth century, culminating in Robert Tressell's *The Ragged-Trousered Philanthropists* in the early twentieth century, in which women appear only in domestic roles, if at all.[35]

Perhaps because of this, it is within her social investigative writings that Black develops her most complex and heroic representation of working-class subjectivity, and working women and girls increasingly become the focus of her finest writing. In the same year that *An Agitator* came out, she published an essay coauthored with Stephen N. Fox, "The Truck Acts: What They Do and What They Ought to Do."[36] This early work is mostly a rather dry economic and social analysis of the consequences of what Black and Fox argue is a failure to fully implement the Truck Acts (the legislation intended to guarantee workers full financial remuneration for their labor and to prevent abuses such as compelling them to purchase tools or materials from their employers and subjecting them to compulsory deductions for membership of employer-controlled schemes of medical provision). But the essay is significant for the way in which it insists that a substantial part of the problem is caused by an overly narrow definition of the term *workman*, the category invoked by the Truck Acts. In this publication by the Women's Trade Union Association, Black and Fox do not belabor the issue of gender—indeed, many of the examples they give of workers who fall outside the protection of the acts are within predominantly male occupations. But there is a strong insistence, too, on the fact that the injustice affects many women workers, and Black and Fox dwell in detail on the parlous conditions of several groups, both home workers and factory workers. No distinction is made in their analysis of the evil effects of the failure to implement the acts on the basis of gender.

This assumption, of the equality of men's and women's labor and of the equal need to labor of men and women, is also axiomatic to Black's substantial sole-authored study of 1907, *Sweated Industry and the Minimum Wage.* In this text, the female worker becomes fully the emotional and structural center of the analysis. Black transcends the bald empiricism of her Truck Acts essay, or at least relegates it to the later section of the book, where she discusses in more theoretical terms why the establishment of a minimum wage for all workers will promote rather than jeopardize prosperity. In the first half of the book, she develops a powerful emotional identification with the workers who form her case studies. Male and child workers, home workers, factory workers, and street workers are given coverage, but it is the women workers whom Black focuses on most intently—in particular, the intersection of their work with their social, emotional, and family experiences at different stages of their lives. Significantly, Black is not writing a narrative of the negative impact of paid work on the family or maternal experience. Her most powerful portrait, presented with a kind of awe-filled humility and the disclaimer that Black feels herself inadequate to the representation of her subject, is of the young, yet-to-be-married woman worker—"The Factory Girl."

> I have not drawn the factory girl as I have known her and delighted in her, gay to "cheekiness," staunchly loyal, wonderfully uncomplaining, wonderfully ready to make allowances for "the governor" as long as he speaks her fair and shows consideration in trifles, but equally resolute to "pay him out," when once she is convinced of his meanness or spitefulness. Her language is devoid, to a degree remarkable even in our own undemonstrative race, of any tenderness or emotion. She accepts an invitation with the ungracious formula: "I don't mind if I do." Upon the "mate" of her own sex, to whom she is so much more warmly devoted than to her "chap," she never bestows a word of endearment. "Hi, Liza, d'y' think I'm going to wait all night for you?" is the tone of her address to the friend with whom she will share her last penny or for whom she will pawn her last item of pawnable property. She speaks roughly to her relatives and aggressively to

the world at large; she is no respecter of persons, and her eye for affectation or insincerity is unerring. Condescend to her and she will "chaff" you off the field. But meet her on equal terms, help her without attempting to "boss" her, and within a month or two you will have won her unalterable allegiance. . . . Two qualities, in particular, mark the factory girl of from sixteen to twenty: her exuberant spirits and energy, and the invariable improvement in manner and language that follows upon any sort of amelioration in her position.[37]

These assertive, feisty girls, brimming with self-esteem and generosity, are the emotional center of Black's texts. This celebration of a socially and sexually autonomous adolescent female working-class identity seems to me to be groundbreaking and an interesting addendum to the kinds of autonomous subjectivity that Levy was trying to envisage for her middle-class heroines. Perhaps the most radical aspect of Black's depiction in *Sweated Industry and the Minimum Wage* is her refusal to hold out marriage and motherhood as a reward or release for these girls. Indeed, their passage away from this female-centered social and working world into maturity is presented by Black as anything but a happy ending:

A few years pass, a very few, and these bright girls become apathetic, listless women of whom at 35 it is impossible to guess whether their age is 40 or 50. They are tired out; they toil on, but they have ceased to look forward or to entertain any hopes. The contrast between the factory girl and her mother is perhaps the very saddest spectacle that the labour world presents. To be the wife of a casual labourer, the mother of many children, living always in too small a space and always in a noise, is an existence that makes of too many women, in what ought to be the prime of their lives, mere machines of toil, going on from day to day, with as little hope and as little happiness as the sewing machine that furnishes one item in their permanent weariness. (*Sweated Industry*, 137)

Presciently skeptical, here and in other writings, about the notion of the "family wage" and the wife as secondary earner, Black identifies the plight of homeworking mothers as the most dire of all workers: "[A]bove all, a cruelly heavy burden rest[s] on the shoulders of the woman who tries to be at the same time a mother, housekeeper, and bread-winner, and who in return for her endless exertion seldom receives enough even to keep her properly fed, and never enough to satisfy her own very modest standards of comfort" (*Sweated Industry*, 3). In her accounts of even her married working women, Black offers curiously little description of their relations with men, either emotional or economic. Working-class men in these studies are disempowered figures, downtrodden and defeated by the conditions of their labor. Black insists always upon the power and heroism of women: "[E]very defect of spending power has to be made good by the toil of woman's muscles."[38]

This portrait diverges sharply from the images of the "factory girl" produced in most writing of the period. As Chris Willis has pointed out, after the match girls' strike, the factory girl exerted a strong pull over the popular cultural imagination, but she was represented through a very limited set of stereotypes, "as a combination of an exploited innocent, a sexual threat and a violent virago."[39]

Always using a variant of the same name—Eliza, Liz, or Liza—a rash of short stories such as "Lizerunt," the first of Arthur Morrison's *Tales of Mean Streets,* and poems such as W. E. Henley's *London Type,* "Liza," appeared at the very end of the 1880s. They established a stereotype of the factory girl as, in the final line of Henley's poem, a "stupid, straight, hard-working girl," who has no conception of self-protection or her best interests and inevitably goes to the bad because of a combination of her inauspicious family background— an absent or abusive father and drunken mother—a penchant for blowing her wages on fancy clothes and hats to wear on bank holiday trips to Wanstead Flats and, most perilously, an obsession with getting and holding on to a man, violent, drunken, and impecunious though he will inevitably be.[40] At the end of Morrison's text, Lizerunt's husband (who has not done a day's work during the whole of his life, has watched his mother work herself to death, and has stolen the money she had saved for her funeral) pushes his wife out into the street and orders her to earn money for him from prostitution.

The most extensively developed example of the genre (and in the period, perhaps the most notorious) was W. Somerset Maugham's heroine of his 1897 novel *Liza of Lambeth.* It is worth drawing a brief contrast between Maugham's representation and Black's, for although Black picks up on the conventional name for the factory girl in the texts of the late nineteenth and early twentieth centuries, the distance of her account from Maugham's is striking. Liza of Lambeth's first appearance in Maugham's novel is not at work or even in post-shift solidarity with the other factory girls; instead, she appears as a lone figure, in a highly sexualized self-display, parading up her street in a new outfit.

> It was a young girl of about eighteen, with dark eyes and an enormous fringe, puffed out and curled and frizzed, covering her whole forehead

from side to side, and coming down to meet her eyebrows. She was dressed in brilliant violet, with great lappets of velvet, and she had on her head an enormous black hat covered with feathers.

"I sy, ain't she got up dossy?" called out the groups at the doors, as she passed.

"Dressed ter death, and kill the fashion; that's wot I calls it!"

Liza saw what a sensation she was creating; she craned her back and lifted her head, and walked down the street, swaying her body from side to side, and swaggering along as though the whole place belonged to her.[41]

In response to the suggestion that she has obtained the dress from the pawn-broker's shop, Liza reveals her talent for scolding:

"Garn!" said Liza indignantly. "I'll swipe yer over the snitch if yer talk ter me. I got the mayterials in the West Hand, didn't I? And I 'ad it mide up by my Court Dress-maker, so you jolly well cry up, old jelly-belly."

"Garn!" was the reply. (9)

So Liza's vanity, dizzy disposition, and sexual availability are indicated from the outset. The one prospect of salvation the novel holds out for her is marriage to her boring but reliable boyfriend. But she quickly dumps him and takes up instead with a married man, Jim Blakeston, whose courtship consists primarily in nights, and indeed days, of heavy drinking—Liza goes through much of the plot (including her shifts at the factory) with a violent hangover. He impregnates her and then abandons her. After punch-ups with Jim's estranged wife and with Jim himself, Liza goes back to her mother, whose comfort consists of the dispensing of yet more alcohol. Liza suffers a miscarriage after an especially heavy night—to the horror and scandalization of her mother, who does nothing to assist her. Liza dies soon after. So Liza's circumstances are a grim concatenation of maternal neglect and cynicism, physical violence, complete cultural impoverishment, and appallingly ugly dialect. Maugham makes no suggestion that the workers, either male or female, have any kind of analysis of the exploitative conditions of their labor, let alone the intellectual or political resources to set about doing anything about them.

So as far as Maugham is concerned, Liza's only chance of improvement in her life is via judicious disposition of her sexuality in a respectable marriage. Because she rejects this, Maugham sacrifices her on the altar of her sexuality, with even her mother offering no support or sympathy in her dying moments. As we have seen, Clementina Black absolutely refuses this trajectory. Indeed, her later text, *Married Women's Work*, which published research conducted under the aegis of the Women's Industrial Council, focuses in particular on the working mother; here Black makes some radical suggestions to alleviate problems identified in *Sweated Industry and the Minimum Wage*. She places strong emphasis on women's wage-earning activity and radically undermines any faith in either maternal vocation or a male provider as the basis of financial competence for women and their children. She advocates the rearing of infants in state nurseries to free women up to return to paid work on a full-time basis: "The assumption . . . that the existence of babies must and should in all cases and for ever prevent the mother of them from going out to work would be rash. It is by no means always true that a mother is the person best qualified to take care of her infant."[42] Once again, ascribing a dignity and self-awareness to her subjects that Maugham could not conceive of, she also emphasizes working-class women's recognition of the importance of their economic autonomy: "[T]he woman who said, 'a shilling of your own is worth two that *he* gives you,' spoke the mind of many of her sisters" (*MWW*, 4). Most significantly, Black insists on a definition of unpaid domestic labor as being of equal importance to paid work and as equally in need of regulation and intervention in the context of maternity. Taking on the question of the desirability of excluding mothers from the paid labor market—the predominant view within social theory of the time—she says, "The horrible boast, 'I never missed but one week's wash with any of my babies'—which has been made to me more than once—tells its own tale; and the law which forbids the return of women to the factory, does not prevent the washing and wringing of sheets, the carrying of coals and water and the scrubbing of floors" (*MWW*, 10). Perhaps this contrast with *Liza of Lambeth* helps us to understand why Black's most powerful and subjectively authentic portraits of working women, their voices, and their desires are contained within Black's sociological writing rather than her novels. The novel form, being so wedded to the European *Bildungsroman* drive toward marriage and maternity as the happy ending for women, could not contain the truth of what Black discovered about the impact of what "fulfilling" her sexual and maternal destiny did to the woman worker. Rather than the pitying revulsion of Somerset Maugham, Black's sociological writings delineate huge respect for and even adoration of the factory girl. For Black, this is the (comparatively) blessed state, and the transition to sexual maturity is a tragic fall: "One thing I have not succeeded in picturing—and it is the thing which seems to me perhaps the most terrible of all: the change of the working girl into the working woman."[43]

In one of Amy Levy's late stories, "Eldorado at Islington," something of these issues of working-class life do perhaps start to impinge.[44] The story describes the strain caused to the life of the middle-class Lloyd family by the collapse of their fortunes. Despite their suffering, the family's father refuses a legacy that comes their way from his brother, because he knows the money to have been made from exploited labor:

> "Wife, children, you must put to-day and yesterday out of your heads. It has all been a mistake."
>
> Half-imploring, half-defiant he swept the dismayed circle of faces with his glance; then, dropping his eyes, went on—
>
> "The money was never ours, never could be ours. It was the fruit of cruelty and extortion; it was wrung from the starving poor. It is money that no honest man can touch." (230)

But still Levy's focus does not stray from bourgeois subjectivity. There is no detail in the story as to precisely what the nature of the exploitation was and the emphasis throughout is on the disappointment and difficulty the Lloyds will continue to suffer. The story is told from the perspective of Eleanor, the grown-up daughter of the house, who has been compelled to find work as a governess. Significantly, Eleanor makes no connection between the continued curtailment of her opportunities caused by impoverishment and the fate of the working-class women she sees around her: "[S]he held her father's decision as absolutely without alternative, as he had done himself . . . [and] directed [her anger] against Fate" (231). Instead, the working woman is reinscribed as an object of exoticism and of envy, from whom Eleanor can only measure her distance:

> Eleanor Lloyd, from her window in the roof, could see not only the wall and the plane-trees, but, by dint of craning her neck, the High Street itself, with its ceaseless stream of trams and omnibuses. There was a public-house at the corner, and, as the door swung backwards and forwards, Eleanor caught glimpses of the lively barmaid behind her tall white tap handles. A group of flower-girls, with uncurled feathers and straight fringes, stood outside on the pavement, jesting with the busmen and passers-by. Eleanor, who was a "lady," (Heaven help her!) used sometimes to envy the barmaid and the flower-girls their social opportunity. (227)

WE need to chasten our celebration of Levy with the knowledge of what she squandered politically and perhaps aesthetically in her relationship with Clementina Black. Levy clearly was committed to assisting Black's work and Liselotte Glage suggests that Levy gave her money as well as her time to the WPPL.[45] It is impossible to know the extent to which this was attributable to her personal attachment to Black or how much and what kind of identification with or analysis of the plight of working-class women motivated her. I think Black is deserving of our attention in her own right as an important actor at the interface of feminism and socialism in her period. Considering her as Levy's closest friend perhaps helps us to understand a little more the things that Amy Levy did not know, chose not to know, about her political moment. Levy killed herself in September 1889, two months short of her twenty-eighth birthday. As with so many aspects of her work—her development of a lesbian poetics, what appears to be her prefiguring of the Symbolism of the 1890s, even, perhaps, her protomodernism (she was twenty-one years older than Virginia Woolf —imagine a 1920s Bloomsbury that contained them both)—the way in which she might have engaged with socialism had she lived to develop a mature oeuvre is a tantalizing question.

Notes

1. Some important recent studies of Levy that locate her as a "feminist heroine" include Joseph Bristow, "'All Out of Tune in This World's Instrument': The 'Minor' Poetry of Amy Levy," *Journal of Victorian Culture* 4 (1999): 76–103; Deborah L. Parsons, *Streetwalking the Metropolis: Women, the City and Modernity* (Oxford: Oxford University Press, 2000); Ana I. Parejo Vadillo, "New Woman Poets and the Culture of the *Salon* at the *Fin de Siècle*," *Women: A Cultural Review* 10, no. 1 (1999): 22–34.

2. Linda Hunt Beckman, *Amy Levy: Her Life and Letters* (Athens: Ohio University Press, 2000), 6; Edward Wagenknecht, *Daughters of the Covenant: Portraits of Six Jewish Women* (Amherst: University of Massachusetts Press, 1983).

3. Warwick James Price, "Three Forgotten Poetesses," *The Forum* 47 (1912): 367–68.

4. Letter to Isobel Levy from Amy Levy, quoted in Beckman, *Amy Levy*, 233–34.

5. Letter to Isobel Levy from Amy Levy, quoted in ibid., 234.

6. Israel Zangwill, *Children of the Ghetto: A Study of a Peculiar People* (1892), ed. Meri-Jane Rochelson (Detroit: Wayne State University Press, 1998), 73.

7. Carolyn Steedman, "Fictions of Engagement: Eleanor Marx, Biographical Space," in *Eleanor Marx: Life, Work, Contacts*, ed. John Stokes (Aldershot, UK: Ashgate, 2000), 23–39, quotation on 26.

8. Beckman, *Amy Levy*, 79.

9. Steedman, "Fictions of Engagement," 29–30.

10. Max Beer, *Fifty Years of International Socialism* (London: Allen and Unwin, 1935), 72.

11. Olive Schreiner, *Woman and Labour* (1911; reprint, London: Virago, 1978).

12. Ibid., 14.

13. Deborah Epstein Nord, "'Neither Pairs Nor Odd': Female Community in Late Nineteenth-Century London," *Signs* 15 (Summer 1990): 735–36.

14. Beatrice Webb, *My Apprenticeship* (London: Longmans Green and Co., 1926), 395.

15. Ibid., 399.

16. Ruth Livesey, *Socialism, Sex and the Culture of Aestheticism, 1880–1914* (Oxford: Oxford University Press, 2007).

17. Yvonne Kapp, *Eleanor Marx*, vol. 2, *The Crowded Years* (London: Virago, 1979), 268.

18. Liselotte Glage, *Clementina Black: A Study in Social History and Literature* (Heidelberg: Carl Winter Universitätsverlag, 1981), 30–31.

19. Eleanor Marx, letter to the *People's Press*, 31 August 1890, quoted in Kapp, *Eleanor Marx*, 2:394. Marx was incensed at her exclusion from the Trades Union Congress of September 1890 on the grounds that she was not a "working woman" (Black was admitted). One can hardly resist the observation that Marx is at high risk of bringing the words "pot," "kettle," and "black" to mind.

20. Glage, *Clementina Black*, 25. Working with a very scientific political definition, the German writer Glage argues that identifying Black as a socialist may be problematic: "It is probably safest to say she was bourgeois and pro-Labour, and not to attempt further identification" (36). I would be less cautious (perhaps because of my background within the British Left)—my definition of socialism is certainly broad enough to include her.

21. Glage, *Clementina Black*, 20; Beckman, *Amy Levy*, 131.

22. Glage, *Clementina Black*, 47.

23. Ibid., 46.

24. Glage lists, as an example, Black's activities of 1888, taken from the *Annual Report of the General Meetings of the WPPL*. They included her speaking at a meeting of the Scientific Press Cutting Association on how to turn their organization formally into a trade union; addressing meetings of working women in Chelsea, Pimlico, Walsall, Walthamstow, and Westminster; encouraging and advising on the process of unionization; and conducting extensive investigative fieldwork on women's living and working conditions in poor communities in London (and the writing up of her findings for publication)—in addition to her role in the match workers' strike and its aftermath, in which Black took a leading role in the establishment of a consumer's league, which aimed to encourage consumer boycotts of goods produced in exploitative circumstances (Glage, *Clementina Black*, 28–33).

25. Beckman, *Amy Levy*, 179.

26. Amy Levy, "Women and Club Life," *Woman's World* 1 (1888): 364–67; reprinted in Amy Levy, *The Romance of a Shop* (1888), ed. Susan David Bernstein (Peterborough, ON: Broadview Press, 2006), 219.

27. Ibid., 214.

28. Levy, *Romance of a Shop*, ed. Bernstein, 53. Subsequent references to this edition appear parenthetically in the text.

29. George Gissing, *The Odd Women* (1893; reprint London: Virago, 1980). Although I have been unable to find documentary proof that Gissing had read Levy's novel, the similarity between the two plots is so striking that to leave it unremarked would seem to me to be intellectually negligent. As Levy's impact on late-nineteenth-century literary culture

becomes more evident, perhaps the conditions will be created for a Gissing scholar to uncover such evidence.

30. Amy Levy, *Reuben Sachs* (1888), ed. Susan David Bernstein (Peterborough, ON: Broadview Press, 2006).

31. Clementina Black, *An Agitator* (London: Bliss, Sands and Foster, 1894), 58–59.

32. Lynne Hapgood, "The Novel and Political Agency," *Literature and History*, 3rd ser., 5, no. 2 (1996): 49. Black's article is "Women and Work," *New Review* 5 (1891): 213–21.

33. Hapgood, "Novel and Political Agency," 44.

34. See, for example, Stokes, *Eleanor Marx*. Hapgood's essay in this volume, "Is This Friendship? Eleanor Marx, Margaret Harkness and the Idea of Socialist Community" (129–44), addresses the crucial intellectual and political influence these two women had on the socialist cultures of late-nineteenth-century London.

35. Robert Tressell, *The Ragged-Trousered Philanthropists* (London: G. Richards, 1914). However, in *Working Class Fiction: From Chartism to Trainspotting* (Plymouth: Northcote House, 1997), 17–18, Ian Haywood points to the existence of a story, Allen Clarke's "The Daughter of the Factory," published in *Northern Weekly* in 1898, which has as its central figure the factory worker Rose Hilton. Rose is inspired by a "female agitator" into becoming a feminist and trade union leader. Rose writes a weekly newspaper column about factory conditions, physically assaults a male overseer who has seduced one of the workers, and sparks a riot by singing "Le Marseillaise" at a rally. This would seem to indicate that Black's novel and her social investigative writings about working women had achieved some measure of cultural penetration by the end of the nineteenth century.

36. Stephen N. Fox and Clementina Black, "The Truck Acts: What They Do and What They Ought to Do" (London: Women's Trade Union Association, 1894).

37. Clementina Black, *Sweated Industry and the Minimum Wage* (London: Duckworth, 1907), 134–35. Subsequent references to this edition appear parenthetically in the text as *Sweated Industry*.

38. Clementina Black, *Married Women's Work* (London: G. Bell and Sons, 1915), 9. Further references to this edition will appear in the text.

39. Chris Willis, "Victim or Virago? Popular Images of the Victorian Factory Girl," http://www.chriswillis.freeserve.co.uk/factory.htm, 8.

40. Arthur Morrison, *Tales of Mean Streets* (London: Methuen, 1901); W. E. Henley, *London Types* (London: William Heinemann, 1898).

41. W. Somerset Maugham, *Liza of Lambeth* [1897] (Harmondsworth, UK: Penguin, 1967), 8. Subsequent reference to this edition appears parenthetically in the text.

42. Black, *Married Women's Work*, 6. Subsequent references to this edition appear parenthetically in the text, abbreviated as *MWW*.

43. Black, *Sweated Industry*, 134.

44. Amy Levy, "Eldorado at Islington," *Woman's World* 2 (1889): 488–89; reprinted in *Romance of a Shop*, ed. Bernstein. Subsequent references to this edition appear parenthetically in the text.

45. Glage, *Clementina Black*, 24.

3

Between Two Stools

exclusion and unfitness in
amy levy's short stories

—

Gail Cunningham

FOLLOWING her submission of "The Recent Telepathic Occurrence at the British Museum" for the first issue of *Woman's World,* Oscar Wilde wrote to Levy, "I hope you will send me another short story. I think your method as admirable as it is unique."[1] Though Levy referred dismissively to her short stories as "potboilers,"[2] Wilde's assessment is both perceptive and accurate. The short story form seems to me to suit her as a prose writer better than the novel. The quality that, in his obituary for Levy, Wilde praised in her prose writing—her "extraordinary power of condensation"[3]—can appear as mere perfunctoriness when stretched over a full-length novel, even those as brief as hers. And Harry Quilter makes an interesting point when he criticizes her novels for what he calls their "detachment of mind," a quality he considers "the most fatal possession of the story-teller."[4] His argument is that Levy's novels exhibit a certain flatness or uncertainty in their construction of narrative voice. Whereas this may create fruitful tensions in, for example, *Reuben Sachs,* in *Miss Meredith*—the work that primarily provokes Quilter's comment—Levy's apparent detachment from the first person narrative voice can fatally undercut the novel's emotional thrust. In her short stories, by contrast, she employs a variety of confidently controlled narrative voices ranging from bitter cynicism through ironic detachment to elegiac lyricism. Her frequent use of the first person (male as well as female) and of the epistolary form enables her to adopt a range of confessional stances that both reveal and disguise the narrator, drawing the reader into active interpretative engagement with even the most apparently slight descriptive sketches.

The aspect of Levy's short story "method" that particularly interests me here is the way she plays with issues of confession and self-revelation. Relations between narrator (or narrators), reader, and author, and between the fictive and the real, form a recurrent feature of the stories. Levy's devices for highlighting these relations vary. In "Between Two Stools" and "Sokratics in the Strand," for example, she takes two conventional narrative forms—epistolary and third person omniscient—which she destabilizes by the unexpected interpolation of an unknown first person narrator. In the first of Nora's effusively emotional letters in "Between Two Stools," Levy interpolates a sudden narrative comment: "[Here follow several pages which, for the reader's sake, we have thought best to omit.]"[5] "Sokratics in the Strand" similarly contains a single intervention from an otherwise hidden narrator, though this time at the end: "Opinions differed . . . but my own belief is . . ."[6] In other stories, names or places are what provoke implicit enquiry from the reader. For example, "Cohen of Trinity," a story whose narrator displays bafflement, attraction, and repulsion toward the eponymous protagonist, would be a very different story if its authorial signature did not disclose that its author (though not its narrator) is Jewish. Levy's travel sketches are habitually narrated by and addressed to characters from Tennyson's *Princess*[7] but are set in locations that are identified within the story as not merely realistic sounding but as actually real—names and addresses of inns, for example, where she had stayed (and which in some instances still exist). Virtually all her stories are laced with quotation and reference, inviting readers to share her emotional and intellectual framework. And in "Griselda," Levy adopts the highly unusual practice of using her own elder sister's name for the story's somewhat unpleasant fictional elder sister, a device that would have carried embarrassing—even aggressive—implications to friends and family while remaining entirely opaque to most of the story's first readers.

These narrative methods engage the reader in a dynamic interrogation of the relations between narrator and author, between the imaginary, the realistic, and the real. Many of the stories, in particular those relating to travels in Germany, Switzerland, Italy, and—especially—Cornwall, are of course closely based on Levy's personal experience. And though a reductive reading of fiction as veiled autobiography is likely to impoverish rather than enrich, Levy's method inevitably suggests elements of confession withheld or disguised, revelation teasingly hinted at through allusion. Certainly her readers, from contemporaries to the present, have responded to a literary distinctiveness of voice and mind that provoke questions about their author, and the degree to which Levy as both woman and author embodies characteristics of difference from her society particularly interests modern readers. Levy frequently asks her readers to note the presence or question the nature of author behind narrator and thus to engage with a figure whose existence outside her work can read significantly back into it. Ana Parejo Vadillo notes that "after a century of critical demotion" Levy "has been elevated back into the canon" and that the publication by Linda Hunt Beckman of the first full-length biography of Levy has been "vital in this revival."[8] And as Cynthia Scheinberg argues, this revival of interest rests largely on the degree to which Levy speaks "to concerns of the contemporary critical moment: Jewish Diasporic identity, lesbian identity, women's emancipation."[9] Her contemporaries, however, approached these concerns within a significantly different cultural context. Beatrice Webb, for example, in reflecting on Levy's depressive character and ultimate suicide, argued that "in these terrible days of mental pressure it is courage to *live* that we most lack, not courage to die."[10]

The deep-rooted pessimism that is an informing feature of all of Levy's work was noted by Quilter as a veritable "habit of mind,"[11] and Linda G. Zatlin, reviewing Melvyn New's collection of Levy's work, asks, "[W]hy do sadness and pessimism thread insistently through Levy's writing?"[12] Socially or politically determined pessimism was, of course, a recurrent feature of feminist writing at the fin de siècle, and many fictional New Women were represented as driven by the intractability of male hegemonic society to untimely deaths either by their own hand or as a more or less direct outcome of their societal difference.[13] Though her fiction (novels as well as short stories) largely avoids this trope, her most notable suicides—in "Sokratics in the Strand" and "Cohen of Trinity"—being male, to an almost extreme degree Levy embodied difference in her very person. Set apart from societal norms by race, education, gender, political conviction, and perhaps sexuality, the conditions of both body and mind encouraged her self-construction as the paradigmatic outsider. Acutely sensitive to physical appearance, she clearly felt that her classically Jewish features rendered her unattractive in the largely gentile, intellectual circles to which her education introduced her. The sketches and doodles that decorate many of her manuscript notebooks include pages of vividly drawn female profiles with exaggerated Semitic noses. The catalogue of bodily ailments recounted in her letters to friends and family attest to the "lack of physical robustness" that Clementina Black cited as one cause of the "fits of extreme depression"[14] that finally drove Levy to suicide. And the recurrent theme in her short stories of an idealized, lost world of pure learning ("Camford" or "Princess Ida's")[15] attests to the difficulty experienced by the highly educated woman seeking integration into late-nineteenth-century society.

Levy's short stories, then, give consistently vivid expression to the sense of exclusion and unfitness that formed an essential part of feminist discourse at the fin de siècle, a sense that Levy more than any of her contemporaries embodied in her own life and person. Turning to the short story form explicitly as a money-earning enterprise, Levy's letter on the subject to her sister Katie interestingly draws on images of both exclusion and unfitness: "Are we going to be in a very bad way financially all this winter? . . . I have sent my tale 'perisonally' to . . . Clementina & asked if she thinks it is any good fr. a magazine point of view. I believe being educated has taken away all chance of my producing 'potboilers'—wh. is a grim reflection."[16] While the reference to her education rendering her unfit for the highly market-driven world of popular magazine story-production is readily comprehensible, the significance of writing "perisonally" to Clementina Black for advice is perhaps less so. Indeed, Linda Hunt Beckman transcribes the word as "periwinkles" and notes that no Levy story with this title is traceable.[17] Levy's handwriting in this letter, however, seems to me perfectly clear, and the allusion particularly important. It refers to the second book of Thomas Moore's *Lalla Rookh*, "Paradise and the Peri," in which the Peri laments the exclusion of her race from Heaven:

> One morn a Peri at the gate
> Of Eden stood, disconsolate. . . . .
> She wept to think her recreant race
> Should e'er have lost that glorious place.[18]

That this reference to the pain of exclusion (racial or otherwise) is sufficiently familiar and shared to be dropped punningly into a letter to her sister is significant, particularly because it is a reference that Levy used more than once in her fiction. In *Reuben Sachs*, for example, the Montague Cohens—Reuben's sister and her husband, who spend their lives "in pursuit of a shadow which is called social advancement"[19]—are characterized as "those two indefatigable Peris at the gate."[20] Here the Peri image is enlisted as a weapon in a passage of comparatively light social satire. In the unpublished short story "Three Times," however, Levy's protagonist, Anne, is a "Peri at the gates of Paradise," from which she is cruelly excluded by class and background. Though this is "rather a dull Paradise, if she had only known it," it nevertheless contains the object of her unrequited love, and her exclusion creates bitter pain. In describing Anne's desolation, Levy's voice lurches abruptly from the third to the first person, shifting the narrative from exposition of the particular to an inclusive generalization of a state that both narrator and reader are forced to share: "We fight so desperately, the blood flows so freely from our wounds, it is hard to recognise our own impotence, the insignificance of our woe. Then follow the long days, the grey days when there is a vague ache in our hearts tho' the battle cry is silent within us. We had pictured much possible misery; but nothing like this ragged, undramatic ending to our little tragi-comedy."[21]

Levy's use of the Peri image acts as a focus for her recurrent interest in themes of exclusion. Her identification of education as a determinant of general unfitness, though, may be appropriate to a perceived difficulty in adjusting her writing to the less elevated end of the literary market. A common trope of antifeminist discourse of the time was the notion that education denatured women, rendered them unfit for their proper sphere of emotion and nurture. Indeed, a year after Levy's death, Grant Allen somewhat brutally evoked Levy as an indicator of misguided educational energies, seeing what he terms "the Higher Instruction of Women" as a prime cause of modern woman's unfitness for life in general and motherhood in particular: "Colleges have been opened; High Schools have been started; Senior Classics have been led like lambs to the slaughter. . . . All life and spontaneity . . . has been crushed out in the process; but no matter for that: our girls are now 'highly cultivated.' A few hundred pallid little Amy Levys sacrificed on the way are as nothing before the face of our fashionable Juggernaut. Newnham has slain its thousands, and Girton its tens of thousands."[22] In her short stories, though, Levy adopts a broader view of unfitness as either biologically determined or rooted in a social-Darwinist struggle for survival in a hostile environment. In two stories —"Out of the World" and "Cohen of Trinity"—she quotes the same passage from Browning's "Caliban upon Setebos":

> . . . hath spied an icy fish
>
> That longed to 'scape the rock-stream where she lived,
>
> And thaw herself within the lukewarm brine
>
> O' the lazy sea. . . .
>
> Only she ever sickened, found repulse
>
> At the other kind of water not her life,
>
> Flounced back from bliss she was not born to breathe,
>
> And in her old bounds buried her despair
>
> Hating and loving warmth alike.[23]

A longing for other worlds is a recurrent theme of Levy's short stories; but just as Browning's icy fish yearns for warmth but is repulsed from an environment "she was not born to breathe," so too does Levy construct fictional characters whose despair is caused by their naturally engendered unfitness for the worlds they desire.

"Out of the World" is a particularly interesting example, not simply because it stands on the margin between fiction and autobiography but also for its extraordinary control of a narrative voice that brilliantly combines lightness of tone with pervasive hints of a darker subtext. Characterized somewhat misleadingly by Melvyn New as "describing her pastoral vacation in Cornwall,"[24] though written in a surface tone of breezy humor the story is seeded throughout with indications to the reader of a deep malaise that the narrator both reveals and conceals. It is one of several pieces that Levy wrote ostensibly as travelogues, given distance and a veneer of fictionalization by a narrative framework taken from Tennyson's *Princess*.[25] In these stories, Levy writes as "Melissa," addressing either Blanche or Psyche and constantly invoking—wherever the traveller happens to be—the lost haven of Princess Ida's palace of learning.[26] In "Out of the World," Melissa writes to "Dearest Psyche" with an account of her holiday on the Cornish coast, in a country inn consciously presented as a series of clichés: "A kind hostess . . . a charming room . . . a log fire blazing merrily in the grate. . . . A dimpled maid . . . bearing on her tray a dainty meal wherein home-made bread and clotted cream figured largely, and where a fragrant teapot crowned the whole."[27] Add to this a landlady who instructs the narrator in "bread-making and cream-scalding" while discussing Matthew Arnold, a countryside bathed in the "autumn glory" of "russet leaves, red berries, gleaming blackberries and purple sloes" and a trip to the sea where Melissa confesses to "quite a little rapture," and we find Levy ostensibly inviting a reading of uncritical engagement with an English idyll. Simultaneously, however, the same voice suggests a different narrative. Melissa's letter, as the first line of the story tells us, is prompted by a "meagre little note" from Psyche, announcing her arrival in a London that Melissa has already left. This leads to a wry reflection on the fatal mismatching of desire and circumstance based on an image drawn from a child's weather-house: "Alas, my friend! we seem fated never to meet, like the pathetic little man and woman in the weather-prophet toy of one's youth; I used to feel so sorry for the poor woman as she emerged from her gay house, prophesying sunshine, only to find that her mate, in obedience to some cruel and inscrutable law of his being, had withdrawn at her approach!" Melissa confesses that after "the engagement and marriage of [her] sister," she is left, by contrast, a "seedy and penurious spinster," and a "great blankness fell upon [her] soul." Seeing the sea, unmediated by the conventions of family holiday or channel crossing, she understands for the first time what "poets mean" in writing of the "'great sweet mother, mother and lover of men, the sea' whose . . . 'large embraces are keen like pain.'"

Clearly the story demands a more complex reading than its surface narrative suggests. Far from being a light piece describing a pleasant holiday, "Out of the World" resonates with Levy's recurring preoccupations with exclusion, unfitness, depression, and suicide. Appropriately to a narrative framed by Princess Ida's academy, Melissa writes largely through literary reference and quotation. The story's title is taken from Thomas Hood's "Bridge of Sighs," and lest the reader assume that the phrase is merely a commonplace of English idiom, Levy quotes directly from the poem: "'Anywhere, anywhere out of the world,' I cried." Hood's poem is a tale of a young woman driven by circumstance to kill herself by drowning:

> Mad from life's history,
> Glad to death's mystery,
> Swift to be hurl'd—
> Anywhere, anywhere
> Out of the world![28]

Similarly, Melissa's "little rapture" over the sea must be read on a different level in the light of Levy's quotations from Algernon Charles Swinburne's "Triumph of Time" that accompany it. Here the rejected lover first longs to be out of the world linked in death with the beloved:

I wish we were dead together today,
Lost sight of, hidden away out of sight,
Clasped and clothed in the cloven clay,
Out of the world's way, out of the light.

(lines 113–16)

When this is denied, he seeks solitary oblivion in the sea's embrace:

I will go back to the great sweet mother,
Mother and lover of men, the sea. . . .
Thy sweet hard kisses are strong like wine,
Thy large embraces are keen like pain.
Save me and hide me with all thy waves,
Find me one grave of thy thousand graves. . . .

(lines 265–66, 275–78)[29]

Taken together with the "icy fish" quotation from Browning's "Caliban upon Setebos" that concludes the piece, these literary references and the running images throughout the story to personal disappointment and isolation construct an underlying reading of a narrator who is as unfit to be out of the world —whether through simple escapism or suicidal impulse—as in it.

Christine Pullen argues that "Out of the World" was written in the autumn of 1885 after one of the two suicide attempts referred to by Constance Black following Levy's death.[30] Harry Quilter, whose reminiscence of Levy was prompted by his stay at the same Falcon Inn that features in the story, tells how the landlady revealed to him that Levy "had come down there ill . . . and had been nursed," though he is careful to add that she gave him no details of the illness.[31] Pullen identifies two events in the summer of 1885 that could have caused Levy severe personal suffering. First, in July 1885, Karl Pearson—to whom, Pullen suggests, Levy had been peculiarly close—formed the second Men and Women's Club, from whose membership he specifically excluded her.[32] Second, and particularly significant in view of the reference in the story to "the engagement and marriage of my sister," in August 1885 Levy's sister Katie had married after a short engagement. This wedding provided the subject matter for some of Levy's caricatured sketches of Jewish figures and appeared to confirm the superior claims to personal attractiveness of the elder sister. Writing to Katie at her honeymoon address, Levy's comical exaggerations cannot wholly conceal a note of pained bitterness: "The latest thing is your great beauty—

started by 'the aunts' to while away the August hours in London, I suppose. Such terms as 'very beautiful'(!), 'sweetly pretty,' 'her great big eyes,' float about freely & goad me into paroxysms of envious madness."[33] Perhaps now thinking of herself as a "seedy and penurious spinster," it is appropriate that Levy has Melissa visit the local convent, where her guide "spoke with enthusiasm" of the cloistered life—a life from which she is excluded through lack of vocation. Melissa then wanders through the churchyard as the sun sets, observing a cast of archetypal English rural characters (an idiot boy, children playing "by the gold-tinted brook," the "wisely passive" village policeman, the rector's wife with basket on arm) and amidst this pastoral idyll seems to hear a newsboy "calling out Special Editions and terrible catastrophes!" And she concludes that, despite the "superior peace, simplicity and beauty of a country life," her own place "is among the struggling crowd of dwellers in cities." She is, explicitly, "like Browning's 'icy fish,'" yearning for a world she is unfit to inhabit. Whether or not the circumstances of Levy's life at this point had led to anything as extreme as attempted suicide, it is clear that "Out of the World" draws directly on personal experiences that find imaginative expression in recurrent images of exclusion and unfitness.

The "struggling crowd of dwellers in cities," to which Melissa feels herself fatally to belong, is often constructed in Levy's stories as a ballroom or similar place of social gathering. Here women are locked in an evolutionary struggle in which their faces and bodies determine their fitness for survival. "A ballroom is like a battle-field, where it is *væ victis* . . . and the weakest goes, very literally, to the wall," says Nora in "Between Two Stools." In "Wise in Her Generation," Virginia notes cynically how the young girl, fresh from the schoolroom, is "arrayed gorgeously, whirled through a gas-lit city, and finally let loose in a crowded ball-room, there to sink or swim."[34] And in "The Diary of a Plain Girl," the narrator evokes the pain of exclusion caused by physical unattractiveness, in which a waltz becomes "torture music" and "the happy people dancing round are torturers, exquisitely cruel torturers."[35] Interestingly, Levy's depiction of a woman's sexual allure is not absolute but relative; her female protagonists habitually assess themselves by comparison with (most often) a sister or, for example, in the unpublished "Lallie,"[36] an older friend and role model. In "Griselda,"[37] Levy actually gives her comparatively plain heroine a beautiful older sister with the same name—Katie—as her own sister. "The Diary of a Plain Girl," though essentially trite in plot, contains some vibrantly effective writing on appearance, as the "plain" Milly steels herself to a confrontation with her own image: "I made up my mind to face the worst, and take a long, long look in the glass. . . . At first it wasn't so bad as I expected. I saw an ordinary little girl enough in a plain hat and frock; nothing to excite notice one way or the other. And then Dahlia came in behind and put her head over my shoulder, and my face looked grey—positively grey—like a mouse, and I seemed to shrivel up into a sort of dwarf." Levy vividly images the beautiful older sister literally outshining and diminishing her younger sibling. Alone, Milly is ordinary but acceptable; her face can be effaced—"nothing to excite notice one way or the other." Doubled with her sister, however, her reflection is actively altered; her color changes and she shrinks in stature to the point of freakishness.

In both "Griselda" and "The Diary of a Plain Girl," Levy rescues her plain heroines and rewards them with unexpected but fulfilling marriages. Other, darker, stories depict exclusion from the yearned-for paradise of requited love that ends either in death ("Lallie" and "The Recent Telepathic Occurrence at the British Museum") or in protracted pain and bitterness ("Three Times"). In both cases, however, Levy's love-seeking female figures are essentially passive, victims of a struggle in which their fate is determined by others. Perhaps this denial of agency is what lends these stories a sense of self-indulgence, a hint that Levy, like Horace in "Sokratics in the Strand," sometimes "liked to nurse and dandle . . . sorrow." Her strongest stories, by contrast, pitch agency against fate, interrogating the nature of (un)fitness in a society of social-Darwinist struggle and desire.

Two early examples, in which pain is leavened by ironic distance, are "Between Two Stools" and "Sokratics in the Strand." "Between Two Stools" takes the case of a young woman, fresh from Cambridge, precipitated into the London social world of dressmakers, balls, and the marriage market. Nora writes from London to her Cambridge friend Agnes, recounting in a series of letters her nostalgia for the lost world of aesthetics and scholarship where "we puzzled over Plato on the lawn, and read Swinburne on the roof in the evenings." This is comically contrasted with London society in which "it is not young-ladylike to have one's facts right or one's sentences logical," and "a woman is held to have no absolute value; it is relative, and depends on the extent of the demand for her among members of the other sex." Nursing a hopeless passion for the Cambridge scholar Reginald Talbot, Nora loftily rejects the advances of a decent society suitor to preserve the purity of her intellectual ideals. When she discovers, meeting Talbot again in London, that her love for him is illusory, she finds that between the two stools of Cambridge and London, intellect and emotion, feminism and subjection, she has "fallen most woefully to the ground." Levy's assured control of narrative voice encourages a reading beyond the wry humor of Nora's tone toward interpretation that broadens the individualistic into the gender politics of the fin de siècle. Nora may affect distance from social struggle, claiming to regard life "solely from the spectator's point of view," and may attribute her position to the "irony of fate," but in the contested territory she occupies as an educated woman she is inevitably granted agency. Her newfound ability to make choices results ironically in self-exclusion from two contrasting worlds and leaves her unable to exist in either of the elements available to her.

"Sokratics in the Strand" is prefaced by two quotations advocating suicide as a means of escaping an intolerable world. The first, from Aeschylus's *Prometheus Bound*, is cited in the original Greek and could be translated, by readers with a classical education, as "What gain have I then in life? . . . Better it were to die once for all than linger out all my days in misery." The second, from W. S. Gilbert's *Tom Cobb*, is more accessible: "I do assure you, Whipple, that if I knew a safe and perfectly painless way of popping out of this world into some comfortable quarters in the next, I'd do it." This tonal contrast on the subject of suicide is continued in the main text as the "Sokratics" of the title are played out in discussion between the despondent writer Horace—an "unfortunate victim of the 'poetic temperament'"—and the bracingly cheerful barrister Vincent. Seeing himself as "a striking instance of the Irony of Fate," Horace plays gloomily with the idea of suicide, while Vincent counters with dismissive lightheartedness: "Oh, so it's Waterloo Bridge is it? There's a want of originality about the scheme which I should not have expected of you." Levy constructs the formal contrasts between the two on criteria of convention; Vincent is commonplace but professionally successful, Horace exceptional (with "singularly beautiful" head and hands) but struggling as a writer and with "an undue share of the common anguish." Vincent's suggested remedies for Horace's *anomie*—hard work, application, and a sense of proportion—are standard prescriptions for the Victorian gentleman and have served him well. Significantly, though, Horace's inability to inhabit this clubbish and conventional world is expressed in Levy's familiar terms of alienation. Groping for appropriate expression, Horace comes up with a self-diagnosis of "unfitness for life. Yes, a haunting sense of unfitness—that's the phrase I've been wanting all along." The story appears at first to invite a conventional reading of fine poetic sensibility contrasted with the crassly insensitive, as exemplified in

Vincent's riposte: "Unfitness for life! You are so awfully greedy, you poets, you expect too much from life, and when you don't get it think all the world has gone wrong. Of course life is a disillusion, a disappointment for most of us. The only way is to treat it as a game. . . . I'm playing the game of barristering, of success in life. . . . And now . . . I must be off to take my turn at that pretty little pastime called Flirtation." But Levy destabilizes the reader's instinctive responses, stepping in at the end of the story with a hitherto unheard authorial voice that undermines the obvious conclusion that Horace has killed himself: "[M]y own belief is . . . that he did nothing to hasten [his end]. . . . Poets, and those afflicted with the 'poetic temperament,' although constantly contemplating it, rarely commit suicide; they have too much imagination. The click of the self-slaughterer's pistol . . . is oftener heard in Mincing Lane and Capel Court than in the regions of Grub Street and Parnassus Hill."[38] Levy's unexpected conclusion serves to clarify the locus of the story's bitterness and irony. It is not, as the reader has been led to infer, straightforwardly in the doomed sensitivities of the artistic soul but rather that the very qualities that render the artist unfit for life are the ones that prevent him from acting to counter it.

In her two final, and probably strongest, stories, "Cohen of Trinity"[39] and "Wise in Her Generation," Levy rewrites the themes of "Between Two Stools" and "Sokratics in the Strand" into works of bleak despair. Both focus on central figures on the margin of their social worlds: Cohen, a Jewish student at Cambridge; and Virginia in "Wise in Her Generation," a jilted woman who regards society life from a position of world-weary cynicism. Like the "greedy" Horace in "Sokratics in the Strand," Cohen is a suicidally inclined writer with "insatiable demands." And just as Vincent engages in the struggle for survival in his sphere by belittling it as no more than "playing the game of barristering," so too does Virginia's experience of society's marriage market lead her to having "no intention of playing a losing game a second time." And Levy constructs both Cohen and Virginia as characters whose apparent triumphs ironically convince them that they are unfit to survive.

"Cohen of Trinity" announces itself through its very title as a study of discordance. The obviously Jewish "Cohen" is (mis)matched with the essentially Christian "Trinity," and similarly the narrative voice of the story engages with a subject with which it has no natural mode of contact. As a Jew at Cambridge, Cohen is a beneficiary of the University Test Acts of 1871 that abolished exclusion on religious grounds, and he is thus a figure who attracts close individual attention by virtue of distinctiveness and rarity. Levy's male narrator, however, is a fellow student of anonymous conventionality. He has no name, no face, and no origin, and though located in physical proximity to Cohen in both Cambridge and London, the narrator is distanced from him by social, racial, and characterological difference. As readers we know the narrator largely by contrast with Cohen—he is not Jewish, not alienated, not struggling, not a genius—and Levy positions us in a similar locus of secure yet puzzled anonymity. Of course, Levy's authorial signature distances her in turn from her narrator (as author, she is manifestly Jewish, a woman, a writer) and thus sets up a multilayered set of interpretative activities between reader, narrator, and subject that mimics the story's focus on discordance.

Levy's nameless narrator—self-characterized as a "curious observer"—gives largely unanalyzed expression to the contradictions in Cohen's nature: his brutishness and idealism, his arrogance and self-deprecation. The descriptive terms that are laced through the text force the reader into the position of active, if puzzled, interpreter of both Cohen and the narrator. For the narrator, Cohen is at once "ungainly," "awkward," "unattractive," and "coarse," while at the same time possessing "magnificence," "radiance," "exuberance," and "robustness." The story opens with the news of Cohen's death by suicide and the narrator's comment that Cohen "had often declared suicide to be among the characteristics of his versatile race," and the narrative continues with the retrospective account of his first sight of Cohen as "he came across the meadows towards the sunset, his upturned face pushed forwards catching the light, and glowing also with another radiance than the rich, reflected glory of the heavens." The younger Cohen, whom we know by this point in the narrative to be dead by his own hand, walks out of the sunset holding a book and "a few bulrushes and marsh marigolds"—Christian symbols of the Church faithful and perfect Marian love. In the face of such immediate discordance, the narrator's attempts to account for Cohen become similarly unstable: "His unbounded arrogance, his enormous pretensions, alternating with and tempered by a bitter self-deprecation . . . impressed me, even while amusing and disgusting me." Rejected by the Cambridge Jewish community on the grounds that his "family were not people that one 'knew,'" and excluded by race and class from the sophisticated gentile circles to which he aspires, Cohen falls fatally between two stools. Like Melissa in "Out of the World," he uses Browning's icy fish as signifier of his unfitness, but here Levy extends the passage's essentialist resonances by quoting it at greater length and leaving its relevance—that the self cannot change its relation to the world—unremarked or uncomprehended by the narrator. Only toward the end does Cohen reveal that what has driven him is a desire for recognition of selfhood: "They *shall* know, they *shall* understand, they *shall* feel what I am." But at the moment of success, when his book *Gubernator* has become the triumph of the season and "'they' do know," Cohen experiences the full force of Browning's lines: "Nothing . . . can alter the essential relations of things—their permanent, essential relations." This perception is what leads Cohen, unlike Horace, to "[send] a bullet through his brain."

In "Between Two Stools," Levy had approached the question of woman's struggle in the marriage market in a comparatively light vein. Nora is thoroughly foolish and self-deceiving but not fatally damaged. By contrast, "Wise in Her Generation," published by Wilde the year after Levy's death, is altogether darker in tone and works to a conclusion that can be read as a summation of her philosophy. Indeed, according to Levy's obituary in the *Lady's Pictorial*, it is the story "in the pages of which her pathetic death [is] foreshadowed."[40] The story's title is taken from the biblical parable in Luke 16: the unjust steward, who, dismissed for cheating his wealthy master and unable to earn a living, has to determine how to secure his future. This he does by colluding with his master's debtors in altering the books to show reduced debts, thereby ensuring that "they may receive [him] into their houses." His master praises this action because it shows that "the children of this world are in their generation wiser than the children of light."[41] In this passage, widely acknowledged as one of the most obscure parables, the behavior of the unjust steward appears to favor underhanded cleverness and to commend worldly self-interest at the expense of morality. Biblical interpreters have naturally worked hard, though not always convincingly, to circumvent this reading.

Levy, though, apparently reads the parable with a freethinker's common sense. Her story invites the reader's participation from the start in a cynical worldview for which the marriage market stands as signifier, within which women must use whatever means they can find to secure a mate. The narrator, Virginia, is a seasoned campaigner, "arriving at years of discretion" after being jilted by her first love, Philip, in favor of an heiress. Encountering Philip at a party a year later, she exchanges light conversation whose subtext sets the ground for the story's emerging narrative. Philip hints at excuses for his behavior: "In a civilisation like ours . . . it's the old story of the survival of the fittest." Virginia's immediate agreement with this—"[F]or a thorough-going, untiring support of one's own interest, there is, after all, no one like oneself"—is received as shocking: "[I]t doesn't do for a woman to talk like that!" For Virginia, however, the reverse is true. In a world of perpetual struggle, it is the young woman "let loose in a crowded ball-room" who is the prime exemplar of the need for protective self-interest and a carapace of cynicism. Levy allows Virginia an interesting generalization on the position of the ingénue in love:

> She does not know why she is so happy. All day long she dreams, dreams, or gossips of the night to come. If she thinks at all about it, she thinks prim thoughts such as have been instilled into her, and which have nothing to do with what she feels. The natural promptings of her modesty she mistakes for resistance to this unknown force, which is drawing her to itself as inevitably as the magnet draws the needle. With her prudish defences, she believes herself equipped for any fray; she feels so strong, and, O God, she is so weak! One day a bolt falls from the clear sky; he is going to be married to a woman of fortune, of good connections; he is away in the country wooing his rich bride. . . . Pshaw, what a rhodomontade! . . .
> All the girls, nearly, have gone through it.

Levy constructs Virginia's experience as the paradigm for the young girl's sexual awakening (the "prim thoughts" and "prudish defences," which are inappropriate to the true nature of her feelings) and the inevitable disillusionment that follows. "I wonder, sometimes, that we do not go oftener to the bad, we girls of the well-to-do classes," muses Virginia. Levy's implication—familiar enough in the discourse of late-Victorian feminism—is that "we" do go to the bad, "though the badness is not of the sort which demands the attention of philanthropists." The jilted young girl learns to play the game, and she survives by marrying for wealth and security rather than love. Virginia, more reflective and cleverer than most, plays a more sophisticated hand, reawakening Philip's interest by annexing a wealthy suitor: "I am acquiring such skill with games generally that Philip begins to respect me as he never respected me before." But at the moment when she wins her game, where she has become truly wise in her generation and the rich Sir Guy Ormond proposes, Virginia catches sight of herself in the mirror: "The reflection of my face caught my vision: its expression was scarcely one of triumph. And surely there must be some mistake in the calendar, some trick in the sand and quicksilver; I was not twenty, with smooth cheeks—I was a hundred years old, and wrinkled!" As with Milly in "The Diary of a Plain Girl," Levy uses the experience of literal reflection to redefine her subject's sense of selfhood as grotesque. But unlike Milly, for Virginia there is no external agency that can save and reclaim her. The struggle in which she is engaged is at the end of the story extended to universal essence as Virginia leans out of her bedroom window after rejecting Sir Guy's proposal:

> . . . there is no sound save the distant murmur of the Great City.
>   Black, black in its heart is the City; the blackness of man's heart is revealed in its huge, hideous struggle for existence.
>   Better be unfit and perish, than survive at such a cost.

Levy's bleak conclusion—suggesting that the city, civilization, and society stand for and reveal the condition of human life as a "hideous struggle for existence"—recalls her essay on James Thomson. According to Beth-Zion Lask, this essay is "indispensible to any study of . . . Amy Levy,"[42] dealing as it does with a poet tormented by pessimism and the pain of modern life. In it, Levy argues that Thomson's City of Dreadful Night "stands forth as the very sign and symbol of that attitude of mind which we call Weltschmerz, [p]essimism . . . the almost perfect expression of a form of mental suffering which I can convey by no other means than . . . by calling it 'grey pain,' 'the insufferable inane.'"[43] The stories she wrote in the last year or so of her life focus on Levy's recurrent engagement with exclusion and unfitness. Lask argues that Thomson interested Levy particularly as "a martyr to his unhappy lot, a moody being at the mercy of his temperament,"[44] phrases that recall Cohen, though Thomson's death resulted from despair-induced alcoholism rather than suicide. In Thomson, Levy claims, "we hear one note, one cry, muffled sometimes, but always there; a passionate, hungry cry for life, for the things of this human, flesh and blood life; for love and praise, for mere sunlight and sun's warmth. . . . No, this is not the highest utterance, the word of the great artist struggling towards completion; rather is it the under, coarser cry of the imperfect human being, crushed beneath a load which he is not formed to bear." Levy's interpretation of Thomson's pervasive vision of the passionate, struggling, human being crushed under a burden "he is not formed to bear" resonates linguistically with her recurrent references to Browning's fish that strives for bliss "she was not born to breathe." In Cohen, Levy works with the idea of a potentially heroic figure with a "passionate, hungry cry for life," an artist whose triumph in his struggle against exclusion and toward completion merely reveals, finally, his own unfitness to bear the load. And in Virginia she takes a skilled player in the social game who, at the moment of her triumph, fatally perceives the blackness of the game and chooses to be "unfit" rather than to claim her prize.

Levy's concluding summary of Thomson is that his was "a nature struggling with itself and Fate . . . an existence doomed to bear a twofold burden." Her own "twofold burden"—the acute senses of exclusion and unfitness, which, as I have argued, inform all her best short stories—perhaps illuminates the pessimistic "habit of mind" that puzzled Harry Quilter. Yet for Quilter it was not Levy's pessimism in itself that qualified his admiration for her novels; more important was the "detachment of mind" that, he claimed, created a sense of distance—indeed, lofty removal—from her fictional creations that exposed "a flavour of scorn in the telling of each incident."[45] This is an accusation that could not, I think, remotely be levelled at her short stories. On the contrary, that ironic detachment is the controlling device that restrains Levy's stories from becoming self-indulgent in their writing of despair or that adds an additional dimension to her otherwise-light social satire. The ending of "Sokratics in the Strand" exposes this technique almost starkly, as Horace is left alone to confront his anguish: "He flung himself down by the table and taking up a volume of Die Welt als Wille und Vorstellung which lay near, hurled it across the room. There were times when he liked to nurse and dandle his sorrow; to feed it with philosophy; to mature it with metaphysics; but to-night his own despair made him afraid."[46] Levy's prose brilliantly holds the tension between the slyly comic images of maturing sorrow with metaphysics (and shying Schopenhauer across the room) and the chilling evocation of a man terrified by his own despair.

Schopenhauer's work influenced the pessimism of many late-Victorian writers and was, as Melvyn New notes, "a book Levy seems to have known well."[47] As "Sokratics in the Strand" suggests, however, it cannot in itself provide an adequate account of her pessimistic habit of mind. Nor, ultimately, do the conditions of Levy's life—the inevitable displacement of the educated woman at the fin de siècle and the racial, bodily, and sexual aspects that contributed to her personal sense of exclusion—sufficiently explain the recurring fits of depression that led to her suicide. As her short stories brilliantly testify, Levy was always capable of holding existential despair in productive tension with ironic detachment. Wilde's posthumous tribute may claim that her work was "drawn drop by drop from the very depths of her being . . . that it was in truth her life's blood,"[48] and it is certainly true that from the time of her death to the present, Levy as both woman and writer has been appropriated to serve numerous causes: antifeminism and fin-de-siècle degeneration by her contemporaries; feminism, urbanism, and Jewish and lesbian identity by modern critics. We should be cautious, though, about constructing a figure like Grant Allen's "pallid little Amy Levy" who can stand simply for a victim of personal circumstance. At the Ladies' Literary Dinner of 30 May 1889, less than four months before her suicide, Levy was noted by the Star as "the most interesting personage" in a company that included Alice Meynell, Katherine Tynan, and Mona Caird.[49] After her death, Levy's contribution to the event was recalled in the Pall Mall Gazette: "[H]er delicate beauty [was] set off by a dress of cream-coloured satin and coral ornaments. She was rather silent, smoked her cigarette very thoughtfully, but made a brilliant little speech . . . lavish in the praise of other authors and authoresses . . . but also . . . very cynical, and . . . very pointed."[50] Levy's short stories, written with an urbanity and technical assurance that transcend the simply self-expressive, are notably the product of these features: "brilliant," "cynical," "pointed." More than her novels, and possibly more even than her poems, these stories are grounded in an intelligence and imagination that succeed in locating the independent fin-de-siècle woman in a social, political, and cultural, as well as individual and personal, world. Levy's understanding of the conditions of that world, where the existential fate of race or person combines with a society from which women in particular are excluded or that they are unfit to occupy, is what finds expression in her stories.

Notes

1. *The Letters of Oscar Wilde,* ed. Rupert Hart-Davis (New York: Harcourt, 1962), 208.

2. Amy Levy to Katie Levy, Amy Levy material, private collection.

3. Oscar Wilde, "Amy Levy," *Woman's World* 3 (1890): 52.

4. Harry Quilter, "Amy Levy: A Reminiscence and a Criticism," *Universal Review* 24 (1890): 492–507; quotation on 502.

5. Amy Levy, "Between Two Stools," *Temple Bar* 69 (1883): 337–50.

6. Amy Levy, "Sokratics in the Strand," *Cambridge Review,* 6 February 1884, 163–64.

7. Alfred Tennyson, *The Princess: A Medley* (London: E. Moxon, 1847).

8. Ana I. Parejo Vadillo, *Women Poets and Urban Aestheticism: Passengers of Modernity* (Basingstoke, UK: Palgrave Macmillan, 2005), 38.

9. Cynthia Scheinberg, *Women's Poetry and Religion in Victorian England: Jewish Identity and Christian Culture* (Cambridge: Cambridge University Press, 2002), 190.

10. Beatrice Webb, *My Apprenticeship* (London: Penguin, 1938), 447.

11. Quilter, "Amy Levy," 502.

12. Linda G. Zatlin, review of *The Complete Novels and Selected Writings of Amy Levy, 1861–1889, Studies in Short Fiction* 31 (Summer 1994): 512.

13. Examples include Sarah Grand's *The Heavenly Twins* (1893), Emma Brooke's *A Superfluous Woman* (1894), and Grant Allen's notorious *The Woman Who Did* (1895), a novel whose overblown and often silly antimarriage rhetoric probably contributed significantly to the decline of New Woman discourse on the marriage versus free love question.

14. Clementina Black, Obituary, *Athenaeum* no. 3232 (5 October 1889): 457. Black was the elder sister of Constance (later Garnett), with whom Levy went to school in Brighton and to Newnham College, Cambridge. Levy later turned to Clementina as both a friend and a literary advisor. Her will left "all books, papers, letters and documents of every kind" to Clementina.

15. "Camford" is Levy's substitute for the more familiar "Oxbridge," a composite term for the universities of Oxford and Cambridge. "Princess Ida's" refers to Tennyson's palace of woman's learning in *The Princess*.

16. Amy Levy to Katie Levy, Amy Levy material, private collection.

17. Linda Hunt Beckman, *Amy Levy: Her Life and Letters* (Athens: Ohio University Press, 2000), 242–43.

18. Thomas Moore, *Lalla Rookh: An Oriental Romance* (London: Longman, Hurst, Rees, Orme and Brown, 1817), Part 4, "Paradise and the Peri," lines 1–2 and 7–8.

19. Amy Levy, *Reuben Sachs*, in *The Complete Novels and Selected Writings of Amy Levy, 1861–1889*, ed. Melvyn New (Florida: University Press of Florida, 1993), 214.

20. Ibid., 217.

21. Amy Levy, "Three Times," Amy Levy material, private collection. Notably, in this paragraph Levy's handwriting, always subject to wide variation according to her mood, becomes larger and more flowing than in the rest of the story.

22. Grant Allen, "Plain Words on the Woman Question," *Fortnightly Review* 46 (1889): 455–56. As a vociferous advocate of free love and opponent of marriage, most notably expressed in his *succès de scandal* novel of 1895 *The Woman Who Did*, Allen was associated by contemporaries with New Woman feminism. His interest in the woman question, however, was largely based in his enthusiasm for eugenics and focused on freeing women from social convention in order to breed a healthier race; education for women was, in his view, an obstacle to this end. On the issue of women's education, his radicalism converges oddly with Victorian tradition.

23. "Caliban upon Setebos," lines 33–36, 38–43. Robert Browning, *Dramatis Personae* (London: Chapman and Hall, 1864). Levy slightly misquotes, writing "waves" for "brine" and "bonds" for "bounds."

24. New, *Complete Novels*, 35.

25. Other stories by Amy Levy using this device include "In Retreat," *London Society* 46 (1884): 332–35; and "Another Morning in Florence," *London Society* 48 (1886): 386–90.

26. In Tennyson's *Princess*, Princess Ida's closest friend is Psyche. Melissa is the daughter of Blanche, displaced by Psyche in Princess Ida's regard. It is Melissa who inadvertently betrays the presence of men in the palace of learning.

27. Amy Levy, "Out of the World," *London Society* 49 (1886): 53–56.

28. Thomas Hood, "The Bridge of Sighs," lines 67–71, *Hood's Magazine*, May 1844.

29. Algernon Charles Swinburne, "The Triumph of Time," lines 113–16, 257–8, 267–70, *Poems and Ballads*, 1st series (London: J. C. Hotten, 1866). Swinburne's poem is also quoted at length in Levy's *Reuben Sachs*.

30. Christine Pullen, "Amy Levy: Her Life, Her Poetry and the Era of the New Woman" (PhD diss., Kingston University, 2000), 129. After Levy's death, Constance Black wrote to her father-in-law, "I know she had twice made the attempt before." Richard Garnett, *Constance Garnett: A Heroic Life* (London: Sinclair-Stevenson, 1991), 68.

31. Quilter, "Amy Levy."

32. Responding to a letter from Maria Sharpe on the new Men and Women's Club, which mentions the deafness of a Miss Mills, Pearson replied, "What a misfortune with regard to her deafness! It is the very reason which has withheld my mentioning the matter to a Miss Levy, who it seems to me would otherwise have made a useful member." Pearson to Maria Sharpe, 30 March 1885, Pearson Papers.

33. Amy Levy to Katie Levy, Amy Levy material, private collection.

34. Amy Levy, "Wise in Her Generation," *Woman's World* 3 (1890): 20–23.

35. Amy Levy, "The Diary of a Plain Girl," *London Society* 44 (September 1883): 295–304.

36. Amy Levy, "Lallie," Camellia Collection: Amy Levy Archive.

37. Amy Levy, "Griselda," *Temple Bar* 84 (September 1888): 63–96.

38. Capel Court and Mincing Lane are areas associated with business and commerce; Grub Street, of course, with writers.

39. Amy Levy, "Cohen of Trinity," *Gentleman's Magazine* 266 (May 1889): 417–24.

40. "Miss Amy Levy," *Lady's Pictorial*, 21 September 1889, 358.

41. Luke 16:1–13.

42. Beth-Zion Lask, "Amy Levy," *Transactions of the Jewish Historical Society of England* 11 (1928), 172.

43. Amy Levy, "James Thomson: A Minor Poet," *Cambridge Review*, 21 and 28 February 1883, 240–41, 257–58.

44. Lask, "Amy Levy," 172.

45. Quilter, "Amy Levy."

46. Arthur Schopenhauer's *Die Welt als Wille und Vorstellung* (1883), translated as *The World as Will and Idea* (or sometimes *The World as Will and Representation*), argues that the will (and by extension, the world as representation of the will) is essentially mindless and lawless, endlessly struggling to no purpose.

47. New, *Complete Novels*, 557n.

48. Oscar Wilde, "Amy Levy," *Woman's World* 3 (1889): 51–52.

49. Mainly about People, *Star*, 1 June 1889, 1.

50. Today's Tittle Tattle, *Pall Mall Gazette*, 16 September 1889, 6.

Amy Levy and the Literary
Representation of the Jewess

Nadia Valman

HE most blasphemous words in Amy Levy's avowedly irreverent *Reuben Sachs* (1888) are put into the mouth of Esther Kohnthal, the bitter spinster: "Cursed art Thou, O Lord my God, Who has had the cruelty to make me a woman."[1] Esther's curse boldly reverses the words of the blessing recited daily by the Jewish male, thanking God for not making him female. For Levy, this Oriental "pride of sex" lies at the root of the wretched position of Jewish women that is indicted in the novel.[2] But her citation of Jewish liturgy indicates a religious critique too. Indeed, the thanksgiving for masculinity in Jewish daily worship had attracted attention throughout the nineteenth century, from Maria Edgeworth's philosemitic *Harrington* (1817), where it is pointedly left without comment, to the numerous Evangelical tract writers for whom it became a cornerstone of the Protestant polemic against Judaism.[3] By the end of the century, when Levy quoted and rewrote the blessing, Christian critique and feminist protest had become firmly yoked together and ubiquitous in discussions of contemporary Jewish life.

Levy's achievement in *Reuben Sachs* has been recognized in recent years for the audacious challenge she posed to an Anglo-Jewish literary tradition of representing Jews as contented, pious, and obedient citizens.[4] While many critics have rightly pointed to the analysis of gender and power that underpins her denunciation of Victorian Anglo-Jewry, few have noticed the long provenance of such a critique in nineteenth-century Christian culture. This chapter aims to locate Amy Levy's image of the Jewish woman within this literary context—a representational tradition that both preceded and followed her. My discussion explores the relationship between *Reuben Sachs* and a range of popular novels, from the conversion fiction of the early nineteenth century to Levy's late-Victorian contemporaries—all focused on the figure of the Jewess. Tracing the development of this remarkably flexible trope across the century, I consider the opportunities and limitations it presented for Levy's feminist vision.

Reuben Sachs, *Feminism, and Judaism*

Reuben Sachs has finally come into full prominence as one of the first feminist novels by an Anglo-Jewish writer. The novel's central concern with the social, intellectual, and emotional repression of the middle-class Jewish woman has been brought into focus for many critics by the argument Levy articulated earlier for a more limited readership, in her unsigned article "Middle-Class Jewish Women of To-Day," published in the *Jewish Chronicle* in 1886.[5] Here, Levy charges contemporary Jews with a conservative disregard for the capacities of women. "What, in fact," she asks, "is the ordinary life of a Jewish middle-class woman? Carefully excluded, with an almost Eastern jealousy, from every-day intercourse with men and youths of her own age, she is plunged all at once—a half-fledged, often half-chaperoned creature—into the 'vortex' of a middle-class ball-room, and is there expected to find her own level." Protected from any pursuits that might divert their attention from the objective of a lucrative marriage, Jewish daughters are brought up to be ignorant, unthinking, and mercenary. And "in a society constructed on such a primitive basis, the position of single women, so rapidly improving in the general world, is a particularly unfortunate one."[6]

This argument is given narrative form in *Reuben Sachs* in the divergent destinies of the ambitious barrister Reuben and the beautiful, ardent, but dowry-less Judith Quixano. Judith is unable to grasp hold of her life's potential partly because she comes from a poor family and partly because, as a Jewish woman, she has been brought up not to think. "[F]or Judith Quixano," explains the narrator, "and for many women placed as she, it is difficult to conceive a training, an existence, more curiously limited, more completely provincial than hers. Her outlook on life was of the narrowest; of the world, of London, of society beyond her own set, it may be said that she had seen nothing at first hand" (69). The story begins with Reuben succumbing to his attraction toward Judith, but as his career progresses he abandons her, and she too is pressured to prioritize mercenary concerns in a loveless marriage that raises her socially while crushing her emotionally. In the novel's most poignant comment, Levy's narrator laments the passivity that prevents Judith from struggling for what she desires: "There is nothing more terrible, more tragic, than this ignorance of a woman of her own nature, her own possibilities, her own passions" (125). Such passivity, however, is seen as symptomatic of the condition of the middle-class Jewish woman more generally: despite "her beauty, her intelligence, her power of feeling, [Judith] saw herself merely as one of a vast crowd of girls awaiting their promotion by marriage" (68).

Yet Levy's protest against the iniquities of the West End Jewish marriage market resonates beyond this particular setting, echoing the many critiques of modern marriage that animated feminist debate in the 1880s. In her celebrated article, "Marriage," published in the *Westminster Review* in August 1888 when *Reuben Sachs* was still under composition, Mona Caird used similar terms in attacking the social system that denied middle-class women economic and emotional autonomy. She described "the unfortunate girls whose horizon is as limited as their opportunities, whose views of life are cribbed, cabined, and confined by their surroundings, whose very right and wrong, just and unjust, are chosen for them. . . . It is impossible for an outsider to realise the restrictions and narrowness of the average girl's life." The result, she claimed, was a "bewildered being, stunted in intelligence, in self-respect."[7] The institution of marriage was the economic basis of women's repression, according to Caird, and she vigorously challenged its moral authority. "Our common respectable marriage, upon which the safety of all social existence is supposed to rest," she argued, "is . . . the worst, because the most hypocritical, form of woman-purchase." But under the present organization of sexual relations, she insisted, in which women were financially dependent on men, there was "no reasonable alternative" to mercenary marriage.[8]

This dilemma is also the subject of Levy's highly pessimistic, last-published fictional work, "Wise in Her Generation" (1890), which appeared posthumously in Oscar Wilde's *Woman's World*. What particularly interests me about this story is how closely it reworks, this time for a general readership, Levy's description of the plight of the Jewess in "Middle-Class Jewish Women of To-Day": "Take a girl in the schoolroom and see what her life is. A dingy room, dowdy dresses, bread and butter, and governesses! In all the household there is, perhaps, no person of less importance than she. Then, one day, this creature, knowing nothing of the world, and less, if possible, of herself, is launched on the stream of fashionable or pseudo-fashionable life. At what has been hitherto her bedtime, she is arrayed gorgeously, whirled through a gas-lit city, and finally let loose in a crowded ball-room, there to sink or swim."[9] Here, as in Levy's earlier article, the wry, confident female narrator reflects on the emotional vulnerability of women trained in social and sexual naïveté and then abandoned in the jungle of the bourgeois marriage market. As the story unfolds, however, the narrator finds herself equally a victim despite her raised consciousness (or, perhaps, because of it). In a compressed version of the plot of *Reuben Sachs,* the heroine loses her lover to a wealthier catch but is unable to bring herself to perform the charade of affection toward an alternative suitor for whom she feels no passion. Altering the description of the debutante's floundering in the ballroom "there . . . to find her own level," to the darkly Darwinian "there to sink or swim," Levy's later text suggests a far more despairing perspective. At its conclusion, the narrator realizes that women of intelligence and integrity are particularly disadvantaged in the struggle for survival and declares, "Better be unfit and perish, than survive at such a cost."[10]

While "Middle-Class Jewish Women of To-Day" and "Wise in Her Generation" analyze the social conditions that render women powerless over their destinies, *Reuben Sachs* adds a further element. Levy's novel also considers the religious culture that crucially contributes to Judith's failure to develop an interior life. This is subtly illustrated in the scene in which Judith attends the Upper Berkeley Street synagogue on the Day of Atonement. Surrounded by a congregation disheartened by "the rigours and *longeurs* [*sic*] of the day," Judith "went through her devotion upheld by that sense of fitness, of obedience to law and order, which characterized her every action" (89, 91). Judith's pharisaic attention to ritual observance typifies her unacknowledged discontent: "These prayers, read so diligently, in a language of which her knowledge was exceedingly imperfect, these reiterated praises of an austere tribal deity, these expressions of a hope whose consummation was neither desired nor expected [for restoration to Zion], what connection could they have with the personal needs, the human longings of this touchingly ignorant and limited creature?" (91). Here, Levy emphasizes once again the conformism and inarticulacy of the Jewish woman, unable even to recognize her unfulfilled needs. But Levy is also making an implicit link between Judith's mechanical (rather than self-reflexive) thinking and Judaism, the religion of externals.

What is most striking about this passage, therefore, is its manifest resemblance to the nineteenth-century Christian polemic against Judaism—as lawbound and lacking in spiritual sustenance. In particular, while the synagogue service leaves others, like Reuben, "bored, resigned," it is Judith's "longings" as an emotional but repressed woman that reveal the full deficiency of Jewish religious practice. Of the more intellectual, and more bitter, Esther Kohnthal, who refuses altogether to attend synagogue, the narrator archly comments, "She, poor soul, was of those who deny utterly the existence of the Friend of whom she stood so sorely in need" (91). While Levy's feminism, therefore, foregrounds the enforced passivity of women, it does this by way of a longstanding and specifically gendered critique of Judaism. *Reuben Sachs,* in fact, updates in feminist terms the paradigm popularized by earlier nineteenth-century Evangelical novels, in which the Jewish woman was consistently presented as particularly oppressed and particularly in need of salvation.

The Jewish Woman and Jewish Conversion

Impelled by an urgent sense of apocalyptic crisis, millennialist Evangelicals in the 1830s and '40s devoted extraordinary energy to the conversion of the Jews as a goal that would fulfill messianic prophecy and herald the Second Advent. In the numerous popular narratives and pseudo-memoirs produced for an Evangelical readership in this period, such hopes were symbolically expressed in the figure of the young Jewish woman who, through reading and contemplating the Bible, comes to realize the spiritual limitations of Judaism and finds new life in Christianity. The Jewess was portrayed in terms consonant with the elevated rhetorical status of femininity more generally in Evangelical culture. According to this ideology, women's emotionalism and moral superiority rendered them inherently more spiritual than men and more capable of embodying the Evangelical appeal.[11] In the Evangelical imagination, the full feminine capacities of the Jewess were tragically inhibited by her repressive religion.[12]

Charlotte Anley's *Miriam; or, The Power of Truth: A Jewish Tale* (1826) is one of the earliest examples of the genre of Jewish conversion narrative; it continued to be reprinted for three decades and went into at least eleven editions.[13] Set in the improbable location of the Westmoreland wilds, Anley's novel plots the gradual alienation of a young Jewish woman from her male-dominated household and her increasing attraction to the religion espoused by her simple, rural, female neighbors. From the outset, *Miriam* casts the Jewish father and his daughter as temperamental antagonists. The wealthy, misanthropic Imlah Durvan is mysterious, intimidating and "haughty," while his young daughter Miriam "formed a striking contrast to his own melancholy character," exuberant as she is with the "joy of innocence." From the outset, too, the novel suggests that the only redeeming light in the life of Imlah is his daughter, "upon whom alone, Imlah seemed to smile."[14]

Anley's polemic against Judaism in the novel is incarnated in Jewish men and their failings. Imlah's bitterness is the result of his failed attempt at "the restoration of his alienated race; believing, in his mad enthusiasm, that he could overthrow the Christian church and frustrate the designs of an offended God" (4). Brought up in Germany with a raging hatred of Christianity, he inculcates this militancy into his daughter; when the promised day arrives, she vows, "I, woman as I am, shall wave the banners of our faith, amidst the bleeding heaps of those detested Christians!" (11). Imlah is at home with antagonism and finds it unsettling to be in England, where a Jew "may safely rove in unsuspected liberty, to enjoy all the privileges of peace and security" (7). His ambition, instead, for the national restoration of the Jews, points to Imlah's erroneous attachment to worldly existence. He builds a luxurious home for his daughter, buries himself in intellectual study, and in his religious life is equally a materialist, believing that "conformity to the moral laws and ordinances of the ancient prophets, was enough to ensure his salvation" (9). His household is governed by the severe pronouncements of Rabbi Mendez, whose decrepitude, spleen, and fear of mortality dramatize even more graphically the novel's view of Judaism as spiritually moribund. When she discovers another world to compare with that of her own home, Miriam cannot but notice that "Judaism seemed to throw a gloom of mysterious colouring over the one, which darkened not the other" (105).

If Judaism in Anley's novel is associated with the dreariness and dejection of old age, the sunny vivacity of the young Jewish daughter marks her out for a more enlightened destiny. In contrast to her father, Miriam is indifferent to the "dazzling toys of wealth" that surround her (9). The "stern and dictatorial severity" of Mendez, who feels shame at expressing the "weakness" of emotion, throws into relief the spontaneous sensibility of Miriam, whom we see early in the novel listening to a group of village children singing hymns, and responding tearfully to "the sounds which had thus deeply touched her" (47, 45, 30). True religion, the narrator asserts, is no enemy to such feminine feelings; indeed, it "cherishes rather than forbids the tenderness of nature; and though it heals and sanctifies, it cannot exempt the human heart from human sufferings, nor does it always avert its frailties" (72). But the dry, repressive, and academic environment in which Miriam has been educated provides no outlet for her love of humanity or her delight in the natural world around her. She comes to covet the "unsophisticated mind" of Helen Stuart, a young village woman who befriends her, and wishes she could have "exchanged her useless talents and unvalued wealth for the peace and industry which blest the simple cottagers of Glencairn!" (104, 105).

The novel's revelation of the source of such security—Christian faith—is thus also staged as Miriam's journey toward self-realization as a woman. Increasingly alienated from the emotional austerity and strict legalism of her father and tutor, increasingly turning against her former violent hatred of Christians, Miriam finds herself in close affinity with the feminized religion of the heart that is practiced in Glencairn. Reading the New Testament in secret, she learns to find her own voice, independent of her male mentors. But paradoxically, this journey is also cast by the novel as the fulfillment of her *Jewish* identity. Miriam's first lesson in Christian humility is learned from Helen's mother, who faces the illness of her youngest daughter fearlessly. For Miriam, it seems that "the pious mother had, with an Abraham's faith, bared the bosom of her child to meet in unresisting submission the death-stroke which hung over her!" (53–54). Compared with Rabbi Mendez's terror of mortality, Margaret Stuart's obedience to divine will makes her the more authentic inheritor of Old Testament piety. Likewise, as the story approaches its climactic scene of conversion, Miriam herself asserts an ever stronger devotion to Zion. "Oh! Could my death but hasten the deliverance of Jerusalem, even but an hour, gladly would I lay down my life in behalf of our beloved people. Forsake them! No, my father" (269). Spoken in the language of her earlier zeal, Miriam's words have an import that she herself does not understand. In the millennialist plot of the novel, her death at its conclusion—which is the catalyst for her hard-hearted father's conversion and leads to his work as a missionary to the Jews—is indeed seen to hasten the "deliverance of Jerusalem."

In her death scene, therefore, the converted Miriam appears more Jewish than ever:

> Supported by pillows, she lay in an almost upright posture, with no other covering over her shoulders than a large Turkish shawl which her father had laid over her when sleeping. Greatly oppressed, she had thrown off her cap, and her fine hair now hung carelessly about her neck, partly con-cealing her face, the expression of which was almost angelic, for animated with the enthusiasm of her lofty mind—the desire of evincing the happy influences of Christian hope, and the devotional feelings of pious submis-sion; gentleness and beauty combined to throw a peculiar lustre over the whole aspect of the young Jewess. (354)

Miriam's body has become a symbol of Christian supersession—the superior "lustre" that is "throw[n] . . . over" and elevates the old "enthusiasm," harmo-nizing the apparent conflict between her old and new religions. Significantly, Anley continues to refer to her heroine as a "Jewess" despite her commitment to Christianity, clothing her deliberately in Oriental garb and Romantic eroti-cism. This is perhaps the most unexpected feature of conversion narrative: its insistence on the persistence of Jewishness in the convert. In fact, Miriam's Jew-ishness is what makes her such an ideal Christian, her passionate Jewish nature tempered by Christ-like patience.

Such patience, however, is seen as the flowering of Miriam's femininity. The novel underlines its conviction in the special capacity of women to exemplify Christian teaching in the subplot involving Helen's sister Edith and the man by whom she was almost led astray. Morally and financially crippled by gam-bling, he is eventually condemned to death for committing fraud; however, in-spired by Edith's noble forgiveness, he finally dies in penitence, strengthened by faith. Just as this male malefactor is redeemed by female virtue, so too is Miriam's unbelieving father finally roused by her example to see the light. In the story of Edith, and even more so in the story of Miriam, suffering—in Miriam's case the attempt to arrange her marriage against her will, and the physical illness brought on by the anxiety of her conversion—reveals and calls forth women's extraordinary powers of compassion and submission.

The figure of the Jewess in Anley's novel, then, is drawn from the particularly privileged status accorded both to women and to Jews in Evangelical culture. Evangelicalism's new emphasis on Christ as a figure of humility and sacrifice gave the story of the convert battling the hostility of a patriarchal religion exemplary appeal. The critique of Judaism articulated by Evangelicals, intensely attached to the conversion and redemption of the Jews, produced the highly idealized figure of the Jewess.

Allegories of Class and Race:
Secularizing the Conversion Novel

As Michael Ragussis has shown, the ideology of conversion continued to inform representations of Jewish identity in British literature throughout the century.[15] The specifically gendered dimension of this trope, moreover, was equally enduring. The Jewess whose heightened sensitivities render her more susceptible to suffering continued to play a key role in revealing and critiquing the inadequacies of Judaism and the Jews. Emily Eden's *The Semi-Detached House* (1859), for example, offers a secularized version of the Evangelical conversion narrative, focusing on the abhorrent manners and morals of the new Jewish plutocracy. Whereas Anley's tract dramatized the religious controversies of the early nineteenth century, Eden's social satire uses Jews to produce a parable of mid-Victorian class relations. Written in the wake of the financial crisis of 1857, Eden's tale of the rise and fall of Jewish speculators whose fortunes are made by dishonesty and dissembling was to be often repeated during the 1860s and '70s.[16] In Eden's novel, like those of her predecessors, this account of Jewish materialism is brought into sharp focus by the oppositional voice of a young Jewish woman.

The Semi-Detached House is set in the London suburb of Dulham, where the Chesters, down-at-heel aristocrats, come to reside in one half of a house shared with the respectable middle-class Hopkinsons. While the Hopkinsons prepare to gird themselves against "the vices of the nobility," the Chester daughters bemoan their decline to bourgeois suburbia.[17] This class antagonism is triangulated through the Jewish Baron and Baroness Sampson, latest arrivals in Dulham with their "very showy coach . . . such very high noses, and such jet black hair . . . much pleasantry, and infinite want of tact" (40–41). Unlike Mrs. Hopkinson, who knows her place in the social hierarchy, the baroness has aristocratic aspirations yet is unable to recognize the pedigree of the Chester ladies and snubs them, fearing an embarrassing acquaintance. But she is equally incapable of assuming the station to which her wealth has raised her: "her manner of treating her servants was not calculated to excite either their attachment or respect" (104). In juxtaposition with the baroness's vulgarity, the Chesters and the Hopkinsons realize how much they have in common. While they take up their social responsibilities through philanthropy directed toward other women, the baroness allies herself with men, exploiting her social connections in the cause of her husband's unstable speculative ventures.

The novel's critique of the social and financial speculation practiced by the Jews is offered not only through the narrator but also through the Sampsons' niece, Rachel Monteneros. Moody, melancholy, and an avid reader and quoter of poetry, Rachel's name recalls Maria Edgeworth's refined Sephardic heroine, Berenice Montenero, in *Harrington.* Moreover, in the tradition of conversion narrative, Rachel is shown to be disaffected from her Jewish family, wearing an habitual "look of anxiety, as, resting her head on her clasped hands, she seemed to give herself up to deep and painful thoughts" of how she is "treated with neglect" by them (109, 110). Living in constant suspicion of her relatives' plot to embezzle her fortune, Rachel is drawn instead to Mrs. Hopkinson's "honesty" (111). She confesses that her aunt has "made me what I am—cold, distrustful, unloved and unloving" (248). Between them, the gentile women effect a transformation in Rachel: the Chester ladies "were full of pity and admiration" for her, while the Hopkinson daughters introduce her to the ethos of public charity as an escape from her pathological self-absorption (183). The novel thus cements the alliance between middle- and upper-class women not only through their cultural antitype, the vulgar baroness, but also through the young Jewess, whose figurative conversion replicates and affirms a bourgeois model of femininity.

Eden's novel sets solid female integrity and generosity against the aggressive, philistine materialism of the Sampsons—English middle-class femininity against Jews. This conflict is dramatized most of all in the story of the cultured young Jewish woman who stands alone in resisting her family's values: speculators, Rachel declares, "have more to answer for than the pecuniary ruin they have wrought. They have ruined all confidence, all trust, they have made dishonesty the rule, and not the exception" (135–36). Rachel's ability to reflect, her recognition of the shortcomings of her family, and her readiness to open herself up to the world of Englishwomen point to the origins of her character in conversion narrative. The Jewess who reads, like her converting predecessors with their secret Bibles, reveals and transcends the degradation of Jewishness.

At the end of the nineteenth century, the narrative of the converting Jewess remained potent. The popular romance writer Dorothea Gerard, who produced two novels on Jewish themes during her residence in Galicia, Poland, as the wife of an Austrian army officer, displays in her work a more extreme albeit structurally similar version of the mix of philosemitism and antisemitism that I have identified in the literary representation of the Jewess. In Gerard's work, the theological critique of Judaism is brought into tension with a new physiological and racial understanding of Jewish difference. Ultimately skeptical about the possibility of Jewish conversion, Gerard's representations of Jewish life resonate with contemporary concerns about the potential for integration of eastern European Jewish immigrants in contemporary England. Such concerns are articulated in the novels' fascination with and repulsion from the figure of the Jewish woman.

Published in the same year as *Reuben Sachs* but set in Poland, Gerard's *Orthodox* (1888) centers on the tragic passivity of Salome Marmorstein, a poor but, like her biblical namesake, dangerously beautiful Jewess, and her lover, Count Rudolph von Ortenegg, a naïve aristocratic army officer. Narrated as a cautionary tale by Ortenegg's more worldly friend, the story is designed to demonstrate that Polish hostility toward Jews is thoroughly justified. Ortenegg is initially predisposed in favor of the Jews, whom he views with "pity" despite the narrator's attempts to undeceive him. "You have not been in this country long enough yet," warns the narrator, "to estimate fairly the intensity of that fanatical abhorrence of the baptized which rages like a disease in the veins of every Jew who aspires to the title of orthodox. He must be revenged upon you for being what you are, no matter at what personal or even financial sacrifice, for he hates you more than he loves gold."[18] Dodging the military draft, the narrator insists, is one example of the inveterate anti-Polish antagonism felt by Jews that is theological in nature.

Ortenegg's education in the nature of Jews begins when he encounters Surchen Marmorstein, Salome's little sister, who hopes to lure the officer into a romance by which she will profit. When Surchen first points out her sister to Ortenegg, Salome is modeling an evening dress made in the family workshop, where her father blocks the officer's gaze by holding a lamp "in such a position that it left her face in shadow. All this time she had not moved, but stood with her arms straight by her sides. She seemed absolutely and entirely indifferent to Ortenegg's presence; almost unaware of it" (39–40). Marmorstein's jealous protection of his daughter and Salome's own reserve provoke the officer's desire for conquest. He expresses this, however, in chivalric terms, believing himself a "crusader" against the "narrow superstition" of Judaism and longing to liberate Salome from the oppressive customs of her environment, such as the practices of shearing the hair of brides and arranging marriage through male family members—"a deed of sale" that he sees as "a fearful sin against God and Nature" (50–51, 94–95).

In the ways that the novel elicits a response of pity and desire toward the Jewess, we once again see the philosemitic strain that invariably accompanies critiques of Judaism. In this later text, however, the physical rather than the religious nature of the Jewess is what suggests her potential for redemption: "Salome's beauty was certainly of a more uncommon type than that of any of the raven-locked Jewish beauties of the place. Her pure red-gold hair grew thick and low upon an ivory brow; in the grace of her exquisite figure and the pose of her proud head there was something at once severely classical and haughtily indolent" (48). While the gold-crowned Salome is treated by her father as a valuable hoard, her body is invested by the narrator with moral dimensions that suggest her distinctiveness from the craven Jewish men of her community, whom Ortenegg observes with disgust in a scene at the barracks being whipped by officers in the riding ring for money. It is thus by means of the rhetoric of gender that the text conveys its ambivalence about Jewish difference. Even the cynical narrator is forced to recognize that

> she was independent of her surroundings. She could be lifted out of them, as it were. All the sordid littlenesses of her low-born life would drop from her like a cloak, without leaving even their memory to drag her down from the new sphere in which she was to be placed. . . . This conviction of mine must have resulted partly from the recognition that a character so feminine and so flexible as hers must possess an abnormal power of assimilation, partly from my perception of that peculiar lustre, that touch of *race*, which so often distinguishes the Jewish maiden, and which . . . precludes, even in the lowest and most uneducated, all taint of what we generally term vulgarity. (116, original emphasis)

It is Salome's femininity that ensures her capacity for "assimilation" into the Christian community and her "touch of race" that qualifies her for social promotion. By the late nineteenth century, then, the unique sensibility associated with the Jewish woman had shifted once again, this time to reflect the mysticism of racial thinking. Salome's "touch of race," seen in this context, is another secularized version of the distinctive spirituality attributed to the Jewess.

But although her physique and character seem to point to her redemption, Salome Marmorstein is ultimately unable to save herself. Despite Ortenegg's success in persuading her to convert and marry him, at the last minute she allows herself to be taken back into the Jewish quarter, where her father ensures that she is immediately wedded to the nearest available Jewish man. Returning to Salome's house, Ortenegg finds it deserted except for the shorn locks of her red-gold hair: the symbolic violence and prostitution of her marriage.[19] In this story of failed conversion, the greater destiny for which the Jewess is marked out by her "touch of race" is something that she herself fails to fulfill. "You have no idea of the subjection of intellect in which Jewish women are brought up," the narrator tells his friend, "The old bondage of religious terror is upon them still" (83). In Gerard's novel, the Jews' mistreatment of women epitomizes their primitiveness and their incapacity for enlightenment. The Jewess's racial distinctiveness, therefore, is ultimately subverted by her religious subjugation. Gerard's Catholicism may be the reason for her move away, in this novel, from the Protestant narrative of the convertibility of the Jewess; nonetheless, *Orthodox*, like those narratives, insists on her exceptionality.

As the Christian polemic against Judaism articulated early in the nineteenth century expanded to include critiques of the social pretensions or racial atavism of the Jews, narratives of the Jewess were also transformed. Consistently used to point out the failings of the Jews, the Jewess was idealized—as spiritually elevated or as naturally middle class in culture, or as racially superior. It is the doubleness of this literary tradition that I want to emphasize in returning now to Amy Levy's gendered representations of Jews. Levy's work draws on the various aspects of the tradition even as it pushes them in a different direction.

Amy Levy and the Uncertainties of Conversion

Levy's most signal debt to the Evangelical tradition is her idealization of the figure of the Jewess as an agent of redemption for the Jews. Thus, in "Middle-Class Jewish Women of To-Day," her 1886 article for the *Jewish Chronicle*, Levy's critique of Anglo-Jewish life is accompanied by a celebratory strain of optimism focused on "the potentialities of the women of our race." After analyzing the social and moral structure of bourgeois Anglo-Jewry that leads to the restriction of female autonomy, she goes on to argue that Jewish women's greater discontent made them "more readily adaptable, more eager to absorb the atmosphere around them" than men. In this phrase, Levy reiterates the established notion that the Jewess is more open to conversion, but she uses instead the Darwinian term "adaptable." She casts the Jewish woman as having the evolutionary advantage over the Jew, whose conservatism and ease of existence give him no incentive to join the stream of historical progress. The Jewish woman, in contrast, compelled toward the outside world, leads the march into modernity. Yet it is not religious conversion to which Levy's middle-class Jewesses are more amenable; rather they have, she argues, "in many cases outstripped their brothers in culture." Levy concludes the article with a list of examples of contemporary female intellectuals of Jewish origin and in a triumphal, almost millenarian tone anticipates the imminent demise of "our Conservatism with regard to women . . . in the face of modern thought, modern liberty and, above all, modern economic pressure."

This optimism about the future shape of Anglo-Jewish gender relations is all but absent from *Reuben Sachs*, published two years later. But Levy's story of the suppression of female desire and intelligence—set in a milieu dominated by social aspiration, materialism, and philistinism—can also be seen as a direct descendant of the nineteenth-century conversion novel. *Reuben Sachs* portrays late-Victorian Anglo-Jewry apparently on the brink of oblivion, with religious belief waning and family ties weakening as the younger generation "showed symptoms of a desire to strike out from the tribal duck-pond into the wider and deeper waters of society" (69). The religious disputation that characterizes conversion novels takes place here among Jews, with Reuben weakly defending Judaism against his assimilated cousin Leo Leuniger, who prophesies its supersession as a Darwinian process of adaptation and extinction. As Jews take up the opportunities offered by emancipation, he declares, and "the general world claims our choicer specimens for its own," the demise of the "Community" is an "inevitability" (102). For Leo this prospect is welcome because, restating the Evangelical critique, Judaism is "the religion of materialism. The corn and the wine and the oil; the multiplication of the seed; the conquest of the hostile tribes—these have always had more attraction for us than the harp and crown of a spiritualized existence" (100). In *Reuben Sachs*, as in earlier texts, this critique is also articulated through the symbolism of gender, embodied most of all in the cold ambition of the Jewish male, whose inherited "creed" is "that it is noble and desirable to have everything better than your neighbour . . . the sacred duty of doing the very best for yourself" (104). Alongside such familiar features is the figure of the Jewess, who suffers in her quiet, barely acknowledged resistance to this philosophy: her subversive belief in "strong feeling which had not its foundations in material interests" (133).

Levy's Jewess, like her converting forebears, is singled out from those around her. If early Evangelical writers pointed to the joyful temperament and spiritual sensibility of the Jewish woman, late-nineteenth-century texts, as we have seen, expressed her exceptionality in physiological terms. Thus, while Levy's Jewish men are ugly, ailing, and depressive—strong in vitality but afflicted with an array of nervous diseases—Judith Quixano is "in the very prime of her youth and beauty; a tall, regal-looking creature, with an exquisite dark head, features like those of a face cut on gem or cameo. . . . Her smooth oval cheek glowed with a rich, yet subdued, hue of perfect health"; her body has "the generous lines of a figure which was distinguished for stateliness rather than grace" (62). Judith's "regal" air, her "perfect health," and her maternal figure contrast sharply with the degenerate bodies of the West End Jews, the "ill-made sons and daughters of Shem" (114). Her "air of breeding" suggests both her refinement and her reproductive potential, leading Reuben to fantasize about "[c]hildren on his hearth with Judith's eyes" (84, 103). Unlike Reuben and his extended family, Judith is of Sephardic lineage, carrying a legendary heritage of refinement, intellect, and cultural openness.[20] Her true value as an agent of redemption becomes clear to Reuben when, arguing with Leo, he invokes the mystery of affinity among Jews but, subconsciously, "praised her in the race, and the race in her" (102). As Judith is suddenly inspired with "the flame of a great emotion" and "[feels] the love of her race grow stronger at every word," the novel orchestrates a moment highly charged with eugenic expectation (102). In suggesting that Judith holds the potential to regenerate Reuben's decadent stock, Levy's novel casts "race" as the new revelation that will save the Jews. When Reuben's ambition leads him to abandon Judith, therefore, he also squanders her racial resources, continuing the inexorable path to oblivion that Leo has predicted for the Jews.[21]

Instead, however, the conversion narrative structure of *Reuben Sachs* marks out a different path for Judith. Thrown into desolation after Reuben rejects her, Levy's heroine finds an unexpected source of consolation: alone with a book of poetry she experiences a secular epiphany. Swinburne's words on passion unrealized make comprehensible her own thwarted desire; poetry vindicates her attachment to "feelings which had not their basis in material relationships" (133). Even more important is that this moment catalyzes the "awakening" of Judith's self-consciousness (134). Reading, as for earlier Jewesses, takes Judith beyond her narrow bourgeois world, enabling her to judge its values. She moves from being "only vaguely aware of her own discontent" at the beginning of the novel to "hatred of the position into which she had been forced . . . loathing of what was so alien to her whole way of life and mode of thought" (68, 133). Her life thenceforward is lived in the agony of such self-knowledge. In these aspects of Judith's story, the resonances with conversion fiction are striking. Levy's narrative is structured around Judith's unfulfilled longings, her textual revelation, and the suffering that changes her from an "unsentimental," "thorough-going Philistine, . . . conservative ingrain" into a passionate and intelligent woman (71). Like that of Charlotte Anley's Miriam, Judith's conversion paradoxically returns her to her Jewish origins: reading English poetry rather than barely understood Hebrew prayers reconnects her to the tradition of her intellectual, culturally integrated Sephardic family. At the center of this transformation is the development of Judith's interiority, an explicitly feminist reworking of the convert's path to spiritual autonomy.

Where Levy departs from this model, however, is in the extreme tentativeness of her solution to the plight of the Jewess. If Judith's revelation in the company of Swinburne is momentary, the change it effects in her subsequent life is equally minuscule. The novel ends twice: once with Judith "frozen and appalled" at her absolute loss of Reuben; then a second time, in the novel's epilogue, with a more open-ended glance toward her future as a mother (157). The tradition of conversion narrative, in contrast, is stridently confident in its direction and thoroughly final in its conclusion: Miriam's happy death, Rachel's escape from her family, Salome's surrender to hers. Levy's predictions for the subsequent life of her protagonist are not so singular: Judith's prospects include "pain, and sorrow, and tears" alongside "hope and joy" and "that quickening of purpose which is perhaps as much as any of us should expect or demand from Fate" (157). While Levy's final words underline the importance of achieving self-will or "purpose" for Judith (a purpose whose "quickening" coincides with but is nonetheless distinct from that of her baby), such an achievement is expressed in modest, measured, and distinctly uncertain terms.

Afterlives of Reuben Sachs

The close structural affinities between *Reuben Sachs* and the tradition of conversion writing that I have been demonstrating in this essay are most clearly illustrated by a comparison with Violet Guttenberg's conversionist novel *Neither
Jew Nor Greek: A Story of Jewish Social Life*, published in 1902. As with many books
that appeared in the 1890s in the wake of *Reuben Sachs*,[22] the novel is directly
dependent on Levy's work for its critical portrait of contemporary middle-
class London Jewry, focalized through the experience of an alienated, artistic-
ally inclined female protagonist, and thus suggests how readily Levy's text could,
in turn, provide a resource for conventional Evangelical writing.

Neither Jew Nor Greek looks back, as does *Reuben Sachs*, to earlier representations of the Jewess, depicting the cultured, tasteful heroine, Celia Franks, in
contrast to the brash, materialistic Jews around her; her resistance to the practice of arranged marriage; and the growth of her sense of autonomy through
suffering and sacrifice. The novel also, like *Reuben Sachs*, utilizes the racial rhetoric of its period, contrasting the physically repellent Maida Vale Jews with
Celia, whose higher destiny is indicated by "features [that] were distinctly Gre-
cian in type."[23] Guttenberg's debt to Amy Levy is most literally apparent, however, in the scene in which Celia attends a New Year's Day synagogue service
with her aunt. This episode is expanded from *Reuben Sachs* to point even more
clearly to the limitations of Judaism for a woman who "possessed a nature
which was capable of being deeply moved" (66). Brought up in ignorance of
Jewish observance, Celia eagerly hopes for spiritual edification in the synagogue
but finds that the tuneless singing "grated harshly on her well-trained ear" and
the "silk hats, frock coats, and praying shawls in combination, seemed to her
grotesque" (64–65). At first, she concludes in bewilderment that the "sense of
keen disappointment" that she experiences indicates something wanting in her.
But eventually she realizes that piety is absent in the whole congregation: the
men are "either bored or indifferent" and the women concerned only with each
others' festive attire (65).

In *Neither Jew Nor Greek*, Guttenberg reestablishes a clear trajectory that follows from the scene of the Jewess's dawning discontent. From this point in the
novel, Celia moves inexorably forward—from diagnosing her malaise as an
effect of the decadence of modern Judaism; to an active interest in the Anglican service, the "dignity of the Liturgy, the solemn beauty of the music, and,
most of all, the evident sincerity of the worshippers"; to her resistance to her

relatives' hostility; to her outright conversion and marriage to her best friend's brother (174). As in *Miriam*, Celia is most authentically Jewish when she converts, coming to realize that "Christ's religion did not oppose Judaism, but was a fuller, nobler, and grander expansion of the same" (179). Appropriating Levy's portrait of a woman striving to understand her own feelings, Guttenberg answers her questions and fulfils her longings, reinflecting the Jewess's journey to self-consciousness with specifically Christian meaning.

The echo of conversionist discourse also continued to resonate around Amy Levy herself. While Levy's private correspondence suggests that she was lively, witty, and sociable, posthumous accounts of her unfailingly represent her as an anguished Jewess. Thomas Bailey Aldrich's poem on her suicide, published in 1890, describes Levy's writing as "weirdly incomplete" and imagines the poet "with sorrowful vague eyes / Illumined with such strange gleams of inner light," suggesting both her expressive deficiency and her exceptional visionary potential.[24] Harry Quilter's reminiscence of Levy, published in 1892, implicitly links such paradoxes with Levy's race: she was, he says, "a small dark girl of unmistakably Jewish type, with eyes that seemed too large for the delicate features, and far too sad for their youthfulness of line and contour." Like Miriam Durvan or Rachel Monteneros, Levy's Jewish introspection is in tension with her feminine "delica[cy]" and "youthfulness"; Quilter also comments that he "had rarely seen a face which was at once so interesting, so intellectual, so beautiful, and alas! so unhappy."[25] Levy, it seems, was read as an incarnation of her tragic creation Judith Quixano, whose "wonderful, lustrous, mournful eyes"—likewise considered "out of keeping" with the character of their owner —signal her elevated sensitivity while anticipating her miserable destiny.[26] For both Quilter and Aldrich, Levy's startling physiognomy expresses and symbolizes the inner conflicts that she strove unsuccessfully to resolve; for both, this struggle for transcendence is precisely what makes her unique. In these secular, attenuated forms, then, as well as in Guttenberg's return to the original Christian model, the cultural narrative of the Jewess persisted beyond the work of Amy Levy.

Notes

1. Amy Levy, *Reuben Sachs: A Sketch* (London: Macmillan, 1888); modern reprint edition by Susan David Bernstein (Peterborough, ON: Broadview Press, 2006), 129.

2. Ibid., 74. Subsequent references to this edition are given parenthetically in the text.

3. See Nadia Valman, *The Jewess in Nineteenth-Century British Literary Culture* (Cambridge: Cambridge University Press, 2007), 8–9; Michael Ragussis, *Figures of Conversion: "The Jewish Question" and English National Identity* (Durham, NC: Duke University Press, 1995), 39.

4. Bryan Cheyette, "From Apology to Revolt: Benjamin Farjeon, Amy Levy and the Post-Emancipation Anglo-Jewish Novel, 1880–1900," *Transactions of the Jewish Historical Society of England* 24 (1982–86): 253–65; Emma Francis, "Amy Levy: Contradictions?—Feminism and Semitic Discourse," in *Women's Poetry, Late Romantic to Late Victorian: Gender and Genre 1830–1900*, ed. Isobel Armstrong and Virginia Blain (Basingstoke: Macmillan, 1999), 183–204.

5. See Meri-Jane Rochelson, "Jews, Gender, and Genre in Late-Victorian England: Amy Levy's *Reuben Sachs*," *Women's Studies* 25 (1996): 311–28; Susan David Bernstein, introduction to Levy, *Reuben Sachs*, 11–43, esp. 30–31; Francis, "Amy Levy: Contradictions?"

6. [Amy Levy], "Middle-Class Jewish Women of To-Day. By A Jewess," *Jewish Chronicle*, 17 September 1886, 7.

7. Mona Caird, "Marriage," reprinted in Caird, *The Morality of Marriage and Other Essays on the Status and Destiny of Woman* (London: George Redway, 1897), 63–111, quotations on 100–101. For a full discussion of the contours of the marriage question in the 1880s and '90s, see chapter 4 in Lucy Bland, *Banishing the Beast: English Feminism and Sexual Morality, 1885–1914* (London: Penguin, 1995).

8. Caird, "Marriage," 100, 99, 95.

9. Amy Levy, "Wise in Her Generation," *Woman's World* 3 (1890): 20–23, reprinted in *The Complete Novels and Selected Writings of Amy Levy, 1861–1889*, ed. Melvyn New (Gainesville: University Press of Florida, 1993), 486–97, quotation on 490.

10. Ibid., 497.

11. Valman, *Jewess*, 51–61.

12. Ibid., 93.

13. For brief discussions of Anley's novel, see Ragussis, *Figures of Conversion*, 38–41; Miriam Elizabeth Burstein, "Protestants against the Jewish and Catholic Family, c.1829 to c.1860," *Victorian Literature and Culture* 31, no. 1 (2003): 333–57, esp. 339.

14. [C. A.] [Charlotte Anley], *Miriam; or, the Power of Truth: A Jewish Tale*, by the Author of "Influence" (London: John Hatchard and Son, 1826), 3. Subsequent references to this edition are given parenthetically in the text.

15. Ragussis, *Figures of Conversion*, 1–13.

16. Valman, *Jewess*, chap. 5.

17. [Emily Eden], *The Semi-Detached House*, ed. Lady Theresa Lewis (1859; London: Elkin Matthews and Marrot, 1928), 29. Subsequent references to this edition are given parenthetically in the text.

18. Dorothea Gerard, *Orthodox* (London: Longmans, Green and Co., 1888), 11–12.

19. I am very grateful to Naomi Hetherington for this point.

20. See Todd M. Endelman, "Benjamin Disraeli and the Myth of Sephardi Superiority," in *Disraeli's Jewishness*, ed. Todd M. Endelman and Tony Kushner (London: Vallentine Mitchell, 2002), 23–39; John M. Efron, "Scientific Racism and the Mystique of Sephardic Racial Supremacy," *Leo Baeck Institute Year Book* 38 (1993): 75–96, esp. 76–77.

21. Emma Francis, "Socialist Feminism and Sexual Instinct: Amy Levy and Eleanor Marx," in *Eleanor Marx: Life, Work, Contacts,* ed. John Stokes (Aldershot, UK: Ashgate, 2000), 113–27, esp. 122.

22. For a longer account of this genre, see Nadia Valman, "'Barbarous and Mediaeval': Jewish Marriage in Fin de Siècle English Fiction," in *The Image of the Jew in European Liberal Culture, 1789–1914,* ed. Bryan Cheyette and Nadia Valman (London: Vallentine Mitchell, 2004), 111–29, esp. 115–28.

23. Violet Guttenberg, *Neither Jew nor Greek: A Story of Jewish Social Life* (London: Chatto and Windus, 1902), 12. Subsequent references to this edition are given parenthetically in the text.

24. Thomas Bailey Aldrich, "Broken Music," in *The Sisters' Tragedy, with Other Poems* (London: Macmillan, 1891), reprinted in New, *Complete Novels,* 53–54.

25. Harry Quilter, "Amy Levy: A Reminiscence and a Criticism," in *Preferences in Art, Life and Literature* (London: Swan Sonnenschein and Co., 1892), cited in Edward Wagenknecht, *Daughters of the Covenant: Portraits of Six Jewish Women* (Amherst: University of Massachusetts Press, 1983), 58. For a discussion of the contemporary interpretation of Levy's suicide as an effect of her overreaching intellectualism, unsustainable by her female body, see Lyssa Randolph's chapter in this volume.

26. Levy, *Reuben Sachs,* 62.

5

"Such Are Not
Woman's Thoughts"

amy levy's "xantippe" and "medea"

———

T. D. Olverson

I N 1883, Amy Levy published an essay on one of her favorite poets, the recently deceased James Thomson. The essay is not only an attempt to secure Thomson's posthumous reputation as a meritorious "Minor Poet" but also a strong endorsement of Thomson's philosophical pessimism. Levy clearly identified with Thomson, admiring the passion in his work: the "hungry cry for life, for the things of this human, flesh and blood life; for love and praise, for mere sunlight and sun's warmth."[1] Levy also makes clear that Thomson's "nudity of expression" and moments of "absolute vulgarity" threaten his reputation as a truly talented poet. Attempting to redress the balance, Levy suggests that one major failing of Thomson was that he lacked "one graceful finish of our latter-day bards; the pretty modern-classical trick." He had "neither the wit nor the taste" to drape his work "in the garb of ancient Greece or mediæval France."[2] For a writer who supposedly lacked the "classical trick," Thomson was actually well acquainted with classical material. In 1866, Thomson wrote an essay entitled "A Word for Xantippe," in which he examines the reputation of the wife of the ancient Greek philosopher Socrates. Thomson invites respectable Victorian matrons to follow Socrates home to "judge whether Xantippe had or had not the right to scold and rage, and even to pour out vessels of wrath."[3] He concludes that there is only one living writer "with genius and learning and wisdom and fairness enough to picture truly the conjugal life of Saint Socrates and shrew Xantippe" (227). For Thomson, the only suitable candidate was George Eliot. Eliot, a fine classicist, never took up Thomson's invitation, but the young Amy Levy did. Levy had the wit, the wisdom, and the erudition to garb her philosophy in the guise of ancient Greece. After all, like Eliot, Levy's liberal education included ancient Greek philosophy and drama, which provided her with another language, literally and figuratively, with which to explore her philosophical and political concerns. Levy's classical education and appropriation of Hellenic discourse are particularly evident in her two long "Greek" poems, "Xantippe" and "Medea: A Fragment in Dramatic Form," republished in *A Minor Poet and Other Verse* (1884). I argue that "Xantippe" should be read in light of Levy's developing erudition and political awareness, whereas Levy's "Medea" must be seen in terms of its Anglo-Jewish context and Levy's personal concerns regarding her feminism and her Jewish heritage. In both poems, however, Levy employs the "garb of ancient Greece" to powerful political effect.

The place of women within Victorian Hellenism has, until recently, been largely overlooked. Yet as recent studies by Isobel Hurst and Yopie Prins have shown, the proliferation of Greek subjects in women's literature from the middle of the century suggests a collective movement *into* the classical tradition by women writers and scholars, rather than comprehensive exclusion from it.[4] Amy Levy was just one of an increasing number of women who sought to rewrite the ancient past in the Victorian period. Beginning in midcentury, writers such as George Eliot, Augusta Webster, and (later) Michael Field, Vernon Lee, and Mona Caird all adapted "classic" archetypes, which challenged contemporary cultural and ideological conventions. The works that these women produced, as Ruth Hoberman suggests, reflect "their reading, their resistance, and their working through: their repetition of received versions, their hints of alternative visions, and above all the recurrence of gender and sexuality as issues linked to power. These writers thus *gender* classicism, exposing apparently gender-neutral accounts of the past as stories of male experience."[5]

Throughout the Victorian period, knowledge of the classics, especially the language and literature of ancient Greece, was the gold standard of the British education system. However, for much of the nineteenth century it was very difficult for young middle-class girls with academic ambitions to acquire a sufficiently rigorous classical education. As Claire Breay points out, "education for middle-class girls was much less developed than that for boys and rarely focused on classics. Girls who did go to school were taught far less Latin than boys and many were taught no Greek at all."[6] Most girls and young women received their education at home, often under the amateur tutelage of governesses or relatives. It was not until the 1870s that a wave of new schools sought to reform the nature of secondary education for girls. Fortunately for Amy Levy, the pioneering work of the previous generation of ambitious women provided her generation with new opportunities in work and education.[7]

With the support of her literary and intellectually inclined family, Amy Levy received a first-rate education, first at Brighton High School for Girls and later at Newnham College, Cambridge. At home, the Levy children read widely, encouraged by knowledgeable parents and a governess. As a young girl, Levy recorded in her "Confessions Book" the names of her favorite poets.[8] Interestingly, the list includes a number of accomplished Hellenists, such as Swinburne, Robert Browning, Goethe, and Shelley. Levy's admiration was not confined to male writers, however. As a precocious thirteen-year-old, Levy reviewed Elizabeth Barrett Browning's *Aurora Leigh* for the children's journal *Kind Words,* in which she addressed the issue of inequality in the education of women. Levy accuses Browning of "a very common fault"—"that of introducing too many learned allusions" in her work. Levy reasons that "it is perhaps more excusable in a *woman* than a *man*," for "it is only natural that she should wish to display what public opinion denies her sex—a classical education."[9] Clearly, even at thirteen, Levy considered Barrett Browning's classical erudition as a sophisticated form of feminist protest.

At fifteen, Levy left London to attend Brighton High School for Girls. The school, founded by the feminist reformers Maria Grey and Emily Shirreff, was progressive and espoused a philosophy of women's rights. It was here that Levy was formally taught Latin by Mr. Lomus, who complimented the young Amy on "my Latin generally, and on my translation of Ovid, particularly—said worms often go up for exams with less knowledge than I have."[10] Levy dutifully completed her Local Highers exams and continued her education at Newn-ham. Newnham College was one of the newly opened colleges for women and had a reputation for innovation in women's education.[11] As part of her curriculum, Levy attended lectures in Latin and received formal tuition in Greek from "the worthy Mr. Jenkinson."[12]

In 1879, just before she entered Newnham, Levy completed "Xantippe," which became the title poem of her first volume of poetry, *Xantippe and Other Verse* (1881).[13] Published while Levy was still a student at Newnham, *Xantippe* caused quite a stir. *The Literary World* responded to the volume by suggesting that *Xantippe* was proof of Miss Levy's "training and opportunities, that there is hardly a line which will not pass muster in the most rigorously critical examination." Indeed, the poetry reviewer for *The Literary World* perceived Levy's poetry as representative of a "new movement" which, whilst it may strengthen "the antagonism of discordant natures, will deepen the insight and intensify the sympathies of others."[14] "Xantippe" can be seen as representative of a "new movement" in that Levy directly contends with the issues of representation and cultural power in relation to intellectual women.

"Her tender language wholly misconceived": Amy Levy's "Xantippe"

In "Xantippe," Levy, like James Thomson before her, refashions Platonic philosophy, incorporating it into her protagonist's tale of oppression and resistance. An initial reading of Xantippe's monologue may not immediately invite comparison with any of Plato's dialogues; after all, Xantippe does not *exchange* conversation with any of her fellow characters. Yet the central philosophical influences of the poem are, as in Thomson's "A Word for Xantippe" (1866), Plato's dialogues *Phaedo, Symposium,* and *The Republic.* In accordance with Thomson's wishes, Levy's protagonist is the teller of her own tale, the voice of authority and linguistic control. In recent years, critics such as Cynthia Scheinberg have applauded Levy's use of the dramatic monologue as a complex form designed to highlight the psychological and philosophical concerns of a single female speaker.[15] Through Xantippe's monologue and Medea's passionate objections, Levy directly challenges the notion, famously expressed by the Athenian oligarch Pericles, that women's art is the art of silence.[16] Ironically, it is the profound lack of evidence regarding women's lives in antiquity which allows for imaginative (re)constructions of characters such as Xantippe.

The opening scene of Levy's monologue echoes Plato's account of Socrates' final exercise in philosophy before his death by hemlock in *Phaedo*. In "Xantippe," Levy's tragic heroine delivers one last lecture to her maidens in the final few hours before her death. According to the teachings of her husband, Xantippe, denied lessons in philosophy and metaphysics because of her sex, faces death as an ignorant and, therefore, immoral soul. But a life of bitter regret and subjugation has taught Xantippe some valuable lessons that she is more than willing to share with her maidens:

> What, have I waked again? I never thought
> To see the rosy dawn, or ev'n this grey,
> Dull, solemn stillness, ere the dawn has come.
> The lamp burns low; low burns the lamp of life:
> The still morn stays expectant, and my soul,
> All weighted with a passive wonderment,
> Waiteth and watcheth, waiteth for the dawn.
> Come hither, maids; too soundly have ye slept
> That should have watched me; nay, I would not chide—
> Oft have I chidden, yet I would not chide
> In this last hour;—now all should be at peace.
> I have been dreaming in a troubled sleep
> Of weary days I thought not to recall;
> Of stormy days, whose storms are hushed long since.[17]

We can conceive Xantippe's darkened room as comparable with the cave in Plato's *Republic*. In this space, Levy spins her tale of neglect, rejection, humiliation, loneliness, socially sanctioned misogyny, and the wasted potential of an ambitious and intelligent woman. The interior of her bedchamber is a peculiarly "feminine" space, strongly suggestive of women's domestication, the interior spaces of women's bodies, and psychological introspection. The doleful darkness within the chamber also reflects Xantippe's deficiency in terms of (male) knowledge. This Greek woman lacks the intellectual illumination of Greek culture.

Levy frequently depicts the moods or states of mind of her characters in terms of lighting or light effects, and in this case Xantippe wakes to the "dull, solemn stillness" of predawn. The low-burning lamp anticipates Xantippe's imminent death and suggests that she has lived her life in the shadows. Initially, however, Xantippe's reminiscences focus on the "sunny days" of her youth (24).

The ambitious and intelligent Xantippe longs for direct, unmediated experience of the world that is unfolding before her. But it seems that she is unaware of her peripheral place in the rigid hierarchy of the Athenian polis:

> What cared I for the merry mockeries
> Of other maidens sitting at the loom?
> Or for sharp voices, bidding me return
> To maiden labour?
>
> (24)

Xantippe hears yet resists those "sharp voices" that seek to control her; her sense of self is, at this point, strong enough to resist the social pressure to conform to contemporary ideals of "femininity."

Xantippe tells us that as a young woman she had a

> . . . soul which yearned for knowledge, for a tongue
> That should proclaim the stately mysteries
> Of this fair world, and of the holy gods.
>
> (24)

Xantippe's appetite for knowledge and access to the "mysterious" language of advanced learning echoes the aspirations of a growing number of Victorian women who longed to learn Greek, the language of scholarship and the ubiquitous signifier of knowledge. One thinks of the young Elizabeth Barrett Browning's "ardent desire to understand the learned languages" in order for her to be considered, or to consider herself, as a serious woman writer.[18] Or one might recall the pangs of George Eliot's Dorothea Brooke, who longs for a life of intellectual inquiry.[19]

From her deathbed, Xantippe recalls the day when, as a young maiden participating in a public ceremony celebrating the goddess Aphrodite, she first caught sight of Sokrates. At first, and much like Dorothea Brooke's attraction to the unappealing Casaubon, Xantippe's stubbornly optimistic nature persuades her to see "the soul athwart the grosser flesh" (26) in her husband-to-be. Xantippe also feels, again like Dorothea, that she can see the potential for a mutually rewarding relationship of intellectual inquiry and sophisticated debate with her prospective philosopher-husband. In fact, Xantippe's philosophical meditation on finding the beauty within, as opposed to physical attraction and desire, recalls the lesson that Diotima teaches Socrates in Plato's *Symposium.* Xantippe wants desperately to believe that a soul, "found after weary searching in the flesh / Which half repelled our senses, is more dear" than "a brow of beauty" (26). The irony, of course, is that in the *Symposium* when Diotima instructs Socrates to "consider that the beauty of the mind is more honourable than the beauty of the outward form," she is speaking with regard to Socrates' relationships with other men.[20] As Sarah Pomeroy reminds us, in ancient Greece, "vulgar love could be either heterosexual or homosexual, but intellectual love could be found only in a relationship between two males."[21]

Desperate to enter the all-male sphere of intellectual debate, Xantippe deludes herself into believing that the institution of marriage will provide her with the means to satiate her thirst for knowledge. She trusts that a man at the very pinnacle of Athenian society—the same society that refuses her citizenship, education, and personal agency—will in fact be her champion. If Xantippe's hope of a union of intellectual equals echoes Plato's radical suggestions on philosopher-rulers in *The Republic*, then her desire for equitable marriage is strikingly similar to John Stuart Mill's proposals in *The Subjection of Women* (1859). In book 5 of *The Republic*, Plato suggests that the traditional family unit should be abolished and, consequently, equal opportunities given to women. Plato's ideal state would live communally, and the philosopher-rulers would include both sexes.[22] In his groundbreaking work of liberal philosophy, John Stuart Mill, a self-professed pupil of Plato, suggests that marriage should be "a school of sympathy in equality, of living together in love, without power on one side or obedience on the other."[23] However, Mill's approval of the conventional family unit and the attendant roles of women limited the radical potential of his liberal feminism. In *The Subjection of Women*, for example, Mill went so far as to declare that "woman seldom runs wild after abstraction" but displays a "lively interest in the present feelings of persons."[24]

Predictably, Xantippe's marriage to Sokrates is hopelessly conventional. She describes her wedding as "that strange day" of "sacrifice and flowers," a day when her dreams and freedoms are sacrificed on the altar of male social dominance (27). Just when we might expect Xantippe to launch into a bitter tirade against her famously unattractive and indifferent spouse, she tells us,

> Yet, maidens, mark; I would not ye thought
> I blame my lord departed, for he meant
> No evil, so I take it, to his wife.
> 'Twas only that the high philosopher,
> Pregnant with noble theories and great thoughts,
> Deigned not to stoop to touch so slight a thing

As the fine fabric of a woman's brain—
So subtle as a passionate woman's soul.

(28)

Levy reiterates the (fabricated) charge of women's intellectual fragility, but her sardonic tone is now obvious. Sokrates may well have intended "no evil" to his wife, but his lack of insight and rigid adherence to (homo)social codes has had a detrimental effect on Xantippe. In fact, Sokrates' unenlightened attitude toward his wife's desire to acquire knowledge directly contradicts his own fundamental edict, a belief repeated in Plato's *Republic* and *Symposium*, that the dedicated search for knowledge is both virtuous and good.

Levy's application of the adjective *pregnant* with regard to Sokrates' intellectual labors is an unmistakable allusion to Plato's famous image of the pregnant philosopher as envisaged in *Symposium*. In one of the most celebrated passages of Platonic philosophy, Diotima, the enigmatic female sage of Socrates' dialogue, emphasizes the need for reciprocity in any loving relationship: that each partner should cherish and nurture the other to beget and perpetuate their love. Diotima goes on to suggest that one of the highest forms of love is that of "spiritual procreancy." This intense "spiritual" form of love can be achieved only between men, within an exclusively male intellectual coterie. The male citizens who share this intense erotic bond become metaphorically pregnant with meaning:

> Men whose bodies only are creative, betake themselves to women and beget children—this is the character of their love; their offspring, as they hope, will preserve their memory. . . . But creative souls—for there are men who are more creative [are more pregnant] in their souls than in their bodies—conceive that which is proper for the soul to conceive or retain. And what are these conceptions?—wisdom and virtue in general. . . . But the greatest and fairest sort of wisdom by far is that which is concerned with the ordering of states and families.[25]

Levy's monologue suggests that under these circumstances there is simply no place for an intellectual woman. Indeed, as Luce Irigaray observes, Diotima "does not take part in these exchanges or in this meal among men. She is not there. She herself does not speak. Socrates reports or recounts her words. He praises her for her wisdom and her power and declares that she is his initiator or teacher when it comes to love, but she is not invited to teach or eat."[26] In fact, Diotima is merely a linguistic construction for Plato's dialectic on love.

Plato's *Symposium* had a major impact on discussions about the future of liberal England throughout the Victorian period, despite the fact that during the late eighteenth and early nineteenth centuries the expurgators had been hard at work on translations of Plato's dialogue on love. For instance, it was not until 1850, when George Burges translated the works of Plato, that the general reader in Britain was able to appreciate the importance of the same-sex relationships that are fundamental to the argument of Plato's text.

Major midcentury figures such as Benjamin Jowett, Matthew Arnold, and John Stuart Mill felt that Plato's teachings would help to inspire a new generation of liberal thinkers and that this governing elite would help to save an indolent imperial Britain from intellectual stagnation. Yet toward the end of the nineteenth century, Plato's *Symposium* was appropriated as a liberatory discourse for love between men. As Linda Dowling suggests, under the expert tutelage of Benjamin Jowett, the Platonic or Socratic doctrine of *eros* had, for men such as Walter Pater and John Addington Symonds, "already assumed a living reality, as they saw, in the pedagogic institutions of a reformed Oxford."[27] Simply put, the homosocial (and in some cases homosexual) bonds that are reified in the *Symposium* were a matter of fact in the Oxbridge colleges of mid-Victorian England.

This somewhat reverential attitude toward Plato and his teachings was then enhanced by what Richard Jenkyns calls "the cult of Socrates." Mill compared Socrates' "martyrdom" to "the passion of Jesus," and Matthew Arnold declared that, "though Socrates is dead, every man carries a possible Socrates in his breast."[28] Arnold apparently failed to consider that not every woman would be so enthralled with the ancient lover-mentor-hero, Socrates. Indeed, Levy's poem challenges not only the masculine values of antiquity but also the contemporary male writers and philosophers who threatened to reinstate and thereby culturally legitimize the same elitist and prejudicial attitudes in Victorian England.

The homosocial coterie that is depicted in Plato's *Symposium* is (re)created by Levy in "Xantippe." Xantippe recalls a summer evening and a symposium at the marital home. On the threshold of the *oikos*, "half concealed / By tender foliage," Xantippe observes "the gay group before mine eyes" (29). Funnily enough, the "gay" group consists of some of the most famous pederasts of ancient Athens. From her partially concealed vantage point, Xantippe spies the serene figure of Plato. Next, she observes the solemn figure of Sokrates, at whose feet lies "Alkibiades the beautiful," the famous Athenian general. Crucially, Xantippe does not enter or divide this male circle; her peripheral position to this group is indicative of women's estranged relationship to male philosophic discourse and of her lack of influence over political events in the polis. Xantippe listens closely to the group's conversation and overhears her husband speaking about Aspasia, historically and literally the mistress of the great Greek patriarch, Pericles:

> "This fair Aspasia, which our Perikles
> Hath brought from realms afar, and set on high
> In our Athenian city, hath a mind,
> I doubt not, of a strength beyond her race;
> And makes employ of it, beyond the way
> Of women nobly gifted: woman's frail—
> Her body rarely stands the test of soul;
> She grows intoxicate with knowledge; throws
> The laws of custom, order, 'neath her feet,
> Feasting at life's great banquet with wide throat."
>
> (30)

Instead of the open-minded philosopher-hero that Plato seeks to represent in his dialogues, Levy presents Socrates as a racially intolerant misogynist, who is fearful of cultural diversity and female political power and influence. Levy's provocative reference to the historical relationship between Aspasia and Perikles also suggests yet another layer to this complex monologue. This statement by Sokrates contrasts sharply with Plato's representation of Aspasia as Socrates' political tutor in the playful dialogue *Menexenus*. In *Menexenus*, Aspasia outlines the place of women in the civic myth of autochthony. Furthermore, in *Menexenus* Socrates declares his admiration for Aspasia's intelligence and wisdom. We should remember, however, that Aspasia, like Diotima, is a double construct: first of Plato and then of Socrates. Once again, Levy is playing with reputations.

Sokrates' distasteful image of Aspasia gorging herself on knowledge and wisdom can be directly compared to Xantippe's intellectual malnourishment. For Sokrates, Aspasia's position of power and influence is entirely unnatural and goes against his stratified vision—based on ideas of class, race, and gender —of a healthy body politic. He suggests that a woman's "frail" body is simply not designed to withstand the demands of an intellectual life. If women are not rigidly controlled by social "custom," they will trample all over the laws of the polis, causing anarchy. Xantippe, offended and angered by the unjust and blatantly sexist words of her husband, steps forward into the arbor. Her transgression of the threshold anticipates her next violation of a social taboo; she will dare to speak in public and question the wisdom of the Athenian great and good:

> "By all the great powers around us! Can it be
> That we poor women are empirical?
> That gods who fashion us did strive to make
> Beings too fine, too subtly delicate
> With sense that thrilled response to ev'ry touch
> Of nature's, and their task is not complete?
> That they have sent their half-completed work
> To bleed and quiver here upon the earth?
> To bleed and quiver, and to weep and weep,
> To beat its soul against the marble walls
> Of men's cold hearts, and then at last to sin!"

(30)

Levy's reinstatement of a female presence at this particular symposium underlines the lack of a genuine female voice in Plato's dialogue. Moreover, Xantippe's interjection disrupts the male-dominated discourse that marginalizes both her sex and her voice; she has decided to confront the biological essentialism of the male philosophers by using their own language to disprove their reasoning. Xantippe eloquently unravels Sokrates' dubious supposition that women are sent to earth as failed experiments of the gods. As Xantippe suggests, it would seem that with regard to evaluating women's capabilities, the philosophers are again guilty of ignoring their own lessons.

Dismayed by the ensuing silence, Xantippe looks about and finds the face of Plato, who "half did smile and half did criticise" (31). Plato's ambivalent reaction directly reflects his contradictory attitude toward women, as outlined in his texts. Xantippe then finds the scornful face of Alkibiades, who "with laughing lips" shrugs his snowy shoulders, "till he brought the gold / Of flowing ringlets round about his breasts" (31). In this instance, Alkibiades' effeminacy only seems to reinforce Xantippe's exclusion from this male arena and from male structures of power. Her alien status is further underlined when

Sokrates asks, "[P]rythee tell / From what high source, from what philosophies / Didst cull the sapient notion of thy words?" (31).

Xantippe is momentarily "crushed with all that weight of cold contempt," before angrily throwing the wineskins that she holds upon the floor (31). The wine that is spilled over Xantippe's robes indicates that the silenced woman has been sacrificed to ensure the continuity of male social dominance. The (menstrual) wine stain also signifies her exclusion from male discursive practice. Xantippe's social position is too weak to completely disrupt the masculine order. However, Xantippe's reputation as a bitter and dissatisfied wife indicates that Sokrates has failed in his roles as pedagogue and paterfamilias. By his own standards, Sokrates must be viewed as an unsuccessful citizen of the Athenian polis.

Despite the sense of remorse in the closing lines, Levy ends her monologue on a positive note when, like the released prisoner from Plato's metaphorical cave, Xantippe stretches toward the dawn, an enlightened being:

> Enough, enough. In vain, in vain, in vain!
> The gods forgive me! Sorely have I sinned
> In all my life. A fairer fate befall
> You all that stand there. . . .
>   Ha! the dawn has come;
> I see a rosy glimmer—nay! it grows dark;
> Why stand ye so in silence? throw it wide,
> The casement, quick; why tarry?—give me air—
> O fling it wide, I say, and give me light!
>
>   (34)

If there is a moral to Xantippe's cautionary tale, it is for young women to avoid marriage and to become educated critics. As Levy well knew, women have to learn the terms of male discursive practice before they can change it. "Xantippe" also appeals for female solidarity and the need to create new communities, based on education and knowledge. However, Xantippe's verbal assaults against Sokrates mark her out as a figure of angry protest rather than a figure of reform. Yet Xantippe can also be seen as a successfully subversive figure. Refusing to silently acquiesce to her fate, Levy's Xantippe stands as a reminder of women's mental strength, tenacity, and ability to represent themselves. Tragic and transgressive, Xantippe is a worthy precursor to Levy's next Hellenic (anti-)heroine, Medea.

Hellenism and Anarchy: Levy's "Medea"

In 1882, Amy Levy completed "Medea," which she describes as a "Fragment in Dramatic Form."[29] The dramatic fragment forms an integral part of Levy's second volume of poetry, *A Minor Poet and Other Verse*, published in 1884. As a whole, Levy's collection is strongly influenced by German literature, including the work of the notable Hellenists Heinrich Heine and Johann Wolfgang von Goethe. "Medea," however, may well owe a specific debt to the Austrian playwright Franz Grillparzer. Grillparzer's *Medea*, which forms part of his dramatic trilogy *Das Goldene Vließ* [The Golden Fleece] (1821), is a sympathetic portrayal of the Colchian princess, who is derided by the Greeks for her ethnic difference. I suggest that Levy's Medea can be seen as a combination of the powerful personality and psychology of Euripides' Medea and Grillparzer's racially orientated representation. Through the disavowed and disenfranchised figure of Medea, Levy is able to articulate her anxieties concerning her Anglo-Jewish identity and her feminist beliefs.

The subtitle to Levy's "Medea" states that the dramatic fragment is "After Euripides," and as such there are many similarities, as well as crucial differences, between the dramas. The first and most obvious difference is that of form. There are few stage directions in Levy's drama, and the text consists of only two main scenes and has only four main characters. However, Levy does include a couple of conspicuous details in the formal arrangement of the "dramatic fragment." Against tradition, Medea is identified as a citizen of Corinth, and the first scene takes place before "Medea's House," suggesting Medea's agency and subjectivity. Levy also dispenses with many of the visually arresting stage devices, such as the spectacular *deus ex machina*, the golden dragon-chariot, which "rescues" Medea at the end of Euripides' play. Indeed, in keeping with her humanistic approach, Levy resists Euripides' representation of Medea as semi-divine. She also omits the Chorus of Corinthian Women and the crucial figure of the Nurse from her drama. Levy was technically accomplished, so her decision to depart from classical forms should be seen as deliberate and in keeping with her intentions for the volume. Consequently, I suggest that Levy's verse-drama was *not* intended to be performed on stage.

Levy's *Medea* can, however, be situated within the tradition of closet dramas written throughout the nineteenth century, such as those by Lord Byron, Percy Bysshe Shelley, Robert Browning, and George Eliot. Yet Levy's use of the form also anticipates the representational strategies of the Actresses' Franchise

League and of the Women's Social and Political Union, which devised plays in order to explore the social and political disadvantages of women. Levy's "Medea" may therefore be seen not only as an attempt to find a suitable literary form to represent the complex social issues facing contemporary women but also as an attempt to meet the aesthetic challenge of representing women as "determined heroines."[30]

"Medea" is positioned alongside two long monologues in Levy's second collection of verse. "A Minor Poet," "Xantippe," and "Medea" are all character studies, focused on the psychological sufferings of outcast figures. Importantly, the three poems are separated from the "other verse" that follows, forming a sort of triptych of philosophical pessimism. I suggest that Levy retains only the bare essentials of Euripides' drama to highlight the origins of Medea's psychological pain. Indeed, the first act of Levy's dramatic fragment focuses on Medea's ethnicity and Jason's betrayal; the second act relays, through an intermediary, Medea's act of infanticide. What emerges from this dramatic fragment is a sympathetic portrait of a woman compelled by circumstance and her own nature to act against her intolerable maltreatment at the hands of a hostile society.

As an Anglo-Jewish woman writer, Levy was particularly well positioned to examine the difficulties involved in immigration and assimilation. Indeed, from a young age, Amy Levy seems to have struggled with her Anglo-Jewish identity. At times, she firmly and happily locates herself within the Jewish community. At other moments, however, Levy can be seen to be at best ambivalent, if not unsympathetic, toward other Jews. Some commentators have suggested that Levy suffered from Jewish self-hatred, which contributed to her suicide at the age of twenty-seven.[31] Levy may have struggled with her identity as a young woman, but her Jewishness cannot be seen as a major factor in her depression. Levy's re-vision of "Medea" can, however, be seen as an important development in Levy's career. Through the figure of Medea, Levy is able to articulate the difficulties of being both a young intellectual woman and a culturally marginalized Other in the late nineteenth century.

According to various traditions, Medea's saga begins in Colchis, the kingdom of her father Aeëtes. Medea is said to fall in love with the Greek Argonaut Jason, whom she helps, with the aid of magic, to steal the Golden Fleece. After she betrays her father and kills her brother, Apsyrtus, Medea and Jason flee to Corinth, where, while they are living as husband and wife, Medea bears Jason two sons. Jason, who has ambitions toward the throne, resolves to wed the king of Corinth's daughter and to consequently exile Medea and his sons from Corinth. Medea, outraged at Jason's betrayal, determines to take her revenge by murdering the princess and Medea's own two sons. Multiple versions of Medea's story existed in antiquity, but it is the ancient Greek playwright Euripides who has been credited with the "invention" of the mother who killed her children.[32] Levy (re)appropriates Euripides' notorious antagonist, but her drama is also a radical departure from Euripides' version of the Medea myth.

Famously accused by Friedrich von Schlegel and Friedrich Wilhelm Nietzsche for "killing" tragedy, Euripides was denounced by various Victorian moralists for his philosophical complexity and moral degeneracy.[33] Euripides' popularity actually increased throughout the nineteenth century, as testified by the many translations, reproductions, and appropriations of his work. One of the most notable Victorian representations of an enraged Medea was Augusta Webster's acclaimed monologue "Medea in Athens," published as part of her volume *Portraits* in 1870. Webster had also produced a scholarly translation of Euripides' *Medea* in 1868. Other women writers were also eager to rehabilitate Medea as a protofeminist icon. For instance, Vernon Lee, Mona Caird, and Edith Wheelwright exploited the feminist potential of the Medea myth in their portrayals of rebellious women.[34] George Eliot repeatedly returned to the Medea myth in *Adam Bede* (1859), *Felix Holt* (1866), and *Daniel Deronda* (1876). Interestingly, Josephine McDonagh suggests that in *Daniel Deronda*, "George Eliot uses the figure of Medea through which to associate women's righteous anger with their world with their situation as outsiders, the disenfranchised of society, analogous with the Jews."[35] Levy knew Eliot's work well, and she can be seen to echo Eliot in her characterization of the painfully disenfranchised, socially ostracized Medea.

Medea also made repeated appearances on stage during the period. Fiona Macintosh notes that the sudden proliferation of new versions of *Medea*—both tragic and burlesque—in midcentury coincided with public debates regarding the divorce laws and the enfranchisement of women in England.[36] Indeed, after the Divorce and Matrimonial Causes Act was passed in August 1857, Medea, as Edith Hall observes, "became one of the most ubiquitous heroines on the London stage."[37] The Greek sorceress also appeared later in the century when an adaptation of Grillparzer's *Medea* was staged at the Haymarket in London in 1876. On this occasion, the tempestuous Czech-born actress Francesca Janauschek was contracted to play the title role. Unlike the burlesque productions of twenty years earlier, this *Medea* was not played for laughs.

As the nineteenth century wore on, Medea was increasingly appropriated for political purposes. In fact, Medea's famous speech to the "Women of Corinth" formed part of the repertoire of the Actresses' Franchise League at suffragette meetings.[38] Levy actually omits this speech from her drama but includes an extract from the speech as an epigraph. The epigraph can be translated as "Of all those beings capable of life and thought, we women are most miserable of living things."[39] Levy consequently frames Medea's tragedy in terms of moral and social justice, rather than political reform. Nevertheless, Levy's verse-drama should, I think, be seen as a response to the social and political circumstances of her time.

Clearly fascinated by another disreputable and demonized female character, Levy completed "Medea" in Lucerne in the summer of 1882. The previous year Levy had decided, after two years of hard study at Newnham, to continue her education abroad.[40] While in Germany, Levy kept an eye on the reviews of *Xantippe* and continued to study Greek, under the tutelage of a "Cambridge man." At this time, Levy's continued interest in Greek subjects collided with her hyperawareness of and disturbing ambivalence toward other Jews. A letter from Dresden recounts her visit to a "beastly" synagogue: "[T]he place was crammed with evil-looking Hebrews. . . . [T]he German Hebrew makes me feel, as a rule, that the Anti-Semitic movement is a most just and virtuous one."[41] Beckman sees Levy's letter as a "classic instance" of Jewish self-hatred.[42] Levy's reaction does seem to comply with Sander Gilman's analysis of the perceived impact of "the Eastern Jew" on assimilated western Jews. The letter demonstrates not only Levy's difficulties with Jewish identity but also her consciousness of the German anti-Semitic movement. In another letter from Lucerne, Levy describes herself as "sad but infinitely amused" at the sight of other Jews in the resort. Interestingly, Levy chooses to associate the Jewish tourists with her sister Katie, "yr. [your] co-religionists," not with herself.[43] Levy implies that the visitors are readily identifiable as Jewish, which makes her feel both "sad" and detached. It is under these circumstances that, in Dresden and Lucerne, the twenty-one-year old Levy writes "Medea."

Levy was familiar with the work of the Austrian playwright Franz Grillparzer, as she translated his verse-drama "Sappho" in the same year that she wrote "Medea."[44] The similarities between Grillparzer's representation and Levy's are not structural or technical. Rather, Levy shares Grillparzer's interest in and his emphasis of Medea's ethnic difference. As Macintosh observes, Grillparzer's trilogy set a new trend in presenting Medea's cause in a thoroughly sympathetic and humanistic light.[45] Grillparzer's *Medea* is therefore an interesting precursor for Levy, not least because, as Macintosh suggests, his "Hasidic" Medea was written against the background of the pogroms in Austria in 1817–18.[46] In comparison, Levy's drama was written against the backdrop of the mass immigration of Jews from eastern Europe.

In Levy's drama, Medea's ethnic difference is highlighted from the outset. As a native of Colchis, a country that the Greeks believed nestled on the eastern edge of the Black Sea, Medea is frequently described in terms of blackness. Medea is said to be "wild" in her gestures and speech; she has "fierce" black eyes and profuse amounts of untamed inky-black hair. The gross objectification and dehumanization of Medea by Nikias, a citizen of Corinth and supporter of Jason, corresponds with the many late-Victorian representations in art and literature of the Oriental female:

> I like not your swart skins and purple hair;
> Your black, fierce eyes where the brows meet across.
> By all the gods! When yonder Colchian
> Fixes me with her strange and sudden gaze,
> Each hair upon my body stands erect!
> Zeus, 'tis a very tiger, and as mute!

> (38)

As Nadia Valman notes, in nineteenth-century culture the Jewess was "ubiquitously conflated with the Oriental woman, and recognized by her stylized sensual beauty: her large dark eyes, abundant hair and languid expression."[47] Levy taps into this visual economy by endowing Medea with the stereotypical motifs of the Jewess.

Todd Endelman points out that before the 1870s, Jews did not loom large in the political or cultural imagination of the English.[48] The change occurred during the 1870s and 1880s, when there was a significant increase in the number of Jewish immigrants entering England from eastern Europe. It was, Endelman suggests, mass immigration from eastern Europe that focused attention on Jews.[49] And as many critics have illustrated, despite relatively positive Anglo-Jewish relations, the unassimilated Jew was widely felt to pose a threat to the "purity" of the English national character.[50] The arrival of the eastern European Jews also had an impact on established Anglo-Jewish communities. Endelman suggests that the "new immigrant 'ghettos' were both an embarrassment and a threat, with the potential, it was believed, to undo the social and political gains made by anglicized Jews."[51] Native leaders were critical of the immigrants for their "foreign" customs, and many community leaders suggested that the new immigrants go elsewhere. However, anglicized Jews also understood that "the fates of the two communities were linked, that hostility to poor, unacculturated, foreign-born Jews could, and frequently did, become an attack on all Jews."[52] It should be noted that the writing of "Medea" coincides with the first major peak in immigration of eastern Jews into England.

Levy seems to have been acutely sensitive to the cultural impact of the growing number of "foreign" Jews, as her sketches of this period (1876–81) indicate. Beckman observes that "these drawings reveal a new, much more troubled preoccupation with 'racial' difference" and that they bear a striking resemblance to the caricatured Jewish faces in Robert Knox's *The Races of Men* (1850).[53] Knox's work has become the most notorious text of the Victorian pseudo-science of ethnology. It was not, however, the only text. Sander Gilman suggests that "the general consensus of the ethnological literature of the late century was that the Jews were black" or, at least, "swarthy."[54]

Medea's "blackness" is also significant in that it can be interpreted as "a pathological sign."[55] In *The Jew's Body*, Gilman suggests that for many eighteenth- and nineteenth-century scientists the "blackness" of the Jew was not only a mark of racial inferiority but also an indicator of the diseased nature of the Jew.[56] The pathologized Jewish body not only threatened to corrupt the racial "purity" of the English nation but was also perceived to be the carrier of sexually transmitted diseases, contagious infections, and mental illness. In Levy's drama, the "black" character threatens the health of the Corinthian body politic—not only in terms of racial purity but also in terms of infection.

At the conclusion of Levy's play, following the bloody deaths of his mixed-race sons, Jason declares that no Corinthian should seek out Medea lest "we pollute our hands / With her accursèd body" (55). Medea is also conceived as "a festering plague / In our fair city's midst" (55). Importantly, Grillparzer also uses pathological terms to describe Medea's ethnicity. For instance, Grillparzer's Jason tells Medea that it is unlikely that she will be allowed entrance to the city, as "one shuns communion where infection flares" (act 1, p. 14).[57] Furthermore, when Medea looks to embrace Creusa, the princess recoils, to which Medea responds, "Oh draw not back! My hand will not infect!" (act 1, p. 27). King Creon subsequently banishes Medea from his kingdom, telling her, "[G]et you from my father's hallowed town / And make the air you poisoned pure again" (act 2, p. 55). And in the final act, Grillparzer has the king exile

Jason on the basis that he has been infected by his (sexual) contact with Medea: "Pollution all too near, I see, is dangerous" (act 5, p. 114). I suggest that Levy appropriates Grillparzer's racial terminology in her version of the play to reflect continuing debates concerning Jewish immigration and national identity. Indeed, Medea's social isolation and eventual exile suggest the difficulty of maintaining a diasporic identity in the face of a (seemingly) hegemonic culture.

Despite her isolation, Medea has managed to overcome one of the key difficulties of assimilation: the ability to speak the language of the dominant culture. One of the defining characteristics of the ancient Greeks was their sophisticated use of language, as opposed to the non-Greek-speaking barbarians. Levy's Medea is acutely aware of the need to express herself in this culture, "I, an alien here / That well can speak the language of their lips / The language of their souls may never learn" (36). Her inability or unwillingness to adopt "the language of their souls" indicates Medea's different system of ethics and may also signify her religious difference. This is a crucial statement by the immigrant Medea and can be seen to influence much of the later action.

When Jason announces his forthcoming marriage to Princess Glauke, he reveals that he is to become leader of the state that has denied Medea personal agency, liberty, and respect. His is a double betrayal. Medea tells the self-deluding patriarch,

> You never knew Medea. You forget,
> Because so long she bends the knee to you,
> She was not born to serfdom.
>   I have knelt
> Too long before you. I have stood too long
> Suppliant before this people.
>
> (48)

In this fictional setting, Levy can allow her heroine to take definitive action; she will destroy the status quo. Medea instructs Jason, "[B]ehold me now, *your* work, a thing of fear" (43, my emphasis), and she resolves to "move the generations yet unborn" (49) in revenge. As she moves back within the boundaries of the family home, Medea proclaims that there "shall be a horror and a horror in the land" (48). Unlike Euripides' text, there has been no mention of revenge before this point, so we do not feel that Medea is "naturally" vengeful. Conversely, we feel that she has been provoked and that Jason must suffer the consequences of his appalling actions. According to tradition, Medea will exact a terrible revenge by killing her children and Jason's bride-to-be. Levy's Medea is far less conflicted about her revenge than Euripides' protagonist. Following an angry exchange with Jason, Levy's Medea determines to take decisive action, and we do not see her hesitate. Medea tells us that she feels "strong" and "lifted up into an awful realm / Where is nor love, nor pity, nor remorse" (48). Bernard Knox points out that Medea's murderous rage should in fact be considered alongside the actions of other famous Greek "heroes," such as Ajax and Achilles.[58] But how does Levy deal with the ethical difficulties of identifying with a tragic protagonist who is at once heroic, sympathetic, and morally repugnant?

Reading Euripides, Christopher Gill suggests that Medea's act of infanticide should be interpreted as "an exemplary gesture." For Gill, "this gesture despite its horrific character, expresses an ethical stance."[59] The ethical standard of ancient Greek social and political life was, in essence, to be good to your friends and do harm to your enemies.[60] Levy's Medea, shunned by the Corinthians for her ethnicity and her sex and betrayed by her husband for his political ambitions, sees herself as harmed by the people who should be her friends. Jason's unilateral decision to sever their marriage, a union upon which Medea has been totally dependent, can be seen as a violation of the ethics that govern interpersonal relationships. Without her marriage to Jason, Medea and her children will be destitute. Her desperate predicament is one with which many Victorian women could have identified.

By murdering Jason's children and his future wife, Medea not only exposes the potential for violence within the family but also inflicts maximum damage on the state. Intentionally or not, Levy certainly tapped into widespread fears about the increasing prevalence of infanticide in Victorian society.[61] The statistics are unclear and unreliable, but Lionel Rose estimates that the number of inquest verdicts of murder of infants was around two hundred per year in the 1860s.[62] In response to the worrying statistics concerning the infant mortality rate, the government passed the Infant Life Protection Act in 1872. But as McDonagh notes, nineteenth-century child murder cases are sites of extraordinary cultural contests in terms of race, class, and gender. McDonagh suggests that "the very geography and temporality of the modern British nation were at stake; its networks of communication, its hygiene, its moral stature, all were threatened by persistence and primordial stagnancy of child murder."[63] The frequency of child murder cases seemed to threaten the very basis of civilized society.

Levy's Medea not only stabs her children to death but also poisons Jason's bride-to-be, Princess Glauke. Yet Medea does not confess to having committed any crime. She does not speak of her guilt; Nikias does. If she is guilty, as we presume she is, Medea does not enjoy her retribution. "Vanquished utterly," Medea is not a female criminal who revels in the art of murderous revenge. Nevertheless, the citizens of Levy's Corinth are unwilling to accept that Medea's actions could be carried out by any civilized Greek woman. Nikias is quick to denounce Medea as an "alien."

For Levy, Medea's actions testify to the alienating and destructive effects of institutionalized sexism and racism. And like Euripides and Grillparzer, Levy refuses to punish Medea directly. But there is no magic chariot to rescue Medea in Levy's humanistic tragedy. Following Grillparzer's lead, Levy achieves a truly pessimistic ending. The outcast figure is condemned to fulfil her role in exile, as the Wandering Jew of the ancient world: "Thus I go forth / Into the deep, dense heart of the night—alone" (57). In contrast to Euripides, who refuses to provide a clear explanation for Medea's behavior, Levy implicates the sexist, racist, and morally bankrupt Corinthians in Medea's crimes. In this case, Medea's assimilation or conversion fails because the dominant society cannot and will not accept the "Oriental" female as a fully fledged member of the state. Levy ensures that as a result of denying this woman her civil and human rights, anarchy reigns over Hellenic society.

If James Thomson lacked "the classical trick," Amy Levy had classical trickery in abundance. Levy's trick was to combine classical erudition with subversive intent, as Levy knew that often the only way to demythologize is to remythologize. Levy's Hellenic poems can therefore be read not only as cautionary tales concerning the disavowed and disenfranchised but also as forward-looking contributions in revisionist mythmaking.

Notes

This chapter is based on an earlier version, as published in T. D. Olverson's *Women Writers and the Dark Side of Late-Victorian Hellenism* (Houndmills: Palgrave Macmillan, 2010). Reproduced with permission of Palgrave Macmillan.

1. Levy's essay "James Thomson: A Minor Poet" was initially published in the *Cambridge Review* in February 1883. It was recently reprinted in *The Complete Novels and Selected Writings of Amy Levy, 1861–1889*, ed. Melvyn New (Gainesville: University Press of Florida, 1993), 501–9, quotation on 506.

2. Levy, "James Thomson," 508.

3. James Thomson, "A Word for Xantippe," in *Thomson, Essays and Phantasies* (London: Reeves and Turner, 1881), 220–27, quotation on 220–21.

4. See Isobel Hurst's fine survey, *Victorian Women Writers and the Classics* (Oxford: Oxford University Press, 2006); Yopie Prins, "'Lady's Greek' (With the Accents): A Metrical Translation of Euripides by A. Mary F. Robinson," *Victorian Literature and Culture 24, no. 2 (2006): 591–618.*

5. Ruth Hoberman, *Gendering Classicism: The Ancient World in Twentieth-Century Women's Historical Fiction* (Albany: State University of New York, 1997), 3.

6. Claire Breay, "Women and the Classical Tripos, 1869–1914," in *Classics in Nineteenth and Twentieth Century Cambridge: Curriculum, Culture and Community*, ed. Christopher Stray (Cambridge: Cambridge Philological Society, 1999), 48–70, quotation on 49.

7. See Martha Vicinus, *A Widening Sphere: Changing Roles of Victorian Women* (Bloomington: Indiana University Press, 1977).

8. Levy's "Confessions Book" entry is reprinted in Linda Hunt Beckman, *Amy Levy: Her Life and Letters* (Athens: Ohio University Press, 2000), 16.

9. The article won a Junior Prize in the October edition of *Kind Words* (1875). The article forms part of the Camellia Collection: Amy Levy Archive, Kent, UK. Italics in original.

10. Extract taken from an undated letter to Amy's sister Katie, reprinted as letter 5 in Beckman, *Amy Levy*, 219–20.

11. See Rosemary Day, "Women and Education in Nineteenth-Century England," in *Women, Scholarship and Criticism: Gender and Knowledge, 1790–1900*, ed. Joan Bellamy, Anne Laurence, and Gill Perry (Manchester: Manchester University Press, 2000), 91–109.

12. Quotation from an undated letter by Levy to her sister Katie, reprinted as letter 11 in Beckman, *Amy Levy*, 228–29.

13. Levy's notes in her copy of *A Minor Poet and Other Verse* indicate that Xantippe was composed in 1879 in London and Brighton; Beckman, *Amy Levy*, 290n14.

14. The review, "A Newnham Student's Poems," was published in *Literary World*, 5 August 1881, 90–91.

15. See Cynthia Scheinberg, "Recasting 'Sympathy and Judgment': Amy Levy, Women Poets, and the Victorian Dramatic Monologue," *Victorian Poetry* 35, no. 2 (1997): 173–91. See also Scheinberg's chapter on Levy in *Women's Poetry and Religion in Victorian England: Jewish Identity and Christian Culture* (Cambridge: Cambridge University Press, 2002), 190–238.

16. Pericles pronounced the virtue of women's silence in his funeral oration for the fallen soldiers of the Peloponnesian War. Thucydides, *History of the Peloponnesian War*, trans. Rex Warner, intro. and notes by M. I. Finley (London: Penguin, 1972), 2.46.

17. Amy Levy, "Xantippe," *A Minor Poet and Other Verse*, 2nd ed. (London: T. Fisher Unwin, 1891), 23. Further references to page numbers in this edition are made parenthetically in the text.

18. See Alice Falk, "Lady's Greek without the Accents," *Studies in Browning and His Circle* 19 (1991): 92.

19. George Eliot, *Middlemarch* (Edinburgh: Blackwood, 1874; reprint, London: Penguin, 1994), 30.

20. Plato *Symposium* 210c. Lysis, *Phaedrus and Symposium: Plato on Homosexuality*, trans. Benjamin Jowett and selected retranslation and notes by Eugene O'Connor (New York: Prometheus Books, 1991), 143.

21. Sarah Pomeroy, *Goddesses, Whores, Wives and Slaves: Women in Classical Antiquity* (London: Pimlico, 1975), 7.

22. Susan Okin reminds us that Plato valued neither sexual equality nor justice, in the sense of fairness. His idea of dismantling the family actually forced the philosopher to rethink the role of women. Okin, *Women in Western Political Thought* (Princeton: Princeton University Press, 1992), 15–28 (chap. 2).

23. John Stuart Mill, *The Subjection of Women* (London: Parker, 1859), reprinted in *On Liberty and Other Essays*, ed. John Gray (Oxford: Oxford University Press, 1991), 471–583, quotation on 519.

24. See chapter 3 in ibid., 524–57.

25. Plato *Symposium* 209a, 142.

26. See the reading of Diotima's speech in Luce Irigaray, *An Ethics of Sexual Difference* (London: Athlone Press, 1993), 20.

27. Jowett's decision to obfuscate the references to pederasty in his highly regarded and widely read translations of Plato's texts are somewhat incongruous; especially if one considers that Jowett was largely responsible for the "Socratic" tutorials for which Balliol College became renowned. For a full discussion of these issues, see Linda Dowling, *Hellenism and Homosexuality in Victorian Oxford* (Ithaca, NY: Cornell University Press, 1994).

28. Richard Jenkyns, "The Nineteenth Century": Introduction in *Platonism and the English Imagination*, ed. Anna Baldwin and Sarah Hutton (Cambridge: Cambridge University Press, 1994), 201–6, quotation on 205.

29. Parenthetical page citations for "Medea" refer to *A Minor Poet and Other Verse*, 2nd ed. (London: T. Fisher Unwin, 1891).

30. See Susan Brown's absorbing article "Determined Heroines: George Eliot, Augusta Webster, and Closet Drama by Victorian Women," *Victorian Poetry* 33, no. 1 (1995): 89–109, quotation on 104. However, as a genre, closet drama can also be problematic for women writers. As Brown points out, it is often very difficult to know whether an author intended a work to be read as an entirely textual production, or whether other issues determined the work's status as a "closet drama." See Brown, "Determined Heroines," 106nn3–4.

31. See, for instance, Todd M. Endelman's assessment of Levy in *The Jews of Britain, 1656 to 2000* (Berkeley: University of California Press, 2002), 170.

32. For a more detailed explanation, see chapter 1 in Emily McDermott, *Euripides' Medea: The Incarnation of Disorder* (University Park: Pennsylvania State University Press, 1989), 1–24.

33. For a full discussion of Euripides' critical reputation, see Ann Michelini, *Euripides and the Tragic Tradition* (Madison: University of Wisconsin Press, 1987).

34. For a discussion of Caird's *Daughters of Danaus* and Lee's "Amour Dure," see chapter 6 in Ann Heilmann, *New Woman Strategies* (Manchester: Manchester University Press, 2004), 200–233.

35. Josephine McDonagh, *Child Murder and British Culture, 1720–1900* (Cambridge: Cambridge University Press, 2003), 168.

36. See Fiona Macintosh, "Medea Transposed: Burlesque and Gender on the Mid-Victorian Stage," in *Medea in Performance, 1500–2000*, ed. Edith Hall, Fiona Macintosh, and Oliver Taplin (Oxford: Legenda, 2000), 75–99.

37. Edith Hall, "Medea and British Legislation before the First World War," *Greece and Rome* 46, no. 1 (1999): 42–77; quotation on 56.

38. See ibid., 45–46; Fiona Macintosh, "The Performer in Performance," in Hall, Macintosh, and Taplin, *Medea in Performance, 1500–2000*, 1–31, quotation on 18.

39. Translation of *Medea*, lines 230–31, by Ruby Blondell, in *Women on the Edge: Four Plays by Euripides*, ed. Ruby Blondell, Mary-Kay Gamel, Nancy Sorkin Rabinowitz, and Bella Zweig (London: Routledge, 1999).

40. It is worth noting that Levy never traveled to Greece, but she made repeated trips to Europe.

41. See letter 16, dated 4 December 1881, from Levy to her sister Katie, reprinted in Beckman, *Amy Levy*, 235–36.

42. See Beckman, *Amy Levy*, 110. Beckman's use of the phrase is borrowed from Sander Gilman's important study *Jewish Self-Hatred: Anti-Semitism and the Hidden Language of the Jews* (Baltimore, MD: John Hopkins University Press, 1986). See especially chapter 4.

43. See letter 19, dated 18 July 1884, reprinted in Beckman, *Amy Levy*, 241–42.

44. Levy's partial translation "From Grillparzer's Sappho" was published in the *Cambridge Review*, 1 February 1882. Levy's translation of Grillparzer's "Sappho" can be seen in the Camellia Collection: Amy Levy Archive, Kent.

45. See Macintosh, "Performer in Performance," 14.

46. Ibid., 12–14. Hall and Macintosh also call Grillparzer's Medea "Hasidic" in *Greek Tragedy and the British Theatre, 1660–1914* (Oxford: Oxford University Press, 2005), 424.

47. See Nadia Valman, *The Jewess in Nineteenth-Century British Literary Culture* (Cambridge: Cambridge University Press, 2007), 4. Reina Lewis also provides a gendered reading of visual productions of the Orient in British culture in *Gendering Orientalism: Race, Femininity and Representation* (London: Routledge, 1996).

48. See Endelman, *Jews of Britain*, 150.

49. Ibid., 156. For further discussion, see chapter 5, "Tide of Immigration, 1880–1905," in V. D. Lipman, *Social History of the Jews in England, 1850–1950* (London: Watts, 1954).

50. For detailed discussions on the impact of Jewish immigrants on English culture in the nineteenth century, see David Cesarani, ed., *The Making of Modern Anglo-Jewry* (Oxford: Basil Blackwell, 1990); Bryan Cheyette, *Constructions of "the Jew" in English Literature and Society: Racial Representations, 1875–1945* (Cambridge: Cambridge University Press, 1993); David Feldman, *Englishmen and Jews: Social Relations and Political Culture, 1840–1914* (New Haven, CT: Yale University Press, 1994); Michael Ragussis, *Figures of Conversion: "The Jewish Question" and English National Identity* (Durham, NC: Duke University Press, 1995); Endelman, *Jews of Britain*.

51. Endelman, *Jews of Britain*, 171–72.

52. Ibid., 173.

53. Beckman, *Amy Levy*, 112. For reproductions of Levy's sketches, see Linda Hunt Beckman, "Leaving 'The Tribal Duckpond': Amy Levy, Jewish Self-Hatred, and Jewish Identity," *Victorian Literature and Culture* 27, no. 1 (1999): 185–201.

54. Sander Gilman, *The Jew's Body* (New York: Routledge, 1991), 171.

55. Gilman, *Jewish Self-Hatred*, 207.

56. Gilman, *Jew's Body*, 172. For a more gendered reading of this issue, see chapter 6, "The Shadow of the Harem," in Valman, *Jewess*, 173–205.

57. All subsequent quotations of Grillparzer's Medea are from Arthur Burkhard's translation of *Das Goldene Vlies* (Yarmouth Port, MA: Register Press, 1942; reprinted 1956).

58. B.M.W. Knox, "The Medea of Euripides," *Yale Classical Studies* 25 (1977): 193–225, quotation on 197.

59. Christopher Gill, *Personality in Greek Epic, Tragedy, Philosophy* (Oxford: Clarendon Press, 1996), 154.

60. See Patricia Easterling, "The Infanticide in Euripides' *Medea*," *Yale Classical Studies* 25 (1977): 185.

61. For more on this concurrence, see Lillian Corti, *The Myth of Medea and the Murder of Children* (Westport, CT: Greenwood Press, 1998); Macintosh, "Medea Transposed."

62. Lionel Rose, *Massacre of the Innocents: Infanticide in Great Britain, 1800–1939* (London: Routledge and Kegan Paul, 1986), 175.

63. McDonagh, *Child Murder*, 124.

6

"Mongrel Words"

amy levy's jewish vulgarity

———

Susan David Bernstein

*I*N *The Jew in English Fiction,* published in 1889, Rabbi David Phillipson comments, "Because there are some uncultured, vulgar people among the Jews, is this a reason that such are to be specially represented as Jews? Because some Jews have grown suddenly rich, and are loudly ostentatious, is this a cause that the flagrant injustice be done, that they, with these characteristics, be held up by the name of their religion?"[1] In the same year, a reviewer of Amy Levy's novel of middle-class Anglo-Jewry, *Reuben Sachs,* accuses the author of "persuading the general public that her own kith and kin are the most hideous types of vulgarity."[2] Although not explicitly referring to Levy's novel, Phillipson spotlights an entrenched and persistent figure in the representational history of Jewishness: the vulgarity of excessive display, whether of voice, body, or money. That Phillipson qualifies "vulgar people among the Jews" as "uncultured" suggests the fault lines of assimilation, the ways in which Jewish vulgarity works as a marker of difference at a particular time of increasing Anglo-Jewish emancipation.[3] This history typically describes the many "first" Jewish men to hold public office, while Jewish women's role in the equation is slighter and often overlooked altogether. Levy was the first Jewish student to attend Newnham College when both Jews and women were rare presences on campus. Given her affiliations across different cultures and social groups, from her family's congregation at the West London Synagogue of British Jews to Cambridge University and to socialist and feminist clubs and enclaves of late-Victorian London, the figure of Jewish vulgarity in Levy's writing offers a way to untangle the knottiness of modern diasporic identity.

In her 1886 essay "The Jew in Fiction," Levy lambasts the binary depiction of Jews in British literature as depraved or idealized, ranging from Dickens's "bad fairy" Fagin in *Oliver Twist* (1837–38) to the "good fairy" Riah in his last completed novel, *Our Mutual Friend* (1864–65). Calling for more nuance, Levy remarks, "The complex problem of Jewish life and Jewish character . . . this deeply interesting product of our civilisation has been worthy of none but the most superficial observation."[4] Yet reviews in the Jewish press of *Reuben Sachs,* Levy's 1888 novel about the "tribal duck-pond" (as Levy puts it) of London middle-class Jews, construct Levy as a vulgar Jewish woman by protesting her engagement with this very figure. Sometimes Levy's Jewish vulgarity compounds the racialized image of "the Jew" with the social snobbery of class, and in some instances, Levy manipulates vulgarity to shore up her critique of sexism in Anglo-Jewish culture. But more often, these vulgar combinations expose the asymmetrical strands of different equations of Jewishness. As I demonstrate in this chapter, the idea of vulgarity is crucial to the logic of the stereotype, and Levy's multiple uses of vulgarity challenge the discourse of a unified Jewish identity in Victorian culture. For Levy's Jewish vulgarity revolves around the excesses of language, the "mongrel words" by which in-between subjectivities inhabit diverse cultures and systems of meaning. This linguistic rendition occasions a vulgar poetics, although Levy's spare style belies the mongrel writing she otherwise laments.

An Anatomy of Victorian Vulgarity

As Jonathan Freedman points out, Jewish identity at least since the Enlightenment has been "internally contested and quarrelled over" as decentered and variable.[5] Given ambiguous and contradictory meanings as race, nationality, culture, and religion, by definition Jewishness is hybrid and divided, associated with exile, the placelessness of the "wandering Jew." Thus, Jewish identity is necessarily "vulgar" in the sense that a pure, unmediated Jewishness does not exist, a proposition compatible with postmodern and antifoundationalist accounts of subjectivity. While variant notions of Jewishness have worked against a unified, coherent identity, its elusiveness in turn has fueled the repetitive insistence of what Bryan Cheyette calls "the ambivalent Jewish stereotype."[6] The concept of vulgarity foregrounds this unevenness.[7] Pierre Bourdieu's social critique of taste defines vulgarity in opposition to "pure" or specifically cultured aesthetic discernment. Identified with bodily pleasure, vulgarity is equated with untamed nature, as opposed to refined culture. To be vulgar is to be coarse and impure, facile and cheap, to indulge in sheer display without substance, in contrast to the complexities and subtleties of a variantly abundant dominant culture.[8] More than anything, Bourdieu's lexicon makes evident that vulgarity is a relational term. To be vulgar depends on a context of comparison in which, say, a body type with manners and gestures, or a character with linguistic habits, protrudes as a blemish, a gross exaggeration of what passes muster as beautiful form. In his discussion of Kantian pure taste, Bourdieu equates vulgarity with a lack of discrimination between representation and "the nature of the object itself in our sensation."[9]

This lapse of discernment between the artificial and the real, between what is valued and what is demeaned, echoes John Ruskin's discussion of vulgarity. In his chapter "Of Vulgarity" in the fifth and final volume of *Modern Painters,* Ruskin meditates on Victorian vulgarity as "ill-breeding" in contrast to "gentlemanliness" or "high breeding." While Ruskin links "breeding" to race and blood, he emphatically defines vulgarity as an "insensibility"—a cornerstone of Ruskinian vulgarity—to training.[10] Ruskin allows for the force of circumstances: vulgarity as "coarseness of language or manners," he argues, must be separated from impoverished conditions that might produce illiteracy. The crude language of a peasant is not vulgar, but the corrupted speech of an English schoolboy, whose insensibility does not permit him to adapt to the more refined form of speaking to which he is exposed through education, is vulgar.[11] Even while Ruskin understands vulgarity as an intrinsic resistance to social conditioning, his idea of gentlemanliness retains a somatic quality. To this end, Ruskin claims that "a gentleman's first characteristic is that fineness of structure in the body, which renders it capable of the most delicate sensation; and of structure in the mind which renders it capable of the most delicate sympathies."[12] But even an elephant, Ruskin reasons, is capable of delicacy and sensitivity, although only as its "elephantine nature" or its physical qualities allow. Thus, gentlemanliness and vulgarity are not absolute, fixed terms but must be adjusted to suit physical restraints as well. Despite this laundry list of vulgarity's abstract qualities, as a concept it is historically and culturally rooted, a sign of social difference.

Accordingly, Ruskin finds "truthfulness" to be a gentlemanly trait, while "cunning" has an "essential connection with vulgarity" as "the habit or gift of over-reaching."[13] As an example of cunning, Ruskin mentions an illustration of Fagin and one of his urchin street-gang members from *Oliver Twist* with the caption, "The Jew and Morris Bolter begin to understand each other." After sketching out this dichotomy of gentlemanly truthfulness and vulgar cunning, Ruskin further distinguishes truthfulness as "the absolute disdain of all lying" and observes that such truthfulness "belongs to Christian chivalry."[14] Implicitly, then, the opposition of Christian and Jew epitomizes Ruskin's discussion of gentlemanliness, good breeding, and truthfulness in contrast to vulgarity, ill-breeding, and cunning. Offsetting Ruskin's insinuation about Jews through Dickens's Fagin is his earlier example of biblical Hebrews—David, Ruth, and Judah—who all demonstrate "sensitiveness through all flesh and spirit."[15] Ruskin thus differentiates "pure" ancient Jews from Dickens's vulgar and criminal modern Jew, whose cunning is defined by a deliberate desire to deceive.

Ruskin's words on vulgarity appeared in 1860, only two years after the first Jewish man, Lionel de Rothschild, was allowed to take a seat in Parliament—and the year before Levy's birth.[16] As acculturated Jews increasingly gained political liberties and social advantages, representations of Jewish vulgarity also persisted, perhaps in proportion to the success of this mobility.[17] Because this almost, but not quite, complete amalgamation was so frequently the case with middle-class Jews such as Levy in Victorian England, the trope of vulgarity acquired a charged valence in derogatory renditions of so-called crypto or masked Jews attempting to enter the upper echelons of English society. Anthony Trollope's novels are rife with these bounders, such as Joseph Emilius of *The Eustace Diamonds* (1871–73) and Ferdinand Lopez in *The Prime Minister* (1875–76). Although neither character identifies himself as Jewish, this distinction is encoded nonetheless through accents of vulgarity.[18]

Whereas Ruskin and Trollope insinuate a coded Jewish vulgarity, sometimes correlating tropes of race and class, other cultural documents of the day are not as cautious. In *The Races of Men*, for example, reissued in 1862, Robert Knox presents his race science of origins within which immutable signs expose what he terms "the Jewish physiognomy" along with a "willingness to purchase cast-off clothes of others" in order to assume "the air of a person of a different stamp." Despite this habit of masquerade, for Knox the mark of Jewishness remains essentially readable, as he describes the Jewish old-clothes man of London as a fixture of vulgarity: "[L]osing sight of his origin for a moment, he dresses himself up as the flash man about town; but never to be mistaken for a moment, never to be confounded with any other race."[19] Knox typecasts Jews as universally set in body and in culture such that "the real Jew . . . never altered since the earliest recorded period; that two hundred years ago at least before Christ they were perambulating Italy and Europe precisely as they do now."[20] This profile of "the Jewish race" inscribes a paradox: the chameleon-like habits of Jews to take on the camouflage of the culture in which they live offsets Knox's contention of the transhistorical habits and physical features of Jews. As Deborah Cohen has observed, mutability and versatility, qualities understood to be inherited, were key features assigned to Jews in Victorian culture.[21] British Jews were racialized in the course of the nineteenth century "in part as a consequence of assimilation, delimiting difference in a nation where formal legal barriers to Jewish integration had been eliminated and social obstacles largely overcome."[22] Like racialist tropes, vulgar traits, functioning as markers for an inscrutable Jewishness, also suggest the instabilities of identity.

By the same token, definitions of vulgarity rotate around contradictions. For instance, Ruskin specifies, "You shall know a man not to be a gentleman by the perfect and neat pronunciation of his words: but he does not pretend to pronounce accurately; he does pronounce accurately, the vulgarity is in the real (not assumed) scrupulousness."[23] Ruskinian vulgarity is structured by a stubborn, insensate disposition despite superficial adjustments, whereas Knox sees Jewish assimilation as merely a surface counterfeit that barely masks an inability to change.

This combination of fixity and vacillation, of transparency and obscurity, applies to stereotyping as a rhetorical strategy. For Homi Bhabha, the insistence of the stereotype as a "sign of cultural/historical/racial difference" is crucial in "the ideological construction of otherness."[24] Like vulgarity itself, the stereotype is fortified by an ambivalent surplus, a signification that exceeds evidence and logic, as Knox's construction of "the Jewish race" makes manifest. In this sense, the stereotype is "a form of knowledge and identification"[25] that oscillates between what is fixed as indisputable and what must be continually reinforced through anxious repetition precisely because it cannot be proven. The signs of embodied Jewishness, akin to Ruskin's idea of vulgarity and Knox's profile of a "Jewish race," form a network of codes with no explicit identification, because these codes of physical and material excess have become so familiar. This alternation between the visible and the invisible, the stated and the implied is what recapitulates the grammar of the stereotype. Levy's own writing of "mongrel words" confounds the syntax of this typecast Jewishness.

Levy's Jewish Vulgarities

Levy's treatment of Jewish vulgarity turns on a disparity between inside and outside vantage points. Her short story "Cohen of Trinity," first published in 1889 in *The Gentleman's Magazine*, contemplates the difficulties of Jewish acculturation. Describing his subject's physicality through the stereotyping familiar from Knox, Levy's narrator endows Alfred Lazarus Cohen with "full prominent lips, full, prominent eyes, and the curved beak of nose with its restless nostrils."[26] A fellow student who knew Cohen only barely at Cambridge, the narrator parrots the usual litany about vulgar Jews. Yet Levy does open up space for a different kind of reckoning of these traits. From the start, the narrator's intense curiosity about Cohen's class-blended traits predominates, although the narrator does recognize his insubstantial perspective: "I cannot quite explain my interest on so slight a knowledge; his manners were a distressing mixture of the bourgeois and the canaille."[27] The story pivots on the narrator's struggle as a naive reader attempting to decipher Cohen as a freak curiosity: "I was struck afresh by the man's insatiable demands, which looked at times like a passionate striving after perfection, yet went side by side with the crudest vanity, the most vulgar desire for recognition."[28] Because Levy makes evident the limited insights of a privileged-class Englishman about the frustrated aspirations of his Jewish classmate, "vulgar" here remains at best a relative term.

While the narrator assesses Cohen's character and body as vulgar, he likewise finds Cohen's writing a corruption of genre and difficult to categorize: "Half poem, half essay, wholly unclassifiable, with a force, a fire, a vision, a vigour and felicity of phrase that carried you through its most glaring inequalities, its most appalling lapses of taste, the book fairly took the reader by storm."[29] Given that this *Gentleman's Magazine* story is narrated by an English gentleman, the vulgarities of Cohen—from his tasteless half-bred book to his shoddy manners and "ungainly figure"—establish a reversal whereby the narrator is the outsider, the one who can only read Cohen superficially. Although limited, this assessment is necessarily commonplace. Encapsulated in the syntax of the story's title, "Cohen of Trinity," representations of Jewish culture and character cannot be detached from dominant, generalized, or gentile and gentlemanly, expectations.

Anticipating this grammatical consciousness is Levy's 1886 essay "Jewish Humour," in which vulgarity signifies a matter of linguistic marking that cannot be entirely effaced. Whereas "Cohen of Trinity" mimics the perspective of a gentile Cambridge graduate for the readers of *The Gentleman's Magazine,* in this essay Levy addresses her co-religionists in the *Jewish Chronicle,* the flagship newspaper of established Anglo-Jewry. Much of the article centers on the wit of Heinrich Heine, the German Romantic poet who converted from Judaism as required for professional and social advancement. Levy glosses what she calls Heine's "tribal humour" as it appears diversely to outsiders and insiders: "The world laughs, and weeps and wonders; bows down and worships the brilliant exotic. We ourselves, perhaps, while admiring, as we cannot fail to admire, indulge in a little wistful, unreasonable regret, for the old cast clouts, the discarded garments of the dazzling creature; for the old allusions and gestures, the dear vulgar, mongrel words; the delicious, confidential quips and cranks which nobody but ourselves can understand."[30] While "the world" fetishizes Heine as an Orientalized spectacle, Levy expresses nostalgia for the price of acculturation, "the discarded garments" of Heine's lost Jewishness, a trope for Jewish vulgarity figured by the cast-off costumes of the stock-in-trade old clothes man of London. As Cynthia Scheinberg has noted, Levy bewails to her *Jewish Chronicle* readers Heine's betrayal of Jewish humor by converting it into terms accessible to non-Jews.[31] Yet Levy implies that Heine's conversion is inevitably incomplete. From the viewpoint of "the world," he nevertheless remains "the brilliant exotic," while only from the perspective of someone "born a Jew" is Heine's "peculiar and delicate quality of the tribal humour" audible.

The logic of the passage suggests that this failure of full assimilation works on the level of language. If Levy regrets that Heine has "cracked the communal joke, as it were, in the language of culture, for all to enjoy and understand," at the same time she treasures elements of Jewish humor that defy translation, "the dear vulgar, mongrel words" that only the "we" of her *Jewish Chronicle* audience can comprehend. Although "vulgar" is usually set against what is valuable, Levy's ironic twist reverses this equation, whereby a cornucopia of unspecified wordplay, including the "mongrel words" of hybrid Yiddish (or "Jüdisch-Deutsch," as Levy puts it), conveys a special humor that non-Jews cannot disparage because they cannot "crack" its language. Insiders, Levy implies, regard Jewish vulgarity in a way that outsiders, such as the narrator of "Cohen of Trinity," are unable to fathom. This doubleness of vulgarity accentuates the duplicity of a self-gaze that mingles outsider perspectives of a crass Jewish difference with an interior view of a recondite uniqueness.[32] In a sense, Levy suggests that the ear trumps the eye, that the common "world" view of Jewish vulgarity is a dubious visual calculus whereas hybrid Jewish difference is auditory, but a difference that nettles assimilated Jews, who become outsiders to their lower-class co-religionists. Thus, Levy regards Jewish humor as a rare language endangered under the pressures of Anglicization. In *Reuben Sachs*, the more acculturated members of the extended Sachs family refuse to understand their less-refined cousins who speak "a jargon not recognized by the modern culture of Upper Berkeley Street," the address of the West London Synagogue of British Jews, where reformed services included a modified prayer book, sermons in English, and shorter hours of worship compatible with secular timetables.[33]

At the close of "Jewish Humour," Levy ponders the possibilities of a linguistic Jewish difference in the face of acculturation:

> The old words, the old customs are disappearing, soon to be forgotten by all save the student of such matters. There is no shutting our eyes to this fact. The trappings and the suits of our humour must vanish with the rest; but that is no reason why what is essential of it should not remain to us a heritage of the ages too precious to be lightly lost; a defence and a weapon wrought for us long ago by hands that ceased not from their labour. If we leave off saying Shibboleth, let us, at least, employ its equivalent in the purest University English. Not for all Aristophanes can we yield up our national free-masonry of wit; our family joke; our Jewish humour.[34]

For her *Jewish Chronicle* readers, Levy juxtaposes the threatened "mongrel words" of Jewish humor with their seeming opposite, the comedies of classical Western culture. This pairing recalls Matthew Arnold's privileging of Hellenism over Hebraism in *Culture and Anarchy*, an ordering that Levy contests by her reversal.[35] By "saying *Shibboleth*," Levy alludes to a biblical test of nationality to identify Jews on the basis of a verbal pronunciation. Where Levy exhorts her co-religionists to blend linguistically into elite Oxbridge culture, she also advises them to retain a semblance of Jewishness through the use of verbal wit that only other Jews can work out. If acculturation means the disappearance of the obvious traces of Jewish difference, Levy implies the presence of some "essential" element that ought not to be effaced and thus should be cherished as "a heritage of the ages too precious to be lightly lost." However, there is a strain of uncertainty about whether such verbal Jewish vulgarity *can* be preserved through "its equivalent in the purest University English," or even whether special accents encoded in "saying *Shibboleth*" are wholly a matter of choice. The essay intimates a kind of nostalgia for this linguistic hybridity that is becoming increasingly unavailable to further generations of acculturated Anglo-Jewish writers, such as Levy herself.

By extolling Jewish vulgarity as a chameleon-like lingua franca, Levy also exploits what Sander Gilman describes as a longstanding stereotype of the hidden language of "the Jew,": "a strong tradition of the myth of a homogenous language that defines the Other as possessing a different tongue."[36] According to Gilman, it is in the final stages of the process of linguistic colonialism, whereby the dominant gradually overtakes the suppressed language, that any "slight difference [whether in accent, intonation, or vocabulary] becomes a positive sign" as "speakers use this slight difference to stress their necessary separateness, a separateness initially imposed upon them by their reference group and now a sign of their identity."[37] The vulgarity of "mongrel words" here becomes an ambivalent hook on which to attach Jewishness in the throes of modern acculturation.

Jewish Vulgarity for Vulgar Readers? *The Case of* Reuben Sachs

A Jewish novel of manners, *Reuben Sachs* exemplifies Levy's most versatile and complex depiction of vulgarity within "the tribal duck-pond" of middle-class London Jewry. Here she also explores the gendering of Jewish vulgarity through two sets of male and female characters, Reuben and Bertie Lee-Harrison, and Judith Quixano and Esther Kohnthal. The ambiguity around Jewish vulgarity in *Reuben Sachs* might reflect Levy's encoded presumption of a more mixed audience in contrast to the *Gentleman's Magazine* story and her *Jewish Chronicle* essays.[38] Whereas "Cohen of Trinity" models a non-Jewish reading of Cohen's vulgarity through the narrator and "Jewish Humour" portrays with affection the "dear vulgar, mongrel words" within the publication's frame of Jewish writer and readers, the narrator and implied audience of *Reuben Sachs* remain unfixed, as does the significance of vulgarity within the narrative.

The reviews of *Reuben Sachs*, especially in the Jewish press, make evident the extent to which Levy was accused of reinforcing some unsavory stereotypes of West End Jews. The *Jewish World* construed Levy as a vulgar, unfeminine author because she did not display "a saving remnant of decency" by adopting "a Gentile pseudonym" as Julia Frankau had done, hiding her Jewish and female identity beneath the name of "Frank Danby" on the title page of her scurrilous *Dr Phillips: A Maida Vale Idyll* (1887).[39] The reviewer accuses Levy of "playing the *role* of an accuser of her people. . . . She apparently delights in the task of persuading the general public that her own kith and kin are the most hideous types of vulgarity."[40] Shortly after Levy's death, Israel Zangwill defended her depictions of vulgar Jews by indulging in his own crass trope: "She was accused . . . of fouling her own nest; . . . what she had really done was to point out that the nest was foul and must be cleaned out."[41]

These assessments may assume that Levy's opinions are identical with her narrator's views in *Reuben Sachs.* Yet Levy presents vulgar, hybrid portrayals of acculturated Anglo-Jewry, a mixed representation for a mixed audience by a writer caught by the in-between condition of middle-class Victorian Jews.[42] Crediting *Reuben Sachs* as the first modern Jewish novel, Bryan Cheyette has analyzed ambivalent Jewish stereotyping by Victorian Jewish authors who vacillate between apology and revolt, between rendering Anglo-Jews as pious good citizens or casting them as hostile aliens linked to finance capital and the press.[43] As with the structure of the stereotype, Levy wavers between fixity and its undoing, even while her most concerted attention in *Reuben Sachs* to the contradictions of Victorian Jewish identity emerges through the idea of vulgarity. Just as vulgarity assumes different valences, so too does the novel both cringe about and cling to Jewish difference. Whereas Ruskin defines vulgarity as a natural resistance to acculturation that circumstances make possible, Levy's interest in the social barriers to such refinement suggests that Jewish and other sorts of vulgarity can never be wholly a matter of intrinsic disposition apart from questions of power.

As a collection of material signs that bespeak the impossibility of complete assimilation, the Leunigers' drawing room connotes an overcompensating style of upscale Englishness with a hint of vulgar excess: "a spacious apartment, hung with primrose coloured satin, furnished throughout in impeccable Louis XV, and lighted with incandescent gas from innumerable chandeliers and sconces."[44]

This attempt at interior décor that is the equivalent of "purest University English" reveals the uneasy pretensions of Levy's upwardly aspiring Jewish characters. At the same time, the narrator qualifies this space as "the great, vulgar, over-decorated room, with its garish lights, its stifling fumes of gas."[45] This Kensington domestic scenery resonates with what Ruskin takes as a "great sign of vulgarity . . . the undue regard to appearances and manners, as in the households of vulgar persons, of all stations, and the assumption of behaviour, language or dress unsuited to them, by persons in inferior stations of life."[46] Yet Levy submits that so-called overreaching is a consequence of the equivocal social condition of Anglo-Jews endeavoring to prove their worthiness through the gaze of a wider culture: "The Jew, it may be remarked in passing, eats and dresses at least two degrees above his Gentile brother in the same rank of life."[47] The "two degrees" of excess signify a vulgarity that forecloses the social passing that it is also an attempt to achieve. Levy also visualized this vulgarity in her sketches of two women at the theatre, figures as garish and "over-decorated" with jewels as the Leuniger home furnishings. Linda Hunt Beckman designates these ornately dressed women as "Jewesses" and reads the pictorial excesses as reflecting derogatory racialist attitudes.[48]

Although some forms of Jewish difference are rendered visible, Levy is especially interested in the aural marks of social positions. Linguistic acculturation—as Levy discovers in "Jewish Humour"—is a sign of education, a privilege of both class and gender: the upwardly and outwardly aspiring Reuben speaks in a manner "free from the cockney twang which marred the speech"[49] of his mother and sister. An even greater contrast is the vulgarity attributed to the tongues of the Samuel Sachses. This lower-middle-class branch of the extended Sachs family from the Jewish neighborhood of Maida Vale speak "the popular tribal phrases" such as "shool" and "bar-mitz-vah" which their Kensington cousin Lionel regards as "very bad form indeed."[50] Unlike the safe yearning after Yiddish-inflected English in the *Jewish Chronicle's* "Jewish Humour," *Reuben Sachs* evinces little fondness for "dear vulgar, mongrel words," here recast as "popular tribal phrases." Whereas "mongrel words" betoken an ambivalently cherished tongue, the phrasing in *Reuben Sachs* indicates little nostalgia for the losses that accompany acculturation. But even while linguistic vulgarity is an anachronistic blemish, it marks the racialized class inferiority of these old-fashioned Jews, who "managed to retain the tribal characteristics, to live within the tribal pale to an extent which spoke worlds for the national conservatism."[51]

Instead of the more harmonious insider perspective on Jewish diasporic speech that appears in "Jewish Humour," the narrator of *Reuben Sachs* dissects the social scene with a clinical, detached tone: "The humours of the Samuel Sachses, their appearance, gestures, their excruciating method of pronouncing the English language, the hundred and one tribal peculiarities which clung to them, had long served their cousins as a favourite family joke into which it would have been difficult for the most observant of outsiders to enter."[52] If incomprehensible to outsiders, the "favourite family joke" is more a taunt than a treasure from this vexed vantage point.

In the case of the Samuel Sachses, the narrator disparages the vulgarity that Ruskin labels a "cockney dialect, the corruption, by blunted sense, of a finer language continually heard."[53] But unlike Ruskin's stubborn schoolboy, the parochial Samuel Sachses have been, as Levy writes, "educated at Jewish schools, fed on Jewish food, brought up on Jewish traditions and Jewish prejudice."[54] On the one hand, the narrator claims that this unassimilated portion of the family stubbornly resists change in "an age and a city which has seen the throwing down of so many barriers, the levelling of so many distinctions of class, of caste, of race, of opinion."[55] On the other, the novel makes clear through the dilemmas of Reuben, who aspires to serve in Parliament but suffers social snubbing, and of his cousin Leo, who has been to Cambridge (where he never really fitted in), that such "levelling" does have its glass ceiling beyond "the tribal limits," even in modern London.

Levy uses vulgarity at times to delineate a prescription for "too-Jewishness," for the uneasily marked difference of the novel's "tribal duck-pond" characters, who are incapable of dissolving into the larger ocean of Victorian culture. Much like the "distressing mixture of the *bourgeois* and the *canaille*" of manners in "Cohen of Trinity," the snobbery in these various descriptions derives from the melding of class-specific tastes. Unlike that of "Cohen of Trinity," the narrator of *Reuben Sachs* cannot readily be identified with an English gentleman but instead seems a "distressing mixture" of outsider censure and insider perspicacity.

Oscar Wilde observed that Levy "gradually ceased to hold the orthodox doctrines of her nation, retaining, however, a strong race feeling."[56] The role of gender difference in Levy's treatment of Jewish vulgarity in fiction illuminates this contradiction of attachment and disavowal. As with "Cohen of Trinity," vulgar excess accrues more often and in multiple ways around male characters in *Reuben Sachs*—most strikingly in portrayals of Reuben Sachs and Bertie Lee-

Harrison: one, the Jewish man pursuing a career that depends on successful assimilation; the other, the novel's representative member of the gentile gentry, a reverso-converso[57] angling his way into London Jewish culture. The initial description of Reuben explores an embodied vulgarity, yet only partially so:

> He was . . . of middle height and slender build. He wore good clothes, but they could not disguise the fact that his figure was bad, and his movements awkward; unmistakably the figure and movements of a Jew. And his features, without presenting any marked national trait, bespoke no less clearly his Semitic origin. His complexion was of a dark pallor; the hair, small moustache and eyes, dark, with red lights in them; over these last the lids were drooping and the whole face wore for the moment a relaxed dreamy, impassive air, curiously Eastern, and not wholly free from melancholy.[58]

The passage asserts the stereotyping of Jewish physiognomy despite the trappings of "good clothes" that do not obscure Reuben's fundamental identity, much like Robert Knox's "flash man about town," whose sartorial flourishes become wedded to an inescapable "Semitic origin." While Ruskin's gentleman is distinguished by a "fineness of structure in the body," Reuben lacks this anatomical delicacy. However, the novel endows Reuben with fine sensibilities that trump any physical traits; as Ruskin observes, "personal defects" do not make vulgar persons, except those "which imply insensibility or dissipation."[59] Still, Reuben's sensitive nature, similar to Leo's, recalls a nervous "melancholy" that draws on an arsenal of Jewish stereotyping, what Gilman has called "the Jewish disease," the nineteenth-century medical construction that diagnosed a pathological tendency, often among acculturated Jews, to physical infirmities such as debilitating nervousness.[60]

For Levy, the stereotype of vulgarity functions as a trope for the problematic of diasporic Jewish identity, since what is deemed vulgar by definition is aligned with the impure and mixed. Levy renegotiates the terms of a *Jewish* vulgarity as stereotype by transposing its profile onto Bertie, who enters the novel through the excesses of his name: "a howling swell . . . with a double-barrelled name . . . gone over body and soul to the Jewish community."[61] *Reuben Sachs* presents Bertie's zeal for Judaism as a comical version of ultimately outsider knowledge. As one character notes, "Mr Lee-Harrison was staying at our hotel one year in Pontresina. He was a High Churchman in those days, and hardly knew a Jew from a Mohammedan."[62] Bertie's attraction to Judaism is a fickle infatuation, a superficiality that implies a gentile vulgarity through the eyes of Reuben and his extended family: "He says himself . . . that he has a taste for religion. I believe he flirted with the Holy Mother for some years, but didn't get caught. Then he joined a set of mystics, and lived for three months on a mountain, somewhere in Asia Minor. Now he has come round to thinking Judaism the one religion, and has been regularly received into the synagogue."[63]

Bertie's conversion to Judaism is a variation on the theme of vulgarity, an ironic twist for a character whose embodied delicacy echoes Ruskin's ideal of gentlemanliness: "He was a small, fair, fluent person, very carefully dressed, assiduously polite, and bearing on his amiable, commonplace, neatly modelled little face no traces of the spiritual conflict which any one knowing his history might have supposed him to have passed through."[64] A reverso-converso with a "veneer of Judaism," he is devoid of any genuine inner transformation, a sardonic comment on the embodied limits of conversion from the "other" side. With the traditional conversion narrative of English literature following the renovation of Jews into Christians, Levy's Bertie reverses the dominant trajectory. Britain was unusual in that conversion to Judaism was not outlawed, as it was in many European countries in the nineteenth century.[65] Consequently, Bertie's gentile gentlemanliness remains a legibly fixed trait in the culture of West End London Jewry, while his attempt to acquire a Jewish identity comes off as a vulgar enterprise, all surface without substance. Here Levy uses the logic of exceptionalism that is often applied to Jewish converts to Christianity, only in reverse, to suggest that these labels are more than a matter of creed, that they are embodied through birth and upbringing as well.

Bertie's fascination seems a pedantic exercise in the contours of stereotyping: "I am deeply interested in the Jewish character . . . the strongly marked contrasts; the underlying resemblances; the elaborate differentiations from a fundamental type!"[66] If Bertie's words suggest a field ethnologist, perhaps Levy implicates other external or outsider readers of "Jewish character." Although identifying the narrator who mimics such stereotypes with Bertie's converted outsider perspective is difficult, Levy does make clear that only vulgar readings of Anglo-Jewishness can prevail, that a minority self-regard is necessarily corrupted by a dominant gaze. Bertie's attempts to acquire Jewish experience offers a different spin on Ruskin's vulgarity as "the undue regard to appearances and manners." Repeatedly Levy underscores Bertie's inability to reconcile his idealized vision of biblical depictions of Jews celebrating "ancient rites in the land of exile"[67] with the daily lives of modern London Jews, and she uses simplistic phrasing to parody the shallowness of Bertie's perceptions: "Bertie stared and Bertie wondered. Needless to state, he was completely out of touch with these people whose faith his search for the true religion had led him, for the time being, to embrace."[68] A counterpoint to the "dear vulgar, mongrel words" of Levy's earlier essay, Bertie's meticulous speech habits translate into a different manner of linguistic vulgarity to Judith Quixano, the object of his pursuit, in which "his intelligent fluency, his unfailing, monotonous politeness were a weariness to her."[69]

Levy posits Jewish vulgarity as ambiguously and ambivalently embodied from torso to tongue, but both in *Reuben Sachs* and in her essays, Levy more frequently associates vulgarity, whether Jewish or gentile, whether in body or words, with masculinity.[70] Of the two key female characters in Levy's novel, Judith Quixano is cleansed of any of the stereotyped vulgarities aligned to the bodies, speech, or manners of her Jewish "tribe," while Esther Kohnthal speaks the boldest lines of the novel. Esther's voice is wry, satiric, and penetrating, in contrast to Judith's naïve innocence. With her ironic manner, like the serio-comic style Levy demonstrates in "Jewish Humour," Esther is the crux of the novel's feminist double consciousness.[71] Unlike Judith, who is captured within the central marriage plot of the novel, Esther reads the world around her from the margins, a position that allows her the novel's irritating and irate voice of truth. Freed from the need or ability to marry because of her vulgar excesses as "the biggest heiress and the ugliest woman in all Bayswater,"[72] Esther, who has nothing to gain, can afford to be one "of those who walk naked and are not ashamed."[73] When another gentile man comments on "the beauty of Jewish ladies," Esther attributes physical uncouthness specifically to Jewish men: "Yes, we have some pretty women . . . but our men! No, the Jew, unlike the horse, is not a noble animal."[74] In this chapter showcasing the Leunigers' dance, Judith's singular appearance is what catapults Bertie into a quandary about what he has called a "fundamental type," as he observes to himself:

> What a beautiful woman was this cousin . . . of Sachs's! How infinitely better bred she seemed than the people surrounding her!
>
> The Quixanos, as Reuben had told him, were *sephardim*, for whose claim to birth he had the greatest respect. But as for that red-headed young man, her brother—there were no marks of breeding about him!
>
> Bertie was puzzled, as the stranger is so often puzzled, by the violent contrasts which exist among Jews, even in the case of members of the same family.[75]

In Bertie's eyes, Judith glitters through the Sephardic mystique, the notion that Sephardim were the thoroughbred class descended from a tradition of male Jewish scholars of the Iberian Peninsula, such as Judith's father, in contrast to the Ashkenazim of eastern Europe. While the passage seems to replicate the opposition between ideal and vulgar Jews, it also insists on a masculine vulgarity that cuts across the supposed divide of the Sephardic mystique so that Judith's brother in Bertie's eyes presents "no marks of breeding about him." Levy shows how general categories, as with this form of racialized stereotyping, fall apart. In other words, Bertie's attempt to assemble codes of a "fundamental type" of "Jewish character" is a vulgar way of reading.

Ruskin's critique of vulgarity pertains to Bertie's character as well, as Ruskin qualifies certain forms of "excessive neatness" and "precision and exquisiteness of arrangement" as vulgar in someone of "an equality (insensibility) of temperament" and "incapable of fine passion."[76] For Ruskin's final assessment of vulgarity describes an abject "dullness of heart, not in rage or cruelty, but in an inability to feel or conceive noble character or emotion."[77] In fact, Ruskin ultimately defines gentlemanliness as "an intense humanity," a quality of profound, sustained sensitivity. Not only does Bertie seem devoid of such delicacy of feeling, despite his dainty physical appearance and breeding, but the novel's epilogue even hints about a disturbing coldness in Bertie's imposing treatment of Judith, particularly the manner in which he informs her of Reuben's death. Through Bertie's lack of human compassion, Levy suggests a more sinister opposition to an excessive sensitivity aligned with Jewishness.

By using vulgarity in *Reuben Sachs* to question both Jewish and gentile masculine privilege, Levy renders it as a liability against women's freedom beyond the imprisoning sphere of domesticity.[78] This reading of Jewish vulgarity is particularly evident in Levy's *Jewish Chronicle* essay "Middle-Class Jewish Women of To-Day": "Conservative in politics; conservative in religion; the Jew is no less conservative as regards his social life; and while in most cases outwardly conforming to the usages of Western civilisation, he is, in fact, more Oriental at heart than a casual observer might infer. For a long time, it may be said, the shadow of the harem has rested on our womankind."[79] An entrenched resistance to modern gender relations on the part of Anglo-Jewish men again resonates with Ruskinian vulgarity, as a failure to adapt to change as conditions permit. Levy is far more forgiving of Jewish women than of Jewish men on this score, maintaining, "The assertion even of comparative freedom on the part of a Jewess often means the severance of the closest ties."[80]

One of Levy's earliest publications was a series of letters to the *Jewish Chronicle* in response to a correspondent who, in an article titled "Jewish Women and 'Women's Rights,'" exhorted women readers to embrace traditional roles of marriage and motherhood rather than fall under the sway of feminist critiques. In these letters, written when she was a seventeen-year-old student at Brighton High School for Girls,[81] Levy takes issue with the emotional, intellectual, and social suffocation inherent in a life that precluded any aspirations beyond the domestic sphere: "But I doubt if even the great thought of becoming in time a favourable specimen of the genus 'maiden-aunt' would be sufficient to console many a restless, ambitious woman for the dreary performance of work for which she is quite unsuited, for the quenching of personal hopes for the development of her own intellect."[82]

The intransigent responses to these bold letters in the *Jewish Chronicle* anticipate the cool readings of Levy's radically edged vulgarity in *Reuben Sachs.* That the Anglo-Jewish press did not read Levy's Jewish vulgarity as nuanced and pointed is clear from the novel's initial reception. Yet perhaps some non-Jewish readers, who had no personal stake in public presentations of contemporary Jewishness in fiction, did. Wilde, who knew Levy from the London literary salon circuit and as a contributor to *The Woman's World,* which he edited, described *Reuben Sachs* in his notice in the magazine following Levy's death: "Its directness, its uncompromising truths, its depth of feeling, and, above all, its absence of any single superfluous word, make it, in some sort, a classic."[83] These attributes of truthfulness, fineness of emotion, and efficient, spare language rather than verbosity approach Ruskin's profile of vulgarity's antithesis, gentlemanliness. Wilde's equivocation of "some sort" seems extra verbiage that implies a paradox of a qualified—even vulgar—"classic." This ambiguously mixed classification recalls the description of her character's writing in "Cohen of Trinity" as vulgarity with a difference, "wholly unclassifiable, with a force, a fire, a vision, a vigour and felicity of phrase that carried you through its most glaring inequalities, its most appalling lapses of taste."[84] Levy's depictions of Jewish vulgarity, taken together, reorient readers to consider the range, intricacy, and perceptions underpinning such "appalling lapses of taste."

Levy's excessive display of a variety of Jewish stereotyping might seem at odds with her stylistic retreat from overstuffed, lavish language. While Levy's spare style and fragmented viewpoints, including the multivoiced narration, do forecast features of modernism, her writing in *Reuben Sachs* executes her attempt to negotiate what she calls the "complex problem" of imagining Jewishness in

English literature, the very challenge she issued a few years earlier in "The Jew in Fiction."[85] Exploring the divisive triple consciousness of Jewish, English, and gendered identity, the novel rehearses competing ways of representing Jewish women and men in late-Victorian England. Her "truthfulness" and lack of "verbosity" foster her feminist critique that revolves around Judith, whose name means "Jewess" in Hebrew, a character who is nevertheless displaced from the title page on.[86] As formal devices for conveying this cultural tribridity,[87] Levy's innovations include overlapping gazes from "within and without the tribal limits," the fracturing of narrative voice, and the rare, salient use of symbolism, notably, the white chrysanthemums that Reuben plucks from Judith's bodice as they sit in a "crimson recess" at the Leunigers' dance. Promising the "inward turn" of modernism, Levy's stylistic experiments in *Reuben Sachs* also reveal the inadequacy of realism for New Woman writers of the late nineteenth century. As a blurred genre, *Reuben Sachs* falls in between a short story and a novel, and Levy's subtitle, "A Sketch," resonates with her literary impressionism. Levy's impure style replicates formally the predicaments of Jewish vulgarity that her writing otherwise investigates.

Notes

1. Rabbi David Phillipson, *The Jew in English Fiction* (Cincinnati, OH: R. Clarke, 1889), 14.

2. "The Deterioration of the Jewess," *Jewish World*, 22 February 1889, 5. Reprinted in *Reuben Sachs*, ed. Susan David Bernstein (Peterborough, ON: Broadview Press, 2006), 164–66. Subsequent citations are from this reprinted edition.

3. From 1858, when Nathan de Rothschild took his seat in Parliament, through the next several decades, several men became the first Jews to hold different public offices in Britain.

4. Amy Levy, "The Jew in Fiction," *Jewish Chronicle*, 4 June 1886, 13. Reprinted in *Reuben Sachs*, ed. Bernstein, 175–78.

5. Jonathan Freedman, *The Temple of Culture: Assimilation and Anti-Semitism in Literary Anglo-America* (New York: Oxford University Press, 2000), 23.

6. Bryan Cheyette, "From Apology to Revolt: Benjamin Farjeon, Amy Levy and the Post-Emancipation Anglo-Jewish Novel, 1880–1900," *Transactions of the Jewish Historical Society of England* 29 (1982–86): 264.

7. For a more comprehensive analysis of Victorian vulgarity, see Elsie B. Michie and Susan David Bernstein, "Introduction: Varieties of Vulgarity," in *Victorian Vulgarity: Taste in Verbal and Visual Culture*, ed. Bernstein and Michie (Burlington, VT: Ashgate, 2009), 1–13.

8. Pierre Bourdieu, *Distinction: A Social Critique of the Judgment of Taste*, trans. Richard Nice (Cambridge, MA: Harvard University Press, 1984), 485–91.

9. Ibid., 488.

10. John Ruskin, *The Complete Works of John Ruskin*, vol. 5, ed. E. T. Cook and Alexander Wedderburn (London: George Allen, 1905), 344–45.

11. Ibid., 355.

12. Ibid., 345.

13. Ibid., 349.

14. Ibid., 350.

15. Ibid., 346.

16. Elected to Parliament for the City of London four times from 1847 to 1858, Rothschild was finally able to sit in Parliament after he was permitted to omit the words "on the true faith of a Christian" from the Oath of Abjuration.

17. Todd Endelman, *Radical Assimilation in English Jewish History, 1656–1945* (Bloomington: Indiana University Press, 1990), 75.

18. Cheyette, "From Apology to Revolt," 264.

19. Robert Knox, *The Races of Men: A Philosophical Enquiry into the Influence of Race over the Destinies of Nations* (London: H. Renshaw, 1862). Excerpt reprinted in *Reuben Sachs*, ed. Bernstein, 215–18. Quoted on 215.

20. Ibid., 216.

21. Deborah Cohen, "Who Was Who? Race and Jews in Turn-of-the-Century Britain," *Journal of British Studies* 41 (October 2002): 460–83.

22. Ibid., 461.

23. Ruskin, *Complete Works*, 354.

24. Homi Bhabha, *The Location of Culture* (London: Routledge, 1994), 66.

25. Ibid.

26. Amy Levy, "Cohen of Trinity," *Gentleman's Magazine* 266 (May 1889): 417–24. Reprinted in *Reuben Sachs*, ed. Bernstein, 181–88. Quoted on 182.

27. Ibid., 183.

28. Ibid., 188.

29. Ibid., 186.

30. Amy Levy, "Jewish Humour," *Jewish Chronicle*, 20 August 1886, 9.

31. Cynthia Scheinberg, *Women's Poetry and Religion in Victorian Britain: Jewish Identity and Christian Culture* (Cambridge: Cambridge University Press, 2002), 209. Scheinberg reads Levy's discussion of Heine as a rebuttal to Matthew Arnold's Christian perspective on the German Jewish poet.

32. For a discussion of W.E.B. DuBois's theory of "double consciousness" in relation to Levy's writing, see my introduction to *Reuben Sachs*, 11–43.

33. Amy Levy, *Reuben Sachs*, ed. Bernstein, 90.

34. Levy, "Jewish Humour," 10.

35. See Scheinberg's analysis of Arnold and Levy in *Women's Poetry*, 205–12.

36. Sander Gilman, *Jewish Self-Hatred* (Baltimore, MD: Johns Hopkins University Press, 1986), 20. For a discussion about mythical secret language, see Gilman, *The Jew's Body* (New York: Routledge, 1991), 12–13.

37. Gilman, *Jew's Body*, 17.

38. In addition to "The Jew in Fiction" and "Jewish Humour," Levy published three other essays about Jewishness in contemporary culture in 1886 issues of the *Jewish Chronicle:* "The Ghetto at Florence," "Jewish Children," and "Middle-Class Jewish Women of To-Day."

39. "Deterioration of the Jewess," 164.

40. Ibid., 165.

41. Israel Zangwill, "A Ghetto Night at the Maccabaeans: Dinner to Mr. Samuel Gordon," *Jewish Chronicle,* 25 January 1901, 19.

42. For a fuller treatment of Levy's in-between social position, see my introduction to *Reuben Sachs,* 11–43

43. Cheyette, "From Apology to Revolt," 253–54.

44. Levy, *Reuben Sachs,* 61.

45. Ibid., 66.

46. Ruskin, *Complete Works,* 353.

47. Levy, *Reuben Sachs,* 118.

48. Linda Hunt Beckman, "Leaving 'The Tribal Duckpond': Amy Levy, Jewish Self-Hatred and Jewish Identity," *Victorian Literature and Culture* 27, no. 1 (1999): 185–201. Beckman includes these sketches from Levy's papers, now in a private collection.

49. Levy, *Reuben Sachs,* 57.

50. Ibid., 95.

51. Ibid.

52. Ibid., 94.

53. Ruskin, *Complete Works,* 355.

54. Levy, *Reuben Sachs,* 95.

55. Ibid., 94–95.

56. Oscar Wilde, "Amy Levy," *Woman's World* 3 (November 1889): 51–52. Reprinted in *Reuben Sachs,* ed. Bernstein, 167–70.

57. I introduce the term *reverso-converso* to accentuate Levy's implied parody of the enforced conversion of Jews across time and place by her construction of an English gentleman who converts to, rather than from, Judaism. *Converso* is a term referring to Sephardic Jews of the Iberian Peninsula who were forced to convert or risked death or banishment following the outlawing of Judaism in Spain and Portugal in the fifteenth century. Related terms include *crypto-Jews* and *New Christians.*

58. Levy, *Reuben Sachs,* 59. Levy also endows Cohen with this somatic vulgarity: "A curious figure: slight, ungainly; shoulders in the ears; an awkward rapid gait, half slouch, half hobble. One arm with its coarse hand swung like a bell-rope as he went; the other pressed a book close against his side, while the hand belonging to it held a few bulrushes and marsh marigolds" ("Cohen of Trinity," 182).

59. Ruskin, *Complete Works,* 355.

60. Gilman, *Jew's Body,* 55.

61. Levy, *Reuben Sachs,* 63–64.

62. Ibid., 76.

63. Ibid., 64.

64. Ibid., 87.

65. See Michael Ragussis, *Figures of Conversion: "The Jewish Question" and English National Identity* (Durham, NC: Duke University Press, 1995), especially chapter 1, "The Culture of Conversion."

66. Levy, *Reuben Sachs*, 98.

67. Ibid., 97.

68. Ibid., 98.

69. Ibid., 136.

70. Discussed earlier, Levy's unpublished drawings offer a different perspective on this assessment about gender and vulgarity.

71. For an insightful discussion of Esther as "the novel's feminist," see Meri-Jane Rochelson, "Jews, Gender, and Genre in Late-Victorian England: Amy Levy's *Reuben Sachs*," *Women's Studies* 25 (1996): 322.

72. Levy, *Reuben Sachs*, 62.

73. Ibid., 116.

74. Ibid.

75. Ibid., 114.

76. Ruskin, *Complete Works*, 356.

77. Ibid., 359.

78. Levy's use of vulgar masculinity as part of a feminist analysis also figures in "Xantippe," the dramatic monologue of Socrates' wife, to whom the philosopher first appears "all ungainly and uncouth" (line 56).

79. Amy Levy, "Middle-Class Jewish Women of To-Day," *Jewish Chronicle*, 17 September 1886, 7. Reprinted in *Reuben Sachs*, ed. Bernstein, 178.

80. Ibid., 180.

81. Brighton High School for Girls, part of the Girls' Public Day School Company, was founded in 1871 by feminists Emily and Maria Shirreff. That Levy's parents chose to send Levy there for a few years beginning in 1876, when she was fifteen, indicates their progressive beliefs about girls' education. The school implemented a rigorous academic curriculum equivalent to the training that boys received in preparation for university enrollment. Edith Creak, the head of Brighton High School when Levy attended, was in 1871 a member of the first class of five students at Newnham College, one of two colleges at Cambridge University expressly designed to accommodate women. One may reasonably assume that the feminist beliefs Levy articulates in these *Jewish Chronicle* letters were shaped in part by her Brighton education. See Linda Hunt Beckman, *Amy Levy: Her Life and Letters* (Athens: Ohio University Press, 2000), 29.

82. Amy Levy, "Jewish Women and 'Women's Rights,'" *Jewish Chronicle*, 7 February 1879, 5. Levy's second letter, a precursor to "Middle-Class Jewish Women of To-Day" written seven years later, was printed on 28 February 1879. In his letter of 21 February 1879, the original correspondent had speculated on the identity of "Amy Levy" (she was the only one to sign her name): "[S]he is, I presume, an elderly lady who has seen much of the world, and whose grave experience gives weight to her expressions of opinion on this most important subject." Excerpts from these letters, including the quoted passages, are reprinted in *Reuben Sachs*, ed. Bernstein, 171–75.

83. Wilde, "Amy Levy," reprinted in *Reuben Sachs*, ed. Bernstein, 170.

84. Levy, "Cohen of Trinity," 186.

85. Levy, "Jew in Fiction," 177.

86. This entitled displacement mirrors the marginalization of George Eliot's heroine Gwendolen Harleth in *Daniel Deronda*. It is worth noting that Levy explicitly compares Judith Quixano with Gwendolen toward the end of the novel: "Bertie, as Gwendolen Harleth said of Grandcourt, was not disgusting. He took his love, as he took his religion, very theoretically" (*Reuben Sachs*, 146).

87. My gratitude to Dena Mandel, who introduced me to her term *tribridity*, which she uses in relation to the identity constellation of Jewish, Russian, and American in contemporary immigrant literature. I borrow her concept to underscore the third term of gender in Levy's depiction of Anglo-Jewishness.

Passing in the City

the liminal spaces of amy levy's late work

Alex Goody

And you, you passed and smiled that day,
Between the showers.

Amy Levy, "Between the Showers"

She wished to find out about this hazardous business
of "passing," this breaking away from all that was familiar and
friendly to take one's chances in another environment, not
entirely strange, perhaps, but certainly not entirely friendly.

Nella Larsen, Passing

Such a notion of "passing" is not becoming "invisible" but
becoming differently visible—being seen as a member of a
group with which one wants or needs to identify.

Sander L. Gilman, Making the Body Beautiful

THE idea of "passing" still carries a particular resonance for those individuals traversing the difficult ground between polarities of self-identification. In Nella Larsen's 1929 novel of that name, *passing* delineates an ambivalent state, an endless journey between the oppositions of race, of sexuality, and of culture. This experience and the liminal subjectivities it produces are particularly the effect of the transient environment of the modern city. This chapter suggests that the idea of "passing" (and the multiple resonances of the word) can also be used to explore the profoundly ambivalent emotions and subjectivities of Amy Levy's late poetry—poetry that Cynthia Scheinberg describes as exploring, "among other things, a particular affinity for the urban life of Jewish London, an unorthodox spirituality that refuses clear identification with either Christian or Jewish traditions, and her most direct intimations of lesbian sexuality."[1] Reading these poems cross-culturally, even anachronistically, alongside the dynamics of "passing" serves to expose both the potentials and the limits of what could be termed the "nomadic" consciousness of Levy's writing: "the desire for an identity made of transitions, successive shifts, and coordinated changes, without and against an essential unity."[2] The following discussion examines how the ambiguous sexuality and racial awareness of *A London Plane-Tree and Other Verse* (1889), when traced across an urban context, highlight the modernity of Levy's late poetry, an aspect that has been identified by recent critics including Linda Hunt Beckman and Ana Parejo Vadillo.[3] Alongside this orientation toward the modernist experimentation of the next century, the ambiguous urbanism of Levy's poems produces but also endangers radically interstitial, mobile subject positions.

Larsen's *Passing* focuses on two central protagonists: both light-skinned, mixed-race American women. Irene Redfield has stayed true to her "race" by marrying a man darker than her and committing herself to the bourgeois life of cultural uplift in 1920s Harlem. An old school acquaintance, Clare Hendry, has chosen to pass as white, deceiving and marrying a white man who turns out to be an extreme racist (who calls her "nig" as a joke, unconscious of its resonances). The narrative follows Clare's attempts to get in touch with her racial origins by acts of cultural tourism in Harlem, while Irene feels unable to stop Clare's entering her life. Clearly, the transgressive spaces of the city/Harlem are fundamental to the identities that Clare and Irene perform. These two opposite poles of the "passing" divide become increasingly entangled until Clare falls from a window after Irene surmises that Clare is having an affair with Irene's husband.[4]

One way of reading Larsen's novel is as a reworking of the tragic mulatto narrative, with the beautiful Clare unable to exist in a world that would categorize her. Cheryl Wall argues that "for Larsen, the tragic mulatto was the most accessible convention for the portrayal of middle class black women in fiction."[5] The mulatto can thus come to function "as a narrative device of mediation."[6] However, many African American women writers, such as Alice Walker and Ntozake Shange, have recognized the eroticism and complex sexuality of the book.[7] Not only are Irene and Clare both passing in different ways—crossing social, cultural, and economic boundaries—but also there is a dynamic of desire between the two women. They can be read as a split subjectivity recognizing a self in the other but unable to be whole, or be together. This dynamic, traversed by the forces of race, class, and gender, is the murderous force that finally kills one and nearly destroys the other.

Larsen's novel shares with a contemporary modernist text, Virginia Woolf's *Orlando* (1928), an articulation of ambivalent identity that signifies a sexuality outside the confines of rigid heterosexuality. This, in turn, suggests a shared modernist concern with fluctuating or nonfixed subjectivities, a concern that was amplified by the performative possibilities that the modern urban space created. However, the racial dimension of the unfixed identity and sexuality of *Passing* suggests alternative comparisons, which elaborate the anxieties about racial ambivalence that the mobile peoples and races of modernity precipitated.

In a 1997 *Jewish Quarterly* article, Amanda Sebestyen highlights the affinity between the "double-consciousness" that "Black artists in the West have suffered" and the "sharp dividedness . . . associated with the heritage of the European Jew," going on to consider "Black and Jewish Border Crossers" whose "strategies were various and enabled them sometimes to cross over socially to the dominant group, [though] their loyalties could not easily be erased and the process was never without pain."[8] Drawing connections between James Weldon Johnson's *The Autobiography of an Ex-Colored Man* (1912) and the autobiographically "passing" (non-Jewish, nonhomosexual) "I" of Marcel Proust, Sebestyen also points out that "[a]t the turn of the century the 'mulatto' was viewed as refined, over-civilized, artistic, hysterical; all qualities associated with modernity in general and also with an assimilated Jewish avant-garde."[9] She goes on to articulate the similarities between Irene's tensions in *Passing* and the anxieties of the emancipated European Jews when faced with their "primitive" ghetto counterparts.

In a different vein, Sander Gilman's documentation of the discourses around, and origins of, modern aesthetic (cosmetic) surgery reveals its reliance on "the discourse of 'passing,' which comes out of the racialization of nineteenth-century culture."[10] Just as mixed-race African Americans could attempt to "[blend] into the dominant group whose silently taking no notice of one was the key sign of one's acceptance," so too did Jews at the turn of the twentieth century seek rhinoplastic procedures to enable their "vanishing into the visual norm and 'passing' as non-Jewish in appearance."[11] Considering such corollaries does not amount to asserting an essential ambivalence about racial affiliation in turn-of-the-century acculturated Anglo-Jews or mixed-race

Americans; instead, what may be shared in this nexus of associations is a sense of uncertainty that is conjured up by the idea of "passing." In turn, the uncertain space or zone of passing is one of complex identifications and desires: it is both enabling and dangerous—a zone, moreover, where racial ambivalence may also stand as or for an ambiguous set of sexual identifications.

Amy Levy's complex relationship to her sexuality and racial affiliation has formed the impetus of much criticism on her work. This is linked to, and in some cases complicates, the connections that can be drawn between Levy and the figure of the New Woman who preoccupied the fiction and journalism of the 1890s. Levy is often regarded as a "New Woman" poet, with works such as "A Ballad of Religion and Marriage" (undated)[12] and "Xantippe" (1881) articulating a position that is recognizably feminist (from a twenty-first-century as well as late-nineteenth-century perspective). In her novel *The Romance of a Shop* (1888), the protagonists Gertrude Lorimer and her sister Lucy, who find a living as professional photographers, display recognizable New Woman traits. Levy's politics, in association with her network of colleagues (Olive Schreiner, Eleanor Marx, Vernon Lee) and her status as a Cambridge-educated professional writer, serve to connect her with the cultural and behavioral changes that produced the independent women who populated the late-nineteenth-century imaginary: thus, she is endowed with New Woman status in Linda Hughes's 2001 anthology of *New Women Poets*.[13] Admittedly, the concept of the New Woman proper was not identified as such (and even then was much debated) until after the coining of the term in 1893, four years after Levy's death in 1889.[14] However, I use the term in this chapter as does Linda Hunt Beckman in her biography of Levy when "discussing Levy and attitudes towards women's nature and role in the late 1870s and 1880s," basing her usage on the fact that "the ideological and behavioural changes that led to its coinage [the "New Woman"] are already apparent in those periods."[15]

Identifying Levy with the nascent liberated femininity that came to be termed "the New Woman" serves to highlight the importance of the urban in her work: the "Muse" that the epigraph to *A London Plane-Tree and Other Verse* invokes (*LPT*, 7). As Deborah Parsons reiterates, the New Woman "was a specifically urban character, the result of the circumstances and qualities of a growing metropolitan society."[16] What Parsons also makes explicit about Levy is the potential link between "the Jew" as a crucial figure in late-nineteenth-century representations of the city and the increased visibility and presence of "respectable" women (in other words, those who were not prostitutes) in the street. This link is further considered by both Beckman, who argues that Levy's "urban identity . . . stemmed from her conviction that there was a strong historical connection between Jews and city life," and Vadillo, who claims that "the motive of the wanderer allowed Levy to . . . look for a new set of conventions with which to rearticulate the relations between women, Jewishness and the city."[17] As an independent late-nineteenth-century woman and a Jew, Levy has a double affinity with the urban space as the "paven ground" for her subjectivity (*LPT*, 7), an enunciative space that counteracts what some may identify as Levy's triple marginality (as woman, Jewish, and lesbian).

Levy was a member of an assimilated Anglo-Jewish family at a time when Jewishness was becoming an important question in the politics and cultural debates of Victorian England. The emergent "racial science" of ethnology foregrounded the categorization of "Jewishness" rather than the role of Jews in English culture. Robert Knox's popular *The Races of Men* (1850, reprinted in 1862), for example, describes the Jew as having a racial essence comparing him, as an inferior racial type, to the "African." With the increased migration of eastern European Jews to Britain from the 1870s onwards, the growing visibility of these peoples served to reinforce ideas of Jewishness as racial otherness. The Jewish "other" was most in evidence in the poor, crowded urban centers that had long been the arrival point for immigrants, most prominently the East End of London. Todd Endelman describes this racialized stereotype: "When outsiders visited the East End . . . they tended to see its filth, congestion, and bewilderingly foreign character, and often little else. The inhabitants of immigrant districts seemed to be dark, alien, ill-mannered creatures. Their speech, gestures, dress, comportment, shop signs, and wall posters (in Yiddish) revealed their foreign origins. Even the smells encountered there were un-English."[18] The East End European Jew, a racialized other and a stereotype of urban Jewishness, became closely associated with other fears about "outcast London" and (serious and sensationalized) accounts of the moral and physical degeneration of the East End. However, in a *Jewish Chronicle* article published in November 1886, Levy considers and celebrates the urban nature of "the Jew," the "descendant of many city-bred ancestors," while simultaneously reiterating the stereotype of the nervous and highly strung Jew.[19] Levy's prose writing demonstrates a tension between her identifications as urban woman and urban Anglo-Jew. Most obviously in "Middle-Class Jewish Women of To-Day," published two months earlier in the *Jewish Chronicle* in September 1886, Levy articulates a critique of the repressive patriarchal regimes of Anglo-Jewish culture:

Conservative in politics; conservative in religion; the Jew is no less conservative as regards his social life; and while in most cases outwardly conforming to the usages of Western civilisation, he is, in fact, more Oriental
at heart than a casual observer might infer. . . .

In a society constructed on such a primitive basis, the position of
single women, so rapidly improving in the general world, is a particularly
unfortunate one. Jewish men have grown to look upon the women of their
tribe as solely designed for marrying or giving in marriage. . . . If a Jewess
has social interests beyond the crude and transitory ones of flirtation, she
must seek them, perforce, beyond the tribal limits.[20]

In articulating a feminist critique of Anglo-Jewish society here, Levy uses
stereotypes of the primitive, "oriental" Jew. She also draws on a stereotypical
association of "the Jew" with the city in her piece "Jewish Humour," but this
time to identify with it: "[I]ts distinctly urban quality is one of the chief features of Jewish humour. The close and humorous observation of manners (we
use the word in its widest sense); the irresistible, swift transition to the absurd,
in the midst of everything that is most solemn; the absolute refusal to take life
quite seriously, do we not recognize these qualities as common, more or less,
to all bred and born in great cities?"[21]

It is in this article that Levy most explicitly defines a Jewish racial heritage
—"the family feeling of the Jewish race." Here she also writes, "[I]f we leave
off saying *Shibboleth*, let us, at least, employ its equivalent in the purest University English."[22] Though she is from an assimilated family with few active Jewish
connections, the implication here is that Levy identifies, and identifies with, a
Jewishness—"we," "us"—that is located inside an apparently assimilated Englishness, a Jewishness that can be articulated from *within* the dominant culture.
This is not an oppositional politics but a subversive intervention, a tactic that
Scheinberg views as crucial to Levy's negotiation of her Jewish heritage in the
modern world.[23] Scheinberg posits that Levy's "urban lyrics that offer an alternative to the assumptions of pastoral inspiration" function like her interpretation of scripture in poems such as "Magdalen"—as a "challenge to the
conventions of Christian poetry."[24] The difficulties posed by the ambiguity of
Levy's textual position are clearly illustrated by the responses to her novel *Reuben
Sachs* (1888), both at the time of publication and subsequently, which have accused Levy of perpetuating stereotypes and manifesting "Jewish self-hatred."[25]
However, *Reuben Sachs* and the short stories "Leopold Leuniger: A Study" (1880)
and "Cohen of Trinity" (1889) may well, as Beckman argues, reveal a self-

conscious understanding of the phenomenon of Jewish antisemitism and offer the possibility of moving beyond it (of unfixing "tribal limits").[26]

In some of her last work—the poems "Lohengrin" and "Captivity," which appear in the "Moods and Thoughts" section of *A London Plane-Tree and Other Verse*—Levy returns to her racial heritage in a complex set of identifications and longings. These poems, as Scheinberg analyzes, mourn the loss of Jewish roots ("Lohengrin") while acknowledging the impossibility of either a return to Jewishness or a complete rejection of assimilation ("Captivity"). Interestingly, Scheinberg argues that "Captivity" "seems to offer Levy's most Jewish version of being caught between two worlds, a version whose title and references to a lost land position her more directly in line with a tradition of Jewish Diasporic poetry." This poetry mourns the loss of the land of Israel—a "place that is always symbolic of a spiritual state in Jewish literature, rather than mere geographic location."[27] I would highlight how this in-betweenness, which Scheinberg sees as a crucial factor throughout Levy's work in relation to her cultural and sexual as well as religious or racial identity, is a key factor in the nomadic trajectory that she attempts to trace in her writing. Levy does not come to a final resting place either safely within or beyond a racial heritage; her in-betweenness must necessarily persist, for as Gilles Deleuze and Felix Guattari describe it, "[t]he life of the nomad is the intermezzo."[28]

The nascent New Woman and the Jew do offer contradictory identities for Levy as a writer, particularly around the issue of a "feminist" politics, but what they clearly share is their urbanism and their resistance to simple assimilation into the cultural hegemony of fin-de-siècle England. The resulting stereotypes that emerge of both "figures" in the popular culture of the 1880s and 1890s reveal a preexisting anxious need to define their difference from, and thereby their place in, English culture. Levy uses this anxiety to open up a space for articulating an alternative identity that is located in/on the liberating ambiguity of the "changeful" city. Thus, Levy's late work both enables and undermines the Jew and the liberated woman as she inscribes (herself) across the city space. The Jew and the new, urban woman provide some of the multiple launching points for Levy's poems that attempt a radical movement across intelligible subject positions. These works actively seek the in-between, between poles of fixity—which does not mean that they simply pass from one to (an)other: "*Between* things does not designate a localizable relation going from one thing to the other and back again, but a perpendicular direction, a transversal movement that sweeps one *and* the other away, a stream without beginning or end that undermines its banks and picks up speed in the middle."[29] In some senses, the city functions for Levy as just such a nonlocalizable movement-space that sweeps away the self and the other.

In the first section of *A London Plane-Tree and Other Verse*, Levy clearly is celebrating the city and the ability to move through and be immersed in it (a peripatetic rather than a panoramic perspective). The "call" of the city is expressed in "A Village Garden":

> Fain would I bide, but ever in the distance
> A ceaseless voice is sounding clear and low;—
> The city calls me with her old persistence,
> The city calls me—I arise and go.
> Of gentler souls this fragrant peace is guerdon;
> For me, the roar and hurry of the town,
> Wherein more lightly seems to press the burden
> Of individual life that weighs me down.
>
> (*LPT*, 31)

As Beckman states, "the city became central to [Levy's] poetic development" with a poem such as "The Village Garden" expressing a "subordination of self to the power of the metropolis."[30] This poem also clearly evinces what Vadillo terms Levy's "urban aestheticism," in which she "equated London with modernity and urban mobility with revolution."[31] The insistent call of the city in "The Village Garden," expressed through the sibilance of the first stanza, offers an escape from the "burden" of individuality, a manifestation of the opportunities for anonymity that the city of modernity offered. But it additionally suggests that "individual" identity (as a fixed and stable concept) is an encumbrance that disperses in the speed and intensity of the urban space. Moreover, the archaism "guerdon" depicts an old-fashioned, pastoral poetic that is superseded by the multiplicity and "roar and hurry" of the modern. In a similar vein, Levy's "A London Plane-Tree," the opening poem in the collection, rewrites pastoral motifs, associating the speaking-subject, the writer in her garret, with the feminized "plane-tree in the square" (*LPT*, 17). This piece of nature is immersed in and interpenetrated by the "voice" and atmosphere of the city:

> Among her branches, in and out,
> The city breezes play;
> The dun fog wraps her round about;
> Above the smoke curls grey.
>
> (*LPT*, 17)

The uncertain referent of the pronouns here—the "her" in this stanza could easily refer to any of the subjects of the poem—further interconnects speaker, tree, and city, breaking down the singularity of each and opening all the subjects up to each other.

Another poem, "London Poets: In Memoriam," explicitly refers to an urban poetic, calling on the poets who "trod the streets and squares where now I tread" (*LPT*, 29). It likewise evokes the city atmosphere—"smoke," "winds," "breezes"—the breath of the city, which becomes the poets' exhaled voices and, ultimately, the passing breath of the speaker. The speaker recognizes the temporary nature of the urban self, that her existence will indeed become imperceptible. She is empowered to speak by the fact that her sorrows will become part of the palimpsest of the city, a fleeting moment that will leave only a trace with the passing of time.

Levy's interest in James Thomson suggests that his "London" haunts "London Poets,"[32] but perhaps more crucially, as Beckman argues, the symbolist city of Baudelaire stands as a key precursor for the urban poetic that Levy is articulating.[33] The transitory nature of the urban experience (and the urban "self") foregrounded in "London Poets" echo some of the key experiences of Baudelaire's Paris poems—the ephemerality and transience of the cityscape—and other poems from *A London Plane-Tree and Other Verse* describe the chance encounter that is also crucial to the modern city constructed by Baudelaire. Thus, poems from *A London Plane-Tree and Other Verse* in which the beloved is glimpsed, encountered, and subsumed by the city—"Between the Showers," "London in July," and "In the Mile End Road," for example—can be read, as Beckman suggests, as Levy's own form of the symbolist aesthetic, employing "both the city and the figure of a missing woman for whom she searches as symbols of the effect life is having on her."[34] Both the complex relation between the psyche and external space, and the importance of the urban in the French symbolist tradition resonate with Levy's work as Beckman considers. But I would emphasize how, in drawing on this tradition, Levy is rewriting Baudelaire's "À une passante" to perform deliberately masculine *flânerie*: as Deborah Nord claims, Levy expresses the experience of the city, so crucial to her late work, through male personae.[35] However, Levy's poetic persona does not own the objectifying gaze of the male *flâneur*, and thus her performance is also a deconstruction; s/he does not possess the woman or the street she wanders. As Parsons highlights, Levy complicates the "power relationship of observing male, observed female in the city" so that "[r]ather than being at home in the city, an omniscient male observer who can map his landscape, the man [*sic*] [in

"London in July"] wanders lost in its streets."[36] Levy is interested, in poems such as "Ballade of an Omnibus," in celebrating the joys of the city while undermining the traditional gendering of the urban observer and challenging the authority of the *flâneur*. Her urban poems do not offer an identification with masculinity but, I argue, instead utilize this perspective as a way of "passing" in the street. She is, as Vadillo describes, seeking the "construction of a mobile lyric self" and placing herself in a "tradition of urban writers immersed in the production of a nomadic space."[37] Her poems construct view points (and points at which s/he is viewed) that enable her to use the transient city without being fixed and/or recognized as a transgressive woman, becoming "differently visible"[38] to examine and describe desires and identities that exceed the limits of race and gender.

In "Between the Showers," the "changeful" city scene is an ever-changing place/space that allows for the transitory, transgressive encounter:

> Hither and thither, swift and gay,
>   The people chased the changeful hours
> And you, you passed and smiled that day,
>   Between the showers.

(LPT, 26)

The urban space thus functions as a signifier of transgression, both the transgressive acts of the speaker (co-opting the privilege of the male poetic voice, replacing the pastoral poetic idyll with an accelerated urban scene) and the breaking down of boundaries and certainties. The parallelism in these lines ("Hither and thither," "swift and gay") and elsewhere structurally represents how the poem articulates, or attempts to delineate, a state "between" points of fixity; the text is passing between different states as it discovers both the city and the beloved who "passed" by. Just as, in passing from urban woman to urban Jew to *flâneur*, Levy's poetic voice is enabled though its own liminality, so too does *"la passante"* herself come into being in-between ("between the showers"), in a space that is also the enunciative space of the poem.

In emphasizing the movement between that characterizes this "passing," my reading of Levy's urban poetry shares much common ground with the central thesis of Vadillo's account of the urban poetry of four late-Victorian women poets: Amy Levy, Alice Meynell, Graham R. Thomson (Rosamund Marriott Watson), and Michael Field. For Vadillo, mobility and transience are central to these poets' work; moreover, in different ways, forms of urban mass transport (omnibuses, trams, suburban railways, and underground railways) act as metaphor, metonym, and (literal) vehicle for their poetics of the urban. Mass transport offers a way to "transgress the incarcerating ideology of the public/private spheres" and "liberate women to be spectators of modern life."[39] In Levy's work, Vadillo identifies the trope of the "passenger" as having a crucial function in Levy's "poetics of transportation and movement": for Vadillo, "the passenger is a nomad in the modern metropolis" who moves across the boundaries of social space and embodies the flux and movement of the urban space in an essential uprootedness that Levy welcomes "because it was through mobility that the bourgeoisie's Christian patriarchal notions could be challenged."[40] Indeed, there may be poems, such the "Ballade of an Omnibus," that express the female jouissance of the urban woman poet,[41] but clearly the space of passing in the city, the in-between urban space, is not simply positive and enabling in the way Vadillo analyzes it. In her late poetry, Levy signals the grave dangers that beset an "aesthetics of flux and movement . . . at one with the ephemerality of urban life."[42]

Several poems in the first sequence of *A London Plane-Tree and Other Verse* evoke a different sense of the transitory and unstable that is played out across the city. In "Straw in the Street," the speaker passes by and through the uncertain zone between life and death:

> Straw in the street where I pass to-day
> Dulls the sound of the wheels and feet.
> 'Tis for a failing life they lay
>   Straw in the street.
> . . . .
> The hurrying people go their way,
> Pause and jostle and pass and greet
> For life, for death, are they treading, say
>   Straw in the street?
>
>   (*LPT*, 25)

The city street, a place of fleeting encounters and transition and motion, is also, this poem suggests, the liminal space beyond life: the loss of stable identity that the city offers may also be the complete loss of self. Thus, the dangers of transgression are suggested by the other resonances of "passing"—that ironic double sense of "passing" and "dying" that Henry Louis Gates Jr. points to[43]—and foreshadow one of the key dynamics of the second, sexually charged, section of *A London Plane-Tree and Other Verse*.

Just as Levy's simple designation by critics as an independent New Woman elides the problematics of her racial affiliation, so too does such an identification subsume the complexities of Levy's sexuality. In "A Ballad of Religion and Marriage," for example, she imagines a nonheterosexual future where "[f]olk shall be neither pairs nor odd." As Beckman points out, the word *odd* here, a slang term for lesbian, clearly implies nonnormative sexual possibilities[44] and thus complicates an easy assumption that Levy articulates nascent New Woman feminist politics in this poem and elsewhere. Indeed, as her biography suggests (she had a number of unfulfilled romantic attachments), Levy did not easily adopt a position outside her "tribal limits." Her relationship to the liberated urban woman may have been more one of impossible identifications mobilized by a desire *for*, rather than a simple desire to be, this ideal of liberated femininity.

Certain productive ideas emerge if the desires and drives toward the liberated urban woman in Levy's work are explored through a psychoanalytic framework; they can be understood as being both narcissistic and fetishistic, that is, desires both internalized in a fraught way and externalized as a compensatory fantasy. The link between narcissism and lesbianism is clearly made in "On Narcissism" (1914) by Sigmund Freud, for whom such a homosexual libidinal cathexis is a perversion.[45] Leaving such normative classifications aside, there is a recognizably narcissistic, that is, self-identificatory, desire for the beloved that runs through the whole of *A London Plane-Tree and Other Verse* and serves to establish this beloved other as a lost self. This is not to pathologize either Levy or her work but to point to (lesbian) textual relations that disturb the boundaries of the subject, opening her up and multiplying her. Moreover, if we accept Jacques Lacan's extension of the idea of narcissism, in which he aligns it with the imaginary order and makes it a central component of the psyche, the narcissistic textual relations of Levy's work may even gesture toward an imaginary realm outside of symbolic force.[46] Her texts could thus be seen as aspiring to an escape from the symbolic through their narcissistic refusal of stable signification and singular identity.

The unsettling textual relations that can be discerned in Levy's poems surface in the work of later modernist women writers: for example, in the relationship between Hermione and Fayne Rabb in H.D.'s *HERmione*. This text presents a much more explicit exploration of narcissistic desire, lesbianism, and fetishistic disavowal, directly influenced by H.D.'s work with and experience of Freud.[47] As a projection of an ideal ego, the narcissistically desired other-as-self is also a fantasy that is believed in at the same time as its impossibility is recognized: its function is thus fetishistic. So for Levy, the urban woman as fetish—an impossible fantasy—allays the anxieties of the wound, loss, or splitting suffered by the speaking subject. Indeed, if "language . . . is based on fetishist denial ('I know that, but just the same,' 'the sign is not the thing, but just the same,' etc.) and defines us in our essence as speaking beings," as Julia Kristeva claims,[48] then perhaps the fetishized liberated urban woman is that which enables the actual articulation of *A London Plane-Tree and Other Verse*. However, the urban woman as an internal image or self-reflection also figures the narcissistic pull away from exterior objects and symbolic power, and thus away from language and intelligibility. This suggests that as Levy's text comes into being, enabled by a fetishistic fantasy of wholeness and liberation, it confronts the impossibility of this fantasy and so turns back toward hesitancy and inarticulacy.

The ideal of the independent, modern woman is clearly evoked in the dedication poem of *A London Plane-Tree and Other Verse* ("To Clementina Black") in the poem "To Vernon Lee" (both Black and Lee epitomized liberated, educated femininity), and in other poems' reminiscences of Cambridge; additionally, as Vadillo points out, "the book's fourth section [is] dedicated to the figure of New Woman."[49] In the light of these references, one may with little difficulty envisage this new type of woman as the "you" addressed by the love and erotic poems in the volume, particularly those from the second section, "Love, Dreams and Death." The liberated urban woman may serve to authorize *A London Plane-Tree and Other Verse*, but the poem "Impotens" in "Love, Dreams and Death" nevertheless expresses the difficulty of this act of writing in the face of the obstinacy of the symbolic, which is imagined as "The pitiless order of things, / Whose laws we may change not nor break" (*LPT*, 36). Against the wound inflicted by this "pitiless order," some of the poems from this section ("The Dream" and "Borderland") do create an imaginary space wherein a merging with a fetishized female other is possible. In "The Dream," the beloved is "[c]alm and silent," communicating a union with the speaker through touch and glance and persisting after the dream "like faint perfume" that "cling[s]" to the speaker (*LPT*, 38). The speaker in "Borderland" is aroused by an "unseen presence hovering" who "sheds perfume" and brings the speaker to a climax that can be marked only through charged dashes:

My heart in some dream-rapture saith,
It is she. Half in a swoon
I spread my arms in slow delight. — —

(LPT, 42)

However, others of these fantasmic poems express the loss of such joyous nocturnal merging ("In the Night," "At Dawn"), often explicitly as the death of the beloved. The poem "Contradictions," though, is where the hesitancy and inarticulacy that are attendant on the loss of wholeness (figured as the loss of the fetishized other-as-self) are most clearly, and contradictorily, articulated: "That you are dead must be inferred, / And yet my thought rejects the word" (*LPT*, 51). The following section, "Moods and Thoughts," moves on from the erotic, fantasmic poems of "Love, Dreams and Death," but the (narcissistic, fetishistic) other-as-self is evoked again in the opening poem of the section. This time, in "The Old House," "she" is unambiguously a fractured part of the self, the ideal ego projected as a younger self who, in her return, exposes the wound and loss in the speaking subject. There is no shared glance of merging; instead, there is a turning away from recognition and an acknowledgment of the impossibility of unity and reconciliation. The disavowed loss at the core of the subject returns:

She turned,—I saw her face,—O God, it wore
The face I used to wear when I was young!
. . . .
O turn away, let her not see, not know!
How should she bear it, how should understand?

(LPT, 57)

As productive as it might be, such a psychoanalytic analysis is, of course, at odds with the Deleuzian framework through which this chapter deploys the figuration of the nomad and nomadic consciousness to explore Levy's work. But the incompatibility of the two discourses is precisely what highlights the deep rifts in what Levy is attempting in her late work. The in-between, "passing," the nomadic intermezzo are what these poems attempt to write, refusing to fall back onto a site of fixity. Thus, the "paven ground" of the city is crucial as a transitory zone or "state of perpetual flux"[50] in many of the *London Plane-Tree* poems ("London in July," "Straw in the Street," "Between the Showers," "London Poets") in which the speaker traverses rather than locates herself. This resistance to fixity is also a resistance to an intelligible sexual, racial, or gender identity. Thus, although the use of an "urban muse" may signify a Jewish affiliation, as do the poems "Lohengrin" and "Captivity," all of these features are tied to in-betweenness rather than firm identification.

In a slightly different way, the speaker of many of the love and erotic poems passes as a heterosexual man—using androcentric poetic conventions—but attempts to articulate desires that fundamentally disturb the normative gendering and sexuality of such conventions. Simultaneously, though, this in-betweenness is always endangered by a signifying regime that requires intelligibility. At the level of linguistic text and of interpretative act, the necessity of signification sorts out the self and the other, identifies and categorizes, and draws desire back to the solidity of boundaries, borders, and perversions. Levy's poems cannot ultimately mean without a "you" and an "I"; there must be a place of the self; the "Last Words" must be spoken (*LPT*, 44). The pressure of this signifying realm on the voice and subject of her texts forces a splitting and enforces a silence, a silence that is so often figured as (or by) death in *A London Plane-Tree and Other Verse.* That the dangers and ambivalences of the poems' desires, along with the dangers of negating one's racial affiliation, feature as much as the urban landscape in Levy's late work suggests that the city is not simply a space of liberation, "a stream without beginning or end." "Passing" as a (non-Jewish) urban woman, or desiring the passing woman, produces an instability or uncertainty that, while unfixing identity, also threatens its destruction, a threat that is carried by the death that haunts the second section of Levy's last collection.

The uncertain, the transitory, and the in-between are obvious facets of the second sequence of *A London Plane-Tree and Other Verse:* "Love, Dreams and Death." Focusing particularly on this sequence, Emma Francis explores the "emotions of profound ambivalence" in these poems, which she reads as "accounts of separation and encounter, desire and frustration, many of which use death as a lexicon through which the speakers seek to understand their experience."[51] Poems such as "The Dream," "Borderland," "On the Threshold," and "In the Night" do indeed participate in an evocation of ambivalence and liminality while describing imagined erotic encounters with a dead or absent beloved. This is manifest as the scene or setting—dawn, twilight, the threshold—the past time remembered or the fleeting visitation, or, in a poem such as "Contradictions," the actual blurring of self and other, crossing the boundary between life and death. Death is a liminal state in these poems, a "passing on" from which the beloved returns to haunt the speaker (we could recall "Straw in the Street" with its conflation of "for life, for death"). Francis suggests that the dynamics of these poems be read as a manifestation of Terry Castle's "apparitional Lesbian,"[52] and they certainly do seem to call up a repressed or denied subjectivity while articulating the "ghostly" uncertainty of same-sex desires. However, I would further argue that the haunting of (and in) the liminal spaces of these poems is racial as well as sexual, while the presence of death as one aspect of the in-betweenness that Levy evokes hints at the danger of ambivalence and liminality. It suggests that the "passing moments" in Levy's late work are represented with a consciousness of the dangers of the in-between space in which the resistance to oppositional dualisms actually endangers the becoming-subject. The dangers are that this transformative positioning can collapse into a split subjectivity at odds with its-self. This is simultaneously the danger of articulating or representing a multiple lesbian identity and desire and the danger of racial passing.

Conceiving of a narcissistic identification with an uncertain other, a desire for (and desire to destroy) the "passing" self/other helps to shed light on some of the dynamics of Levy's late poetry. As in Larsen's modernist novel *Passing*, the unsettling ambivalence of same-sex desire is also racial ambivalence; on the one hand, these enable a line of flight out of the impossible fixities of molar subjectivity, but on the other, they signal a loss of the stable ground on which the speaking-subject can be constructed. Ultimately, the impossibility of the full enunciation of this ambivalent desire and the potential collapse of subjectivity that it presages are paralleled by race loyalty and a destructive urge to negate ambivalent affiliations. In Larsen's novel, this ends in the violent but ambiguous death of the light-skinned Clare Hendry.

The dilemma of Levy's work, in which she "passes" as an urban woman poet while also attempting to give voice to a Jewish (urban) experience, is also foregrounded through the very act of writing. Levy's comments on the position of Jewish women intellectuals imply an alienation from a racial community that the act of writing creates but also attempts to pass across: Levy writes of "an ever increasing minority of eager women beating themselves in vain against the solid masonry of our ancient fortifications, long grown obsolete and of no use save as obstructions; sometimes succeeding in scaling the wall and departing, never to return, to the world beyond."[53] And the tensions of negotiating between racial milieus through the act of writing are intersected by the fraught desires of a lesbian subjectivity. Existing in the in-between, in a space both inside and outside the "fortifications" of race, is, it seems, impossible. This space can only be passed through and not inhabited; it is not a "localizable relation" and cannot finally negate the tensions between race, sex, and gender that endanger the textual, writing, passing self.

The liminality that is evoked in the first two sections of *A London Plane-Tree and Other Verse* can be read as marked by an ambivalence and a sense of danger— the danger that ambivalence (the inability to accept fixed identity, and the attempt to inhabit a space between poles of fixity) actually incurs an eradication of the self who can no longer inhabit a space of enunciation. Thus, the loved one who is recalled in the "Love, Dreams and Death" poems and is glimpsed in passing in the "London Plane-Tree" section is both an actual object of (lesbian) desire and a part of a (racially/culturally) split and therefore precarious subjectivity. The murderous potential of Levy's refusal to "be" either a (middle-class) Jewish woman or a (queer) urban woman poet, but instead to pass between these identities, is encapsulated in the poem "In the Mile End Road."

"In the Mile End Road," the fourteenth poem in the "Love, Dreams and Death" section of *A London Plane-Tree and Other Verse*, evokes a dead woman who haunts the crowded urban scene of the East End. In doing so, the poem resonates with the reverberations of the Whitechapel murders of autumn 1888 and their attendant racialization: Jack the Ripper was thought in many quarters to be Jewish.[54] That the media representation and public response to the Ripper murders were bound up with antisemitism and Jewish stereotypes highlights the anxieties around the Jewish urban presence in London, particularly with the rise of eastern European Jewish immigration in the last decades of the century.[55] In this context, "In the Mile End Road" cannot be read neutrally. The ghostly presence that haunts the other poems of "Love, Dreams and Death" is manifest here, not in a liminal space between waking and sleeping but in the multiracial city streets of the East End: "How like her! But 'tis she herself / comes up the crowded street" (*LPT*, 50). The poem delays the revelation of the beloved's death until the final line, turning a poem of *la passante* into a disturbing, even uncanny, moment of misrecognition and loss: "I forgot / My only love was dead" (*LPT*, 50). Clearly, tensions similar to those of many of the other "Love, Dreams and Death" poems could be discerned here, or one could again postulate fetishistic and narcissistic drives at work—a lost part of the self is projected outward in a fetishistic disavowal ("For one strange moment I forgot") of the disruption of narcissistic self-containment ("My only love was dead") (*LPT*, 50). Beckman's suggestion that "London *signifies* [Levy's] speaker's state of mind, which is increasingly fragmented and distressed" in poems such as this, is relevant here, for what results, according to Beckman, is that "the self splits and becomes a beloved other": the poem offers what we might read as "an encounter with a part of the self that is dead."[56] Though the poem clearly, as Beckman points out, uses the ballad form to indicate the ballad convention of losing a lover, it moves beyond this to explore a "crisis of self-estrangement." Where Beckman posits an encounter with "Levy's Jewish self" in this poem, "the part of her identity that she was afraid of losing,"[57] I identify subterranean murderous energies, a deliberate sacrificing of the lost part of self that may offer multiple, ambiguous subjectivities but also threatens the possibility of clear identifications. At some level in this poem, the evil Jewish murderer stalks the streets and dispenses with the unsettling presence of the urban woman.

"In the Mile End Road" thus manifests most clearly the implications of the type of mobile subject positions that Levy explores in *A London Plane-Tree and Other Verse*. If, in some sense, there is a nomadic consciousness at work here, writing of or through the intermezzo, or in-between, refusing to rest on a sexual, gender, religious, racial, or cultural point of fixity, it is accompanied by a violence and destructive power that obliterates itself. What this illustrates is that the protomodernism that some critics have identified (quite rightly) in Levy's urban aesthetics, located either in a symbolist examination of the poet's split subjectivity (Beckman) or in the precinematic character of the poetry of the passenger (Vadillo), can never simply be a heralding of the modernist turn in literature. Levy's late work also enunciates the losses that modernism heralds: the destructive ambivalence of modernity and the annihilating vista of a fundamentally inconceivable future.

"In the Mile End Road" presents a dead woman, the woman who passes or has passed on, as the desired subject that the poem addresses and also as a fractured part of an uncertain identity: the new, urban woman that the textual voice ambivalently wants, wants to be, and can never fully attain. The location of the poem implies that speaker is the racial other, the urban Jew, the desiring subject, another fragment of identity and the one who speaks but who for a passing moment goes beyond her/his/its self. Both of them are urban figures, necessarily modern, transient, and self-made, who identify with and through the unregulated space of the city. They are unfixed products of modernity and peculiarly modernist subjects. But instead of an embrace of fulfillment and self-recognition, they are ultimately locked in a space of negation. The tensions between them cannot be maintained, and the between space, the liminal, liberating urban zone, becomes the city of dreadful night.

"In the Mile End Road" is circumscribed by stereotypes that are very difficult to resist; their existence is hinted at by an earlier poem in *A London Plane-Tree*, "Ballade of a Special Edition." The "apocryphal" stories of the Special Edition (*LPT*, 24), the sensational journalism that produced and reinforced negative stereotypes of Jewish otherness and would feed images of monstrous New Womanhood in the 1890s, haunt the edges of Levy's poem about Mile End, itself an easy trope for the horrors of degenerate London. Levy's rejection of sensationalism ("Fiend, get thee gone! no more repeat" [*LPT*, 24]) does not negate her own implication in reductive Semitic representations—the "Oriental" Jew of her essay "Middle-Class Jewish Women of To-Day" and the "evil-looking Hebrews" she describes to her sister Katie in a letter from Dresden (dated 4 December 1881).[58] Nor does it negate Levy's need to textually contain the threat of independent potential New Women by marriage (Gertrude and Lucy Lorimer in *The Romance of the Shop*) or death (their sister Phyllis), or even perhaps to cope with her rejection by the sexually active Vernon Lee. Reading across "In the Mile End Road," one can see the speaker returning as the evil Jew—primitive, vicious, and greedy for Western culture or the Western woman —while the desired liberated urban woman is reduced to dangerous (perverse) sexuality, her liberation the cause of her own destruction. The multiple, non-essentialist, modern subjectivity that Levy strives to write cannot persist in this poem and collapses in on itself in a murderous act.

Poems such as "In the Mile End Road" reveal the double-edged nature of Levy's writing/passing, of her celebration of the space between. The articulation of transgressive racial and sexual identities—of being neither one nor an other—leads to a splitting of subjectivity into disparate fragments. The text is enunciated in the action of traversing and thereby delineating the liminal space between the posed fragments of identity, but the becoming-subject cannot keep circulating, keep passing between; at some point, the self is sacrificed, destroyed as the Other. The idealized "smooth" space that Deleuze and Guattari describe in *A Thousand Plateaus* and elsewhere, which does not have separation, capture, territorialization, or designation, is perhaps what Levy's *A London Plane-Tree and Other Verse* is seeking, but what the poems show is that this ideal is a figuration that cannot be maintained. The between space can be textually evoked but not actually located; as Levy describes, it is "some other where":

Somewhere, I think, some other where, not here,

In other ages, on another sphere,

I danced with you, and you with me, my dear.

("Wallflower," LPT, 85)

Notes

The chapter epigraphs are from Amy Levy, "Between the Showers," in *A London Plane-Tree and Other Verse* (London: T. Fisher Unwin, 1889), 26 (hereafter cited in the text as *LPT*); Nella Larsen, *Passing* [1929], in *Quicksand and Passing* (London: Serpent's Tail, 1989), 157; Sander L. Gilman, *Making the Body Beautiful: A Cultural History of Aesthetic Surgery* (Princeton: Princeton University Press, 1999), xxi.

1. Cynthia Scheinberg, *Women's Poetry and Religion in Victorian England: Jewish Identity and Christian Culture* (Cambridge: Cambridge University Press, 2002), 194–95.

2. Rosi Braidotti, *Nomadic Subjects: Embodiment and Sexual Difference in Contemporary Feminist Theory* (New York: Columbia University Press, 1994), 22. Braidotti is working with a materialist feminist application of a Deleuzian schema of "radical nomadic epistemology" (5) to locate and explore contemporary feminist practice and politics. Her use of the "figuration" of "nomadic subjects" has a specific historical context—the late twentieth century—but my aim here is to show both the pertinence and the limits of such figurations in discussions of work such as Amy Levy's late poetry.

3. See Linda Hunt Beckman, "Amy Levy: Urban Poetry, Poetic Innovation, and the Fin-de-Siècle Woman Poet," in *The Fin-de-Siècle Poem: English Literary Culture and the 1890s*, ed. Joseph Bristow, 207–30 (Athens: Ohio University Press, 2005); Ana Parejo Vadillo, "Amy Levy in Bloomsbury," in Vadillo, *Women Poets and Urban Aestheticism: Passengers of Modernity* (Basingstoke, UK: Palgrave Macmillan, 2005), 38–77.

4. The text is not explicit on this point, and the ambiguity extends into the actual sequence of actions resulting in Claire's death and Irene's response to it.

5. Cheryl A. Wall, *Women of the Harlem Renaissance* (Bloomington: Indiana University Press, 1995), 89.

6. Hazel Carby, *Reconstructing Womanhood: The Emergence of the Afro-American Woman Novelist* (Oxford: Oxford University Press, 1987), 89.

7. For a reading of *Passing* that points to "the more dangerous story . . . of Irene's awakening sexual desire for Clare," see Deborah McDowell, introduction to Nella Larsen, *Quicksand and Passing* (New Brunswick, NJ: Rutgers University Press, 1986), xxvi.

8. Amanda Sebestyen, "Passing Figures: Black and Jewish Border Crossers," *Jewish Quarterly* (Summer 1997): 31–34, quotations on 31 and 32.

9. Ibid., 34.

10. Gilman, *Making the Body Beautiful*, 24.

11. Ibid., 136.

12. Ana Parejo Vadillo offers a very persuasive argument that places the composition of "A Ballad of Religion and Marriage" in 1889: see Vadillo, *Women Poets*, 211n21.

13. Linda K Hughes, *New Woman Poets: An Anthology* (London: The Eighteen Nineties Society, 2001).

14. Michelle Elizabeth Tusan's article "Inventing the New Woman: Print Culture and Identity Politics during the Fin-de-Siècle" (*Victorian Periodicals Review* 31, no. 2 [Summer 1998]: 169–82) offers an important account of the naming of the New Woman and provides the foundation for current debates about this figure in the late nineteenth century. The New Woman remains a contested term in Victorian studies—Lyn Pykett, for example, writes that "*The* New Woman did not exist. . . . 'New Woman,' both in fiction and [in] fact, was (and remains) a shifting and contested term." Pykett, foreword to *The New Woman in Fiction and in Fact: Fin-de-Siècle Feminisms*, ed. Angelique Richardson and Chris Willis (Basingstoke, UK: Palgrave, 2001), xi. The chronology and geography of the New Woman has also been rewritten with the contributions to the volume *New Woman Hybridities: Femininity, Feminism and International Consumer Culture, 1880–1930*, ed. Ann Heilmann and Margaret Beetham (London: Routledge, 2004), spanning a fifty-year period and exploring the phenomenon in Canada, Hungary, Japan, and Ireland as well as Britain and America.

15. Linda Hunt Beckman, *Amy Levy: Her Life and Letters* (Athens: Ohio University Press, 2000), 284n13.

16. Deborah L. Parsons, *Streetwalking the Metropolis: Women, the City and Modernity* (Oxford: Oxford University Press, 2000), 82.

17. Beckman, "Amy Levy," 211; Vadillo, *Women Poets*, 67.

18. Todd M. Endelman, *The Jews of Britain, 1656 to 2000* (Berkeley: University of California Press, 2002), 146.

19. Amy Levy, "Jewish Children," *Jewish Chronicle*, 5 November 1886, 8. Reprinted in *The Complete Novels and Selected Writings of Amy Levy*, ed. Melvyn New (Gainesville: University Press of Florida, 1993), 530.

20. Amy Levy, "Middle-Class Jewish Women of To-Day," *Jewish Chronicle*, 17 September 1886, 7. Reprinted in *Complete Novels*, ed. New, 235, 236.

21. Amy Levy, "Jewish Humour," *Jewish Chronicle*, 20 August 1886, 9–10. Reprinted in *Complete Novels*, ed. New, 521.

22. Ibid., 524.

23. See Cynthia Scheinberg, "Canonizing the Jew: Amy Levy's Challenge to Victorian Poetic Identity," *Victorian Studies* 39, no. 2 (Winter 1996): 173–200, and her *Women's Poetry and Religion in Victorian England*.

24. Scheinberg, "Canonizing the Jew," 190.

25. See the criticism of *Reuben Sachs* as "venomous" in the *Jewish Standard* editorial of 8 March 1889, 6 (possibly written by Israel Zangwill, who caricatures Levy's novel, along with Julia Frankau's *Dr Phillips: A Maida Vale Idyll*, in the same issue). See also Todd Endelman's cursory assessment that "Amy Levy was so depressed and self-hating, which in her case was linked to both her Jewishness and her sexuality, that she killed herself soon after her novel *Reuben Sachs* . . . appeared." Endelman, *Jews of Britain*, 170. "Jewish self-hatred" is Sander Gilman's term for Jewish antisemitism; see Gilman, *Jewish Self-Hatred: Anti-Semitism and the Hidden Language of the Jews* (Baltimore: Johns Hopkins University Press, 1986).

26. "Leopold Leuniger: A Study" was not published in Levy's lifetime; "Cohen of Trinity" was first published in *The Gentleman's Magazine* 266 (1889): 417–23. Both stories are

included in *Complete Novels,* ed. New. For discussion, see Linda Hunt Beckman, "Leaving 'The Tribal Duckpond': Amy Levy, Jewish Self-Hatred and Jewish Identity," *Victorian Literature and Culture* 27, no. 1 (1999): 185–201.

27. Scheinberg, *Women's Poetry,* 232.

28. Gilles Deleuze and Felix Guattari, *A Thousand Plateaus: Capitalism and Schizophrenia,* trans. Brian Massumi (London: Athlone Press, 1988), 380.

29. Ibid., 25.

30. Beckman, *Amy Levy,* 208, 219.

31. Vadillo, *Women Poets,* 4, 39.

32. See, for example, Levy's essay "James Thomson: A Minor Poet," *Cambridge Review,* 21 and 28 February 1883, 240–41 and 257–58. Reprinted in *The Complete Novels,* ed. New. See also Amy Levy, "To a Dead Poet," in *A Minor Poet and Other Verse* (London: T. Fisher Unwin, 1884).

33. See Beckman, "Amy Levy," especially 210.

34. Ibid., 212.

35. Deborah Epstein Nord, *Walking the Victorian Streets: Women, Representation and the City* (Ithaca, NY: Cornell University Press, 1995).

36. Parsons, *Streetwalking the Metropolis,* 98, 97.

37. Vadillo, *Women Poets,* 41, 55.

38. Gilman, *Making the Body Beautiful,* xxi.

39. Vadillo, *Women Poets,* 40.

40. Ibid., 68, 73, 76.

41. Ibid., 73.

42. Ibid., 77.

43. Henry Louis Gates Jr., *Figures in Black: Words, Signs and the "Racial" Self* (Oxford: Oxford University Press, 1989), 202.

44. Beckman, *Amy Levy,* 141. Beckman dates this unpublished poem to early 1888.

45. Sigmund Freud, "On Narcissism: An Introduction" (1914), in *The Standard Edition of the Complete Works of Sigmund Freud,* trans. James Strachey, vol. 14 (London: Hogarth Press and the Institute of Psycho-Analysis, 1975).

46. See, for example, Jacques Lacan, *Seminar,* book 1, *Freud's Papers on Technique* (1953–54), trans. John Forrester (New York: Norton, 1988).

47. See H.D., *HERmione,* ed. Perdita Schaffner (New York: New Directions, 1981). Clare L. Taylor offers a highly theoretical and informed reading of such aspects of H.D.'s text in "'I Am Her': The Cross-Gendered Woman as Fetish Object in H.D.'s *HER,*" in her study *Women, Writing and Fetishism, 1890–1950: Female Cross-Gendering* (Oxford: Oxford University Press, 2003).

48. Julia Kristeva, *Powers of Horror: An Essay on Abjection* (New York: Columbia University Press, 1982), 37.

49. Vadillo, *Women Poets,* 60.

50. Ibid., 74.

51. Emma Francis, "Amy Levy: Contradictions?—Feminism and Semitic Discourse," in *Women's Poetry, Late Romantic to Late Victorian: Gender and Genre, 1830–1900,* ed. Isobel Armstrong and Virginia Blain (London, Macmillan, 1999), 183–204, quotation on 141.

52. Terry Castle, *The Apparitional Lesbian: Female Homosexuality and Modern Culture* (New York: Columbia University Press, 1995).

53. Levy, "Middle-Class Jewish Women," 527.

54. See Sander L. Gilman, "The Jewish Murderer: Jack the Ripper, Race and Gender," in Gilman, *The Jew's Body* (New York: Routledge, 1991), 104–27. I explore this cultural and racial context for Levy's "In the Mile End Road" further in my "'Murder in Mile End': Amy Levy, Jewishness and the City," *Victorian Literature and Culture* 34, no. 2 (2006): 461–79.

55. For a thorough account of the reporting and media representation of the Ripper murders, see L. Perry Curtis Jr., *Jack the Ripper and the London Press* (New Haven, CT: Yale University Press, 2001).

56. Beckman, "Amy Levy," 219, 221.

57. Ibid., 222, 223.

58. Beckman, *Amy Levy*, 238.

"A Jewish *Robert Elsmere*"?

amy levy, israel zangwill, and
the postemancipation jewish novel

———

Naomi Hetherington

I N 1888, the Jewish Publication Society of America was on the lookout to commission a Jewish *Robert Elsmere*.[1] The society was newly formed for the promotion of a modern Jewish literature and culture, and the chair, Judge Mayer Sulzberger, wrote to the journalist Lucien Wolf in London asking whether Amy Levy might "be induced to write a Jewish story for us?"[2] The impetus for this request was the American edition of Levy's novel *Reuben Sachs* (1888), which criticizes Jewish materialism in a world where religion no longer has a strong hold.[3] Levy's suicide in September 1889 led Wolf to recommend the journalist and fiction writer Israel Zangwill, resulting in the society's commissioning of *Children of the Ghetto* (1892), which became, with its British edition, the first Anglo-Jewish best seller.[4] Zangwill's novel is a Jewish response to the religious ferment in Britain at the end of the nineteenth century. It contrasts traditional Jewish piety in London's East End with the spiritual malaise of a younger generation of assimilated Jews. Influenced by late-Victorian attitudes toward Christianity and Judaism, Zangwill appropriated the language and forms of a Christian majority.[5] In particular, *Children of the Ghetto* plays with key elements of the conversion plot in which Jewish survival hinges on a woman's fate.[6] Its central "allegory of Judaism" is the story of Esther Ansell, a brilliant girl graduate from the East End, who, skeptical of the faith of her childhood, publishes a novel critical of contemporary middle-class Jewish life (*CG*, 491). Zangwill's readers have long recognized Levy's influence on the character of Esther, leading to a number of myths that Levy herself came from a poor background and supported her writing through factory work (as Emma Francis's chapter in this volume discusses). This chapter explores the literary relationship between *Reuben Sachs* and *Children of the Ghetto* to reconsider Levy's role within the development of the postemancipation Jewish novel. I read her in relation to contemporary anxieties about the disintegration of Jewish religious and cultural life by using *Children of the Ghetto* as a reception study of her novel. By appropriating *Reuben Sachs* for his narrative of Jewish revival, Zangwill ensured Levy's guiding position within the new direction he signposted for Anglo-Jewish fiction.

Recounting the commissioning of *Children of the Ghetto* on Zangwill's death in 1926, Wolf recalled the "spiritual unrest" of the late 1880s, of which the popularity of *Robert Elsmere* (1888) was a "symptom."[7] The story of an Anglican clergyman beset by intellectual doubt, it became one of the best-selling novels of the nineteenth century.[8] Published the same year, *Reuben Sachs* illustrated, for Wolf, the "intensity" and "dangers" of this atmosphere of "revolt" for Anglo-Jewry.[9] Wolf's term *revolt* has been adopted by Bryan Cheyette in his history of the postemancipation Jewish novel to explain Levy's rejection of an earlier apologetic tradition of Anglo-Jewish fiction.[10] A product of the debates about Jewish emancipation in the mid-nineteenth century, the first Jewish novels portrayed the Jewish community as devout, cohesive, patriotic, and deserving of full civil rights.[11] Protesting against this official version of morality, the "novel of revolt" was characterized by a critique of the rising Jewish middle classes.[12] *Reuben Sachs* plots Jewish civic and social ambition through Reuben's choice of a political career over marriage to Judith Quixano, the poor ward of his aunt and uncle the Leunigers. Cheyette argues that Levy transformed the Anglo-Jewish novel through the character of the Jewish idealist.[13] This is Leopold

Leuniger, a musician and reader of poetry, in love with the daughter of an English aristocrat. He welcomes the "absorption" of English Jews into the "people of the country" on account of their "sickening, hideous greed" and "striving for power" (*RS*, 101). Leo stands for a moral Jewish self, in opposition to "official AngloJewry," which is represented in the novel by his ambitious cousin Reuben.[14] Cultured, earnest, and repressed, Judith likewise provides a moral counterpoint to Reuben's self-serving materialism.[15] She is of Sephardic Jewish lineage, which was commonly believed in nineteenth-century Europe to be racially and culturally superior to Ashkenazi Jews.[16] In betraying their mutual love, Reuben eschews the chance to repair his declining line.[17] Coerced by her guardians into marrying for money, Judith accepts a proposal from Bertie Lee-Harrison, a wealthy convert to Judaism whom she does not love. As Emma Francis explains, her subjection "exacts the price not just of her individual suffering but also that of the degeneration of her people."[18]

Zangwill incorporated the racial and sexual plotlines of Levy's novel into his narrative of religious revival through the story of Esther. Her allegorical role depends on the structure of the conversion plot, which is integral to both novels. Nadia Valman has demonstrated how *Reuben Sachs* "updates in feminist terms" the paradigm popularized earlier in the century by Evangelical novels, which consistently represented the Jewish woman as a particularly oppressed member of her community in special need of liberation.[19] Her vulnerability to proselytization made her the chosen instrument of her people's salvation.[20] She was portrayed as morally and spiritually superior to her male counterparts, in keeping with the elevation of femininity more generally in Evangelical culture.[21] Women's spiritual and moral sensibility was held to derive from an emotionalism that conversionists claimed to be peculiarly inhibited by the ritualism of the Jewish religion.[22] This influence is most striking in *Reuben Sachs* in the narrator's description of a synagogue service for the Jewish Day of Atonement (Yom Kippur).[23] Judith's dutiful attention to ritual observance masks her unmet longings, which find expression unexpectedly in poetry.[24] She borrows Swinburne's *Poems and Ballads* (1866) from Leo's room and experiences a "secular revelation" in its validation of her passionate female sensibility, in opposition to the material interests of her Jewish set.[25] The site of reading was central to the ideology of conversion with the Protestant emphasis on the individual's direct communion with the Word of God.[26] In *Children of the Ghetto*, Esther's dissatisfaction with her Jewish faith stems from her reading of a Christian Testament as a young girl. Though she does not call herself a Christian, she says that she "should like to believe in Jesus" and claims as an adult "to see some relation between Christianity and the truths of experience" (*CG*, 343). She retains a "melancholy" and bitterness against her co-religionists that manifest in her writing of *Mordecai Josephs* (*CG*, 454). Zangwill's relation of the cultural narrative of the Jewish woman to the Jewish novelist depends on its prior association with Levy due in part to her own use of conversionist discourse in *Reuben Sachs*.[27] This provided Zangwill with a powerful model for constructing a postemancipation Jewish future, at the center of which was the role of the Jewish novelist and Zangwill's particular relationship with Levy.

Children of the Ghetto set Zangwill up as an international spokesman for the English Jewry, a position he had previously cultivated through his journalism. Holding editorial roles on both the *Jewish Standard* and the New Humour paper *Puck* (later *Ariel, or the London Puck*), he established himself as a literary personality simultaneously in the Anglo-Jewish and general interest British press.[28] Championing a number of political causes including pacifism and British women's suffrage, he eventually became the leading English spokesperson for Zionism.[29] Zangwill's pacifism led him to propose a universal religious faith, with roots in the ethical systems of Christianity and Judaism, as the foundation for a postnationalist politics.[30] His writings advocate an Arnoldian synthesis of Hebraism and Hellenism in the fusion of "the scientific morality of Judaism" with "the emotional morality of Christ."[31] In an article in the *North American Review* in 1895, Zangwill argued that what Judaism could learn from Christianity is the Hellenic "cult of beauty."[32] He delineated the relation between Judaism and Christianity fictionalized in *Children of the Ghetto* through his reworking of Levy's novel. His essay praises Judaism for its sanctification of "the sensuous," in contrast to which Christianity is "an otherworldly religion" set in opposition to "the material framework of life."[33] It defines Israel's mission to the world as her "tendency towards unification" of which the declaration of divine Unity, said by the dying Israelite and by the congregation on the Day of Atonement, is but the "theological expression."[34] Remarking on Israel's "adaptability" through centuries of persecution, Zangwill maintained that her hope of influencing the future hinges on her "power to absorb the culture of the day."[35] In an early article entitled "English Judaism" (1889), he emphasized the "transition[al]" nature of contemporary Judaism from the traditional faith of the ghetto toward an uncertain future in which it might be unidentifiable externally with what it is now.[36] It was this essay which prompted Wolf to recommend Zangwill to Sulzberger, together with Zangwill's short story "Satan

Mekatrig" (1889), depicting a vital Jewish past and its relation to a Christian context that is both enticing and predatory.[37] It draws on the Christian Faust plot and Jewish folklore in the tale of Moshé Grinwitz, tempted to apostasy by a satanic hunchback, who, it emerges, is the agent of missionaries.[38] Others of Zangwill's short stories connect the aesthetic power of Christian imagery to a forgotten Jewish spirituality.

Meri-Jane Rochelson's study of Christian symbols in Zangwill's short fiction shows how they point up the inexplicable and transcendent in religion, both Christianity and Judaism.[39] Levy's writing is resistant to such a reading.[40] An atheist, she did not share Zangwill's interest in redefining the nature of religious faith.[41] Her ties with the Jewish community were primarily social.[42] She forged her intellectual connections with feminists and socialists whom she met as a student at Newnham, one of the newly opened women's colleges at Cambridge, and through the British Museum Reading Room.[43] She established her writing career in feminist and mainstream journals, only turning to write on Jewish topics in the last three years of her life. Prior to *Reuben Sachs*, she apparently wrote a series of articles for the *Jewish Chronicle* satirizing aspects of middle-class Jewish culture and society.[44] Appearing anonymously, they may have been published through her father's connections with the paper's editor, Asher Myers.[45] Levy's foray into a Jewish publishing market, therefore, differs markedly from Zangwill's cultivation of an Anglo-Jewish literary identity through his journalism. He established a crossover readership for his columns in *Puck* and *Ariel* and the *Jewish Standard,* ingratiating himself with Jewish readers through his attempts to inspire sympathetic views of Judaism in the general public.[46] He presented a humorous Jewish angle on national, political, and cultural events in the *Standard*, while satirizing current controversies in the Jewish community.[47] His stab at Jewish communal complacency is in keeping with the paper's tone, which, though orthodox, was an organ for Jewish intellectuals critical of official Judaism on account of its deference to the wealthy Anglo-Jewish elite.[48] The *Chronicle* was an establishment paper, and Levy's attack on middle-class Jewish values is consistent with the fears about Jewish decadence that were frequently expressed in the paper's editorials.[49] What distinguishes her columns is her use of late-Victorian anthropology and ethnography to signal Jewish primitivism and racial decline.[50] *Reuben Sachs* takes these arguments one step further, incorporating into the contemporary language of heredity and racial degeneration an older Christian anti-Judaism.[51] Leo describes Judaism as a creed of nation rather than faith: "The corn and the wine and the oil; the multiplication of the seed; the conquest of the hostile tribes—these have always had more attraction for us than the harp and crown of a spiritualized existence" (*RS*, 100).[52] While Jewish communal leaders located the roots of contemporary Jewish decadence in increasing secularization, Levy's novel blames the Jewish religion itself.[53] Leo defines Judaism as "the religion of materialism," in contrast to the spirituality and aestheticism of English high culture (*RS*, 100).

Leo's drive for radical assimilation distinguishes Levy's novel from the recuperative stance of her Jewish contemporaries, but Christian criticism of a Jewish fixation with the physical had structured attempts to revitalize Jewish religious and cultural life for much of the century. As David Feldman has shown, the Jewish Reform movement in England and the drive for modernization within orthodoxy in the mid-Victorian period were shaped by an Evangelical critique of Jewish ritualism.[54] Later on in the century, liberal Anglicanism increasingly influenced Jewish self-image with its denigration of Judaism as inherently primitive and lacking in spirit.[55] These charges had ramifications for middle-class Jewish culture far beyond the reform of institutionalized worship. Anxieties about a neglect of the arts pervaded Anglo-Jewish discussions.[56] The *Jewish Chronicle* repeatedly lamented the paucity of Jewish literary life.[57] In America, too, the foundation of the Jewish Publication Society was a response to liberal Christian definitions of Judaism and an attempt to encourage an independent Jewish culture through the promotion of a Jewish literature.[58] This provides one explanation for why Sulzberger thought of Levy in deciding to commission a Jewish *Robert Elsmere*. Yet this was not the context within which the Jewish public received Levy's novel in Britain. *Reuben Sachs* was published a year after another, more virulent, attack on middle-class English Jewry, which similarly implicated Jewish theology in an imbrication of racial and sexual discourse.[59] Appearing under the name of Frank Danby, *Dr Phillips* was soon discovered to be the work of Julia Frankau, the sister of a Jewish society journalist, who had married into a highly assimilated German-Jewish family and increasingly distanced herself from London's Anglo-Jewish community.[60] Grouping Levy's novel together with Frankau's, the *Jewish Chronicle* detected a disturbing new trend in "Jewish criticism of Jews . . . the more deleterious as it is impossible for the general public to know on what superficial knowledge of Jewish society such ill-natured sketches are founded."[61] While the mainstream press looked to *Reuben Sachs* for information about contemporary Jewish life, the Jewish papers were anxious to distance Levy from the debates that raged in their pages.[62] Not surprisingly, the *Standard* stood out in showing some sympathy for both novelists.[63] The editor conceded that "amid much that was gratuitously offensive there was in 'Reuben Sachs' an acute diagnosis of the spiritual blight that has come over well-fed Judaism."[64]

Zangwill concurred with the line of the paper in his column, titled Morour and Charouseth, in arguing that the task of the Jewish novelist was not confined to portraying those Jewish ways and customs most worthy of praise.[65] What he resented about Levy and Frankau was the "undiscriminating hostility" to which they were goaded "by the cramping materialism around them."[66] Parodying both novels together in a satirical poem, he berated their inattention to "ritual details" and "one-sided representations" of Jewish life.[67] On the occasion of Levy's suicide, Zangwill found a particular explanation for her unsuitability as a Jewish novelist in her "morbid" poetic temperament.[68] Preoccupied with suicide and the pain of consciousness, her poetry is indebted to a pessimistic school of British and European poetry, which, Zangwill argued, citing the physician and essayist Oliver Wendell Holmes, is dependent on an extreme sensitivity to external impressions given these poets to "compensate" for "the imperfection of their nature."[69] "[P]enetrating as her glance was within limits," Zangwill claimed, "it is not to such ill-balanced minds as Amy Levy's that one can look for a fair picture of a section of contemporary society."[70] Intending to defend the Jewish community against the charges of Levy's novel, Zangwill drew on a common perception of her writing that owed as much to conversionist discourse as it did to contemporary theories of poetry. In chapter 4 of this volume, Nadia Valman analyzes posthumous tributes to Levy that suggest her elevated sensitivity, her exceptional visionary potential, and the expressive deficiency of her art through the trope of the incomplete Jewish woman. Read in this light, Levy's pessimism in *Reuben Sachs* was deemed but "the reaction from the qualities which she professes to despise."[71] Described as "[p]assionately, almost childishly angry," Levy was not considered "the right person" to impeach her co-religionists, even though her accusations did not strike critics as "much exaggerated or unjust."[72] Even before her death, reviewers faulted the "crude" execution of her novel, while finding it to contain "a moral and a warning. . . . Miss Levy deplores her kinsmen's sordid devotion to material interests and lack of any yearning for a higher life."[73] It is this complex portrait of Levy which Zangwill used to construct the character of Esther in *Children of the Ghetto* and through which he sought to reevaluate the place of the novel of revolt in his own critique of contemporary Jewish life.

Children of the Ghetto plots its relation to the novel of revolt in Esther's publication of *Mordecai Josephs*, which sends shock waves through the novel's West End Jewish community. Like Frankau, Esther publishes her novel under a gentile male pseudonym so that the other characters are free to berate the book in front of her with no idea that she is the author. The novel stages a discussion of *Mordecai Josephs* that replicates the terms in which *Dr Phillips* and *Reuben Sachs* were denounced in the Jewish papers. Anxiety about the damage these novels had done to the public image of Anglo-Jewry is reflected in the opinion of stockbroker Percy Saville that it is "plain treachery and disloyalty this putting of weapons into the hands of our enemies. Of course, we have our faults, but we should be told of them privately or from the pulpit" (*CG*, 329). Mr. Montagu Samuels, a philanthropist and committeeman, claims that the author knows that his book is "all exaggeration and distortion, but anything spicy pays now-a-days" (*CG*, 325). The artist Sidney Graham plays devil's advocate to these "pillars of the community" (*CG*, 326). Defending the "actuality" of the book, he concedes that it is "a crude production, all the same; the writer's artistic gift seems handicapped by a dead-weight of moral platitudes. . . . He not only presents his characters but moralizes over them—actually cares whether they are good or bad and has yearnings after the indefinable—it is all very young" (*CG*, 331). Sidney's speech picks up on the wording of contemporary reviews of *Reuben Sachs*, but in arguing for the author's own "yearnings after the indefinable," it invites the reader to view Levy through the lens of conversionist discourse. This impression is strengthened by the extent to which Esther resembles contemporary vignettes of Levy that use her physiognomy to evoke the inner conflicts of the prototypical Jewish woman. The narrator's description of Esther in this scene is remarkably similar to Harry Quilter's description of a photograph of Levy in his "Reminiscence," published the same year as Zangwill's novel.[74] As Valman's chapter in this volume explains, Quilter's reading of the photograph connects the paradoxes of Levy's art to her Jewish race in evoking her description of Judith's "dark" features in *Reuben Sachs* and her Judith's "wonderful, lustrous, mournful eyes, entirely out of keeping with the accepted characteristics of their owner" (*RS*, 62). This set of associations is strengthened in *Children of the Ghetto* through Esther's secret identity as the author of *Mordecai Josephs* and the additional detail of her "tight-fitting" white evening dress, which is identical to Judith's when she is introduced to the reader (*RS*, 62; *CG*, 338). Capitalizing on the tendency of Levy's critics to elide her with her Jewish heroine, *Children of the Ghetto* co-opts her literary identity for the new direction in which it takes Anglo-Jewish fiction.

Zangwill staked out his place in contemporary debate about Levy's novel through his counterpart in *Children of the Ghetto*, the Jewish journalist Raphael Leon, who becomes the editor of a new Orthodox paper: the *Flag of Judah*.

Raphael is obliged to accept responsibility for a burlesque on *Mordecai Josephs* that appears in his paper, re-creating the curious circumstances surrounding Zangwill's lampooning of Levy and Frankau in the *Standard* when irate readers took his satirical poem literally and the paper was forced to provide an explanation in an editorial leader.[75] Zangwill intertwined his literary relationship with Levy with the romance of Reuben and Judith in *Reuben Sachs* in the love that develops between Esther and Raphael. Raphael slams *Mordecai Josephs* for its "most ignorant" presentation of Judaism (*CG*, 380). Then, when Esther reveals to him that she is the author, his anger melts away into admiration and love. Raphael read "her eager little soul in every line. Now he understood. The whole book was Esther, the whole Esther and nothing but Esther, for even the satirical descriptions were but the revolt of Esther's soul against mean and evil things" (*CG*, 429). Raphael is transfixed by "the great love-scene" of Esther's novel (*CG*, 429), invoking the chapter in *Reuben Sachs* when Judith listens silently to Reuben arguing with Leo for the power of racial "affinity" and learns of his "love" for her for the first time (*RS*, 102). *Children of the Ghetto* restores this lost hope for a Jewish future in Raphael's proposal of marriage to Esther. It contains the novel's description of Esther's life as an "allegory of Judaism, the offspring of a great and tragic past with the germs of a rich blossoming, yet wasting away with an inward canker" (*CG*, 491). The setting is the steps of the British Museum, which, emphasizing Esther's intellectuality and relating it to her flawed vision, particularly connects her with Levy at this point in the novel. Levy's failure to achieve transcendence through her art in popular discourse stands in for the misdirection of contemporary Jewish religious life. Zangwill identified the pessimism of *Reuben Sachs*, its protest against Jewish middle-class values, in Raphael's expression of his desire for Esther: "I want to see you face life courageously, not in passionate revolt, nor in passionless despair, but in faith and hope and the joy that springs from them. I want you to seek peace, not in a despairing surrender of the intellect to the faith of childhood, but in that faith intellectually justified. . . . Be my wife, Esther" (*CG*, 491). The dialectic of "revolt" and "despair" and their synthesis in a "faith intellectually justified" provide my blueprint for the textual analysis that follows.

Children of the Ghetto owes much more to Levy's novel than Zangwill's previous critics have realized. Esther's position of Jewish cultural commentator is that of Levy's sardonic spokeswoman Esther Kohnthal in *Reuben Sachs*. They share a religious skepticism, a love of literature, and an outspokenness, which all contribute in *Children of the Ghetto* to Esther's writing of *Mordecai Josephs*. Esther's history combines details of Levy's life with the story of Judith.[76] She is adopted from a poor East End home by an affluent Jewish family and falls in love with the novel's upwardly mobile male protagonist. Zangwill reworked Levy's love scene in a dinner party at Esther's benefactors, the Goldsmiths, where she meets Raphael for the first time. She listens silently to him debating the future of Anglo-Jewry with Sidney Graham, Leo's counterpart in Zangwill's novel. He is Raphael's cousin and secretly engaged to the daughter of a Wesleyan Member of Parliament. He adopts Leo's role in speaking out against Jewish "isolation" and claiming that his co-religionists "get into little cliques and mistake narrow-mindedness for fidelity to an ideal" (*CG*, 334). Raphael takes Reuben's part in arguing that "[r]ace affinity" is as yet a potent force among English Jews (*CG*, 336). Raphael is Zangwill's idealist championing a Jewish "spiritual revival" in England (*CG*, 336). The "theological passage of arms" that structures his courtship of Esther plays with Leo's definition of Judaism as a religion of materialism devoid of spiritual sustenance (*CG*, 426). Where Raphael argues that "the very theory of Judaism has always been the spiritualization of the material," Esther retorts that "the practice of Judaism has always been the materialization of the spiritual" (*CG*, 343, 344). Referring to *kashrut* (Jewish dietary law), she invokes the trope of universal Christianity transcending a Judaism that is legalistic and earthbound: "The real Judaism is a religion of pots and pans. It does not call to the soul's depths like Christianity" (*CG*, 342). She writes *Mordecai Josephs* out of love for Sidney, hoping to gain his affection by reproducing his views. Her shifting viewpoint changes the narrative center of Levy's novel. Judith is cut off from her people through her marriage to Bertie Lee-Harrison, whose interest in Judaism quickly subsides. Esther, in contrast, refuses a proposal of marriage from Leonard James, an apostate from Judaism who has broken ties with his East End family to pursue a career on the stage. His proposal recalls Esther to the world of her girlhood, and confessing her authorship of *Mordecai Josephs* in a note to the Goldsmiths, she runs away back to the ghetto.

Children of the Ghetto attempts to recuperate a particular Jewish experience, the symbol of which is the Jewish religion. The climax of the novel, cited in full in the *Jewish Chronicle*, is Esther's return to her religious roots on the Day of Atonement.[77] Moved "by an irresistible instinct," she enters the *chevrah*, the traditional East End synagogue of her childhood (*CG*, 498). Witnessing the congregation testify in unison to the Unity of God, she is reconnected to a Jewish past: "[H]er dead self woke, her dead ancestors that would not be shaken off lived and moved in her. She was sucked up into the great passionate wave of faith" (*CG*, 499). In *Reuben Sachs*, the Jewish religion has run its course. The Yom Kippur service occurs early on in the story and is set not in the East but the West End, a place of spiritual bankruptcy in both novels. Together with her cousins, Judith attends the synagogue at Upper Berkeley Street, Britain's first Reform congregation, where Levy's family held seats.[78] The primary concern of the Reform movement in England was to modernize Jewish worship, introducing short services with a choir and organ and an English sermon in the style of an Anglican Church service.[79] In *Reuben Sachs*, "the simplified service, the beautiful music, and other innovations" are insufficient to move the predominantly upper-middle-class congregation (*RS*, 89). Reuben looks "bored" (*RS*, 91). Judith goes through her devotions "unthinkingly," only partly able to understand the Hebrew liturgy with its prayers for the restoration of Zion (*RS*, 91).[80] Levy's narrator questions their relevance to the refined Jewish girl: "These prayers, read so diligently, in a language of which her knowledge was exceedingly imperfect, these reiterated praises of an austere tribal deity, these expressions of a hope whose consummation was neither desired nor expected, what connections could they have with the personal needs, the human longings of this touchingly ignorant and limited creature?" (*RS*, 91). Transplanting the ceremony to the nostalgic setting of the *chevrah*, Zangwill made the archaism of Jewish worship its affective appeal. Upstairs in a separate room, the women follow the prayers through an open window; "only vaguely conscious of the stages of the service," Esther loses herself in the "barren sensuousness" of the sound (*CG*, 499). The sensory appeal of the liturgy unlocks the emotionally repressed Jewish woman. In *Reuben Sachs*, this role can only be performed by poetry, a plotline that Zangwill reserved for Esther's novel.

Berating the book's "ignorant presentation" of the Jewish religion, Raphael complains that "[a]ll the mystical yearnings of the heroine might have found as much satisfaction in the faith of her own race as they find in its poetry" (*CG*, 380–81). Rochelson takes this to refer to *Reuben Sachs*, but there is a crucial difference in that Judith turns not to Jewish poetry but to Swinburne.[81] Thumbing "mechanically" through *Poems and Ballads*, her attention is caught by "The Triumph of Time," which speaks to her feelings of desolation and longing after Reuben has distanced himself from her to begin his campaign for parliamentary election (*RS*, 132). The novel reproduces three verses from early on in the poem that explore the agony of romantic betrayal through a Christian language of passion, idealism, and longing.[82] Denounced as obscene and blasphemous on its initial publication, *Poems and Ballads* exploits the emotional value of Christian symbolism to parody the saving power of Christianity and to sacralize carnal passion.[83] "The Triumph of Time" is one of the tamer poems in the volume, and the verses that capture Judith's attention use the metaphor of an erotic Eucharist to express the speaker's belief at this point in the poem that his lost love had meaning and might have had transcendent power.[84] Deprived of its theological efficacy, Christian language retains a suasive force in Swinburne's poetry, which, in *Reuben Sachs*, Jewish rhetoric cannot. That Zangwill recognized this is evident in Esther's acquisition of a Christian Testament as a girl and the site that reading occupies, not in her novel, but in her childhood. An avid reader, Esther uses literature to construct a rich interior life outside of the harsh material realities of the ghetto. Seeking a change from the romantic and sensational tales she has read over and over again in back volumes of the *London Journal*, she barters the Testament off a school friend in exchange for a slate pencil. The novel's play with the familiar trope of the young woman intrigued with the Christian Bible has fascinated Zangwill's commentators; but in firing Esther's imagination, the Testament reflects the role performed by Christian currency in *Reuben Sachs*.[85] The Testament does not inspire Esther to convert. In fact, she seems unaware of its specific religious significance, asking her brother Benjy why it is so reverenced by Christians. When Benjy tells her that "the New Testament is a wicked book," Esther asks him, "But why do I feel good when I read what Jesus said?" (*CG*, 208). *Good*, here, is not a moral but an emotional signifier. When, years later, Esther tells Raphael that as a little girl she always got her "conscious religious inspiration out of the New Testament," she is contrasting its power to move her with her unthinking recitation of Hebrew prayers (*CG*, 340).

Raphael's criticism of *Mordecai Josephs*, that it replaces religion with poetry, is, therefore, a screen for how Zangwill resolved the central plotline of Levy's novel. In sparring about the relationship between Christianity and Judaism, Raphael and Esther collapse the categories of the religious and the aesthetic. Esther first strikes up a conversation with Raphael by lamenting the lack of a Jewish poetry. Raphael finds the poetry of Browning in the Hebrew prayer book. Persuaded by him to reread the Hebrew Bible, Esther agrees that it contains "great poetry" and takes to reading both Testaments together (*CG*, 425). *Children of the Ghetto* does not promote a new Jewish faith in the way that *Robert Elsmere* reinvents Christianity with the hero's founding of the New Brotherhood of Christ.[86] Indeed, the *Jewish Chronicle* noted approvingly that "the book is not a Jewish Robert Elsmere; the religious interest is strong, but with considerable skill Mr Zangwill has never allowed it to protrude beyond its proper place."[87] Even in the synagogue scene at the end of the novel, the transcendence of Esther's experience is open to question. Her "protestation" of the divine Unity is "half-hysterical," and she faints from "the long exhausting fast, the fetid atmosphere," and the emotional strain of the day (*CG*, 500). What Esther learns from the service is the survival and adaptability of her people through centuries of suffering and persecution. Her hope for Jewish regeneration is the antithesis of Judith's story. In an epilogue to Levy's novel, Judith hears the news of Reuben's death, which, emblematically, closes the possibility of a particular Jewish future. Zangwill's epilogue pays homage to the American commission of *Children of the Ghetto* in suggesting the United States as a possible site for Jewish religious and cultural revival. Esther sails to the New World for her sister's wedding, but the narrator intimates that she will return to marry Raphael. Kissing him goodbye on the pier, she tells him that his "allegory" seems to be turning out in his "favour" (*CG*, 501). Following Esther's return to the religious roots of her childhood, their union represents her search for "peace not in a despairing surrender of the intellect to the faith of childhood, but in that faith intellectually justified" (*CG*, 491). The novel does not resolve theologically what this faith might be, leaving open to question whether Israel's future mission lies in her particular witness to the Unity of God or her absorption into a universal Judeo-centric religion.[88] What Zangwill's ending holds out is the possibility of a particular Jewish future beyond the bleak determinism of Levy's novel.

Appropriating *Reuben Sachs* for his own promise of Jewish revival, Zangwill ensured Levy's guiding role within the new direction he mapped out for Anglo-Jewish fiction. Yet by conflating Levy with her novel, he preserved a contemporary view of her, seen through the lens of the conversionist discourse. It is this cultural narrative of the incomplete Jewish woman which Esther's story subverts, in relation to both Levy's literary career and the story of her Jewish heroine. In Levy's secular rendition of the conversion plot in *Reuben Sachs*, self-realization is momentary and partial, conveyed in the final fragmentary sentences of her novel through the symbolism of a child whom Judith does not yet know she carries. Its quickening in her womb is interpreted allegorically as a moment of insight available to all of Levy's readers: "that quickening of purpose which is perhaps as much as any of us should expect or demand from Fate" (*RS*, 157). This universal note of pessimism is given a particular Jewish history in *Children of the Ghetto*. Esther discovers the "secret of her pessimism" in the poverty of her East End childhood (*CG*, 454). Knowing herself to be "a Child of the Ghetto," she feels "a subtle melancholy joy in understanding herself at last" (*CG*, 454). Esther's coming to consciousness turns around the complement of "pain and sorrow, . . . hope and joy" that motherhood offers Judith (*RS*, 157). The birth of her child no longer signals the perpetuity of the Jewish race, nor, while tempering her grief at Reuben's death, can her self-knowledge materially alter the circumstances of life. That Esther's self-realization leads to a greater understanding of her book is implied through the causal connection the novel establishes between Esther's return to the East End, her revelation of her authorship of *Mordecai Josephs*, and Raphael's recognition of the novel's moral purpose. His vindication of Esther anticipates Zangwill's defense of Levy a decade later, when, speaking at the annual dinner of the Jewish literary and cultural society the Maccabaeans in 1901, he maintained that her purpose in writing *Reuben Sachs* had been misunderstood: "She was accused, of course, of fouling her own nest: whereas what she had really done was to point out that the nest was foul and must be cleaned out."[89] Calling for a reappraisal of her novel, he proclaimed her the "pioneer" of a new "school" of Anglo-Jewish fiction.[90]

Notes

Versions of this chapter were presented at the Midlands Interdisciplinary Victorian Studies Seminar and the Oxford Fin-de-Siècle Seminar, and I wish to thank participants of both seminars for their insightful responses. I am grateful to Bryan Cheyette, Meri-Jane Rochelson, and Nadia Valman for their careful reading of earlier drafts of this article that have contributed toward the development of its final argument.

1. Mrs. Humphrey Ward, *Robert Elsmere* (London: Smith Elder, 1888).

2. Mayer Sulzberger, letter to Lucien Wolf, 30 March 1889, Jewish Publication Society of America Papers, cited in Jonathan D. Sarna, *JPS: The Americanization of Jewish Culture, 1888–1988* (Philadelphia: Jewish Publication Society, 1989), 40.

3. Amy Levy, *Reuben Sachs: A Sketch* (1888), ed. Susan Bernstein (Peterborough, ON: Broadview Press, 2006). All quotations from the novel are taken from this edition and given in the text as *RS*.

4. Bernard Winehouse, "Israel Zangwill's *Children of the Ghetto*: A Literary History of the First Anglo-Jewish Best-Seller," *English Literature in Transition, 1880–1920* 16 (1973): 93–117.

5. For a wider discussion of Zangwill's uses of Christianity in his fiction, see Meri-Jane Rochelson, "'They That Walk in Darkness': *Ghetto Tragedies*: The Uses of Christianity in Israel Zangwill's Fiction," *Victorian Literature and Culture* 27, no. 1 (1999): 219–33.

6. Meri-Jane Rochelson, introduction to *Children of the Ghetto: A Study of a Peculiar People* (1892), by Israel Zangwill (Detroit: Wayne State University Press, 1998), 11–44, especially 33. All quotations from the novel are taken from this edition and given in the text as *CG.*

7. Lucien Wolf, "Israel Zangwill," *Transactions of the Jewish Historical Society of England* 11 (1924–26): 252–60, quotation on 254.

8. For a discussion of the novel's reception and wider cultural significance, see Mark M. Freed, "The Moral Irrelevance of Dogma: Mary Ward and Critical Theology in England," in *Women's Theology in Nineteenth-Century Britain: Transfiguring the Faith of Their Fathers,* ed. Julie Melnyk (New York: Garland, 1998), 113–47.

9. Wolf, "Israel Zangwill," 254.

10. Bryan Cheyette, "From Apology to Revolt: Benjamin Farjeon, Amy Levy and the Post-Emancipation Anglo-Jewish Novel, 1880–1900," *Transactions of the Jewish Historical Society of England* 24 (1982–86): 253–65.

11. Ibid., 253–54.

12. Ibid., 260.

13. Ibid.

14. Ibid.

15. Nadia Valman, "'Barbarous and Medieval': Jewish Marriage in Fin de Siècle English Fiction," in *The Image of the Jew in European Liberal Culture, 1789–1914,* ed. Bryan Cheyette and Nadia Valman (London: Vallentine Mitchell, 2004), 111–29, quotation on 112.

16. Emma Francis, "Socialist Feminism and Sexual Instinct: Eleanor Marx and Amy Levy," in *Eleanor Marx (1885–1898): Life, Work, Contacts,* ed. John Stokes (Aldershot, UK: Ashgate, 2000), 113–27, quotation on 119.

17. Francis, "Socialist Feminism," 122.

18. Ibid.

19. Nadia Valman, *The Jewess in Nineteenth-Century British Literary Culture* (Cambridge: Cambridge University Press, 2007), 191.

20. Michael Ragussis, *Figures of Conversion: "The Jewish Question" and English National Identity* (Durham, NC: Duke University Press, 1995), 38.

21. See Valman, *Jewess,* 51–61.

22. Ibid., 93.

23. Ibid., 191.

24. Ibid., 191–92.

25. Ibid., 192. In this respect, one can trace a trajectory from Levy's novel to H.D.'s use of Swinburne in *HERmione* (New York: New Directions, 1981; written in 1927) to make for a more fluid exploration of sexuality and gender role than is permitted by a modernist poetics of male desire. See Cassandra Laity, "H.D. and A. C. Swinburne: Decadence and Modernist Women's Writing," *Feminist Studies* 15 (1989): 461–84; Dana R. Shugar, "Faustine Re-Membered: H.D.'s Use of Swinburne's Poetry in Hermione," *Sagetrieb* 9 (1990): 79–94.

26. Ragussis, *Figures of Conversion,* 32–33.

27. See Nadia Valman's chapter in this volume for further discussion of this evaluation of Levy's writing by non-Jewish critics. I am grateful to her for sharing this work in manuscript form, which helped to shape my final thinking for this piece.

28. Meri-Jane Rochelson, "Israel Zangwill's Early Journalism and the Formation of an Anglo-Jewish Literary Identity," in *Nineteenth-Century Media and the Construction of Identities*, ed. Laurel Brake, Bill Bell, and David Finkelstein (Basingstoke, UK: Palgrave, 2000), 178–94, especially 178.

29. Rochelson, "Israel Zangwill's Early Journalism," 178. For a detailed account of Zangwill's relation to the British women's suffrage movement, see Meri-Jane Rochelson, "Israel Zangwill and Women's Suffrage," *Jewish History and Culture* 2 (1999): 1–17.

30. Rochelson, "They That Walk," 220.

31. Israel Zangwill, "English Judaism: A Criticism and a Classification," *Jewish Quarterly Review* 1 (1889): 376–407, especially 403.

32. Israel Zangwill, "The Position of English Judaism," *North American Review* 160 (1895): 425–39, quotation on 437.

33. Ibid., 435.

34. Ibid., 436.

35. Ibid., 438.

36. Zangwill, "English Judaism," 396.

37. Wolf, "Israel Zangwill," 255.

38. See Rochelson, "They That Walk," 225–26.

39. Ibid., 230.

40. Cynthia Scheinberg has put forward a different reading of Christian symbolism in Levy's poetry and Jewish prose. See, in particular, chapter 6 in Scheinberg, *Women's Poetry and Religion in Victorian England: Jewish Identity and Christian Culture* (Cambridge: Cambridge University Press, 2002).

41. Linda Hunt Beckman discusses Levy's lack of interest in Jewish religious belief and practice in her biography. See Beckman, *Amy Levy: Her Life and Letters* (Athens: Ohio University Press, 2000), 13–14, 17–18, 128.

42. Ibid., 114.

43. Ibid., 79–81, 84.

44. Beth-Zion Abrahams, "Amy Levy and the 'JC,'" *Jewish Chronicle*, 17 November 1961, 13. These articles are now widely accepted to have been written by Levy.

45. Ibid.

46. Rochelson, "Israel Zangwill's Early Journalism," 178, 191.

47. Ibid., 179.

48. Bryan Cheyette, "The Other Self: Anglo-Jewish Fiction and the Representation of Jews in England, 1875–1905," in *The Making of Modern Anglo-Jewry*, ed. David Cesarani (London: Basil Blackwell, 1990), 97–111, esp. 108.

49. Valman, *Jewess*, 176–77.

50. On Levy's use of ethnographic discourse, see ibid., 176–78, 181–82.

51. Ibid., 181.

52. Ibid.

53. On the reaction of the Jewish leadership to increasing secularization among middle-class Jewry, see Todd M. Endelman, *Radical Assimilation in English Jewish History, 1656–1945* (Bloomington: Indiana University Press, 1990), 96–97.

54. David Feldman, *Englishmen and Jews: Social Relations and Political Culture, 1840–1914* (New Haven, CT: Yale University Press, 1994), 53–61.

55. See Daniel R. Langton, *Claude Montefiore: His Life and Thought* (London: Vallentine Mitchell, 2002), 187–88.

56. Feldman, *Englishmen and Jews*, 61–62.

57. Ibid., 61.

58. Sarna, *JPS*, 23–26.

59. Frank Danby [Julia Frankau], *Dr Phillips: A Maida Vale Idyll* (London: Vizetelly, 1887). For a discussion, see Valman, *Jewess*, 193–200.

60. For the propensity of German-born Jews to disavow their Jewishness, see Endelman, *Radical Assimilation*, 108, 126. Endelman discusses Frankau's family history in further detail in "The Frankaus of London: A Study in Radical Jewish Assimilation, 1837–1967," *Jewish History* 8 (1994): 117–54.

61. "Critical Jews," editorial, *Jewish Chronicle*, 25 January 1889, 11. See also "New Books," *Jewish Chronicle*, 2 August 1889, 12; "The Deterioration of the Jewess," *Jewish World*, 22 February 1889, 5.

62. This was the approach taken by reviewers of *Reuben Sachs* in both the *Athenaeum* (26 January 1889): 114, and the *Academy* (16 February 1889): 103.

63. Cheyette, "The Other Self," 107.

64. Retrospect of the year, *Jewish Standard*, 25 September 1889, 9.

65. See Cheyette, "The Other Self," 107.

66. Marshallik [Israel Zangwill], Morour and Charouseth, *Jewish Standard*, 1 March 1889, 9.

67. Ibid.; see also ibid., 8 March 1889, 9.

68. Ibid., 9 October 1889, 14.

69. Ibid., 9 October 1889, 14. For a discussion of Levy's relation to a British and European tradition of pessimism, see Joseph Bristow, "All Out of Tune in This World's Instrument: The 'Minor' Poetry of Amy Levy," *Journal of Victorian Culture* 4 (1999): 76–103, esp. 89–97; Ana Parejo Vadillo, *Women Poets and Urban Aestheticism: Passengers of Modernity* (Basingstoke, UK: Palgrave Macmillan, 2005), 41–43, 53.

70. Marshallik [Zangwill], Morour and Charouseth, *Jewish Standard*, 9 October 1889, p. 14.

71. Harry Quilter, "Amy Levy: A Reminiscence and a Criticism," in Quilter, *Preferences in Art, Life and Literature* (London: Swan Sonnenschein, 1892), 149.

72. Quilter, "Amy Levy," 149, 147.

73. "New Novels," *Academy* 876 (16 February 1889): 109.

74. See Quilter, "Amy Levy," 138.

75. Rochelson, introduction to Zangwill, *Children of the Ghetto*, 26.

76. Joseph Udelson, *Dreamer of the Ghetto: The Life and Works of Israel Zangwill* (Tuscaloosa: University of Alabama Press, 1990), 103.

77. I. Abrahams, review of Zangwill's *Children of the Ghetto*, *Jewish Chronicle*, 14 October 1892, 8.

78. Lewis Levy to the Membership Secretary of the West London Synagogue, 15 June 1877 and 7 and 8 November 1878; AJ 59 5/4 and 5/9, West London Synagogue of British Jews archive, Parkes Collection, Southampton University, UK.

79. Anne J. Kershen and Jonathan A. Romain, *Tradition and Change: A History of Reform Judaism in Britain, 1840–1995* (London: Vallentine Mitchell, 1995), chap. 2. British Reform differed significantly from its radical counterpart in Germany in its concern for synagogue ritual and practice rather than the theological arguments that motivated Jewish reform on the Continent. See Langton, *Claude Montefiore,* 176–79.

80. In fact, the West London congregation voted to omit the prayer for the restoration of the Temple in 1888, the year in which *Reuben Sachs* was published. Stephen Sharot, "Reform and Liberal Judaism in London, 1840–1910," *Jewish Social Studies* 41 (1979): 215.

81. Rochelson, introduction to Zangwill, *Children of the Ghetto,* 520n140.

82. Levy cites stanzas 4, 5, and 6 of Swinburne's poem, altering "my fruit" to "any fruit" in the first line of stanza 4. Melvyn New suggests that this is to play down the explicitly sexual nature of Swinburne's language. New, ed., *The Complete Novels and Selected Writings of Amy Levy, 1861–1889* (Gainesville: University Press of Florida, 1993), 547n56.

83. For a discussion of Swinburne's use of Christian symbolism in *Poems and Ballads* (1866), see Margot K. Louis, *Swinburne and His Gods: The Roots and Growth of an Agnostic Poetry* (London: McGill-Queen's University Press, 1990), 55–65.

84. See ibid., 55–56.

85. Udelson, *Dreamer of the Ghetto,* 98. In her introduction to the novel, Rochelson comments that Esther's flirtation with Christian ideas here "results in a future that would unsettle both Jews and conversionists" (34).

86. For a discussion of Elsmere in this respect, see chapter 7 in William S. Peterson, *Victorian Heretic: Mrs Humphrey Ward's* Robert Elsmere (Leicester: Leicester University Press, 1976); more recently, see Lynne Hapgood, "'The Reconceiving of Christianity': Secularisation, Realism and the Religious Novel, 1888–1900," *Literature and Theology* 10 (1996): 329–50.

87. Abrahams, review of Zangwill's *Children of the Ghetto,* 7.

88. See Rochelson, introduction to Zangwill, *Children of the Ghetto,* 34.

89. Israel Zangwill, "A Ghetto Night at the Maccabaeans: Dinner to Mr. Samuel Gordon," *Jewish Chronicle,* 25 January 1901, 19.

90. Ibid.

9

Verse or Vitality?

biological economies and
the new woman poet

———

Lyssa Randolph

*A*s an authoritative, establishment discourse, orthodox science could denote modernity and cultural legitimacy for women writers through which to model the presentation of feminist values and goals; yet this was a fraught enterprise, and the ideas these New Women sought to appropriate were used against them. New Woman writers of the fin de siècle met with resistance from critics who subjected their work and persons to socio-scientific scrutiny. In the year 1889, arguments against women's participation in the public, and elite, discourses of science and poetry coalesced around the deaths of two women poets: Amy Levy and Constance Naden. As New Woman figures, their access to education and the cultural and intellectual milieu in which they moved came under discussion. This chapter examines the representation of their identity in relation to their deaths.

Writing on the cultural construction of gender and genius, Christine Battersby has described how, during the earlier part of the century, women writers were disciplined by medical theories that declared that female physiology was unable to withstand the rigors of intellectual creativity that poetic work demanded. For example, the physicians who treated Elizabeth Barrett Browning for the "vapours" believed the impact of the work of female "rhymers" to be detrimental to their health, and the physicians confined her as an invalid to bed; she disputed their diagnosis.[1] In the late nineteenth century, these medical arguments took on a new vitality with the latest findings in both biology and physics. By drawing on the First Law in physics, the limited-energy model of conservation theory posited that the body had finite amounts of energy for its expenditure. This theory became influential throughout the latter half of the century in its implications for what in physiology were the newly integrated healthy bodies and minds.[2]

The law of conservation was integral to Herbert Spencer's synthetic philosophy, and the relation of individuation and fertility, developed in an essay of 1852, was a cornerstone. In this early work, Spencer found that fertility would decrease with the progress of civilization and the application of mental powers it required, while the self-sufficiency and industry of the Englishman entailed a "further enlargement of the nervous centres, and a further decline of fertility."[3] But by the end of the century, the predicted decrease in fertility was colored problematically by numerous socioeconomic and cultural factors and was no longer seen as a positive effect of civilization. In his article "Psychology of the Sexes" (1873), Spencer argued for fundamental psychical differences between men and women, determined by adaptation to maternal and paternal duties, that result "from a somewhat earlier arrest of individual evolution in women than in men, necessitated by the reservation of vital power to meet the cost of reproduction."[4] The arrest of evolution in women is manifested mentally by a "perceptible falling short in those two faculties, intellectual and emotional, which are the latest products of human evolution—the power of abstract reasoning and that most abstract of the emotions, the sentiment of justice."[5] Although he admitted that it was unlikely that "those who wish to change fundamentally the political *status* of women will be influenced by the considerations above set forth on the comparative psychology of the sexes," a rather circular argument only reinforced the maxim that the formation of society is the outcome of underlying psychological patterns of essential difference in the sexes. He stated that "there may be acceptance of the general conclusion, that psychological truths underlie sociological truths,"[6] those "truths" being his own suppositions. He conceded, however, that the differences between men and women's mental abilities could be ameliorated: "[I]t is to be anticipated that the higher culture of women, carried on within such limits as shall not unduly tax the *physique* (and here, by higher culture, I do not mean mere language-learning and an extension of the detestable cramming-system at present in use), will in other ways reduce the contrast."[7]

For British psychologist Henry Maudsley and others of the profession, girls needed to allow their vital energies during adolescence generally, and during menstruation in particular, to be directed toward their reproductive functions; this could not happen if schooling and study became paramount. In his article "Sex in Mind and in Education" (1874), Maudsley claimed that there was "sex in mind as distinctly as there is sex in body,"[8] and on the basis of essential differences between men's and women's brains he argued that women should be denied formal educational opportunity. While Maudsley acknowledged that there are "extraordinary women" of "great mental power," they were anomalous, and only geniuses despite their mental culture, in his view. Unsurprisingly, on the basis of his findings in physiology, Maudsley recommended training for women in their natural life's work: maternity and childcare.

An antithetical relationship between the scholarly (or, in modern parlance, the "Girton Girl") and the maternal woman was endlessly rehearsed by cultural commentators in the decades following Maudsley's influential article—and in no more powerful formulation than in the belief that geniuses could not be found among the female sex because the matter of their bodies could not bear the strain of subsisting with such "demonic influences."[9] As sexologist Henry Havelock Ellis was to reaffirm on the question of genius in women in his autobiography in 1934, "women—though a few attain to the second rank of genius and many possess a streak of it—are entrusted with the preservation of the species, and that is an altogether concrete matter. Here are the central interests of women. We come down to the biological foundation of our world."[10] Havelock Ellis's commentary on women's genius in *Man and Woman* (1894) finds that the fields in which women had succeeded, such as fiction, did not demonstrate the creativity that greater art, such as poetry, demanded. Fiction "makes far less serious demands" than poetry; "[i]t is only when (as in the work of Flaubert) the novel almost becomes a poem, demanding great architectonic power, severe devotion to style, and complete self-restraint, that women have not come into competition with men."[11] The art of poetry "is very rare in women," and where it is written by them, like the female physiology that lacks the robust, muscular vigor and virility of the male body, women's poetry, Ellis suggested, "has a tendency to be rather thin or rather diffuse and formless."[12] Poetry, a literary form steeped in the classical and a privileged intellectual practice, generated specific discourse about the nature of genius in a manner in which the novel, with its relationship to popular (or "low") culture, did not.

The poet and materialist philosopher Constance C. W. Naden (1858–89) combined science with poetry in her career, seeing all disciplines as associated through a synthetic philosophy. Naden was born and brought up in Birmingham, where she studied botany at the Birmingham and Midlands Institute, then modern languages at Mason College of Science, Birmingham. Under the tutelage of Dr. Robert Lewins and the formative influence of his solipsistic, materialist philosophy, she published many articles on "hylo-idealism," a philosophy that was not merely atheistic but also strongly anti-theistic. Derived from Immanuel Kant's early thought in *Critique of Pure Reason*, it was based on the creative principle that each individual self-creates and determines its own universe and existence, and this was to be integral to her thinking. She published two collections of poetry: *Songs and Sonnets of Springtime* (1881) and *A Modern Apostle; The Elixir of Life; The Story of Clarice; and other Poems* (1887), which contains humorous poems on "Evolutional Erotics" and on the New Woman.

In 1887, when Naden had published her second volume of poetry, she was invited to contribute to *Woman's World* by Oscar Wilde, then editor.[13] This suggests that her public recognition was growing; her writing was also reviewed and republished in the feminist journals, which served to bring her work to a quite different audience. In that year, she traveled abroad with her friend Madeleine M. Daniell, visiting first Europe, then India for nine months. On her return, Naden lived and worked in London, where she died eighteen months later from problems relating to ovarian cysts.

In an essay on Naden's feminism, Marion Thain examines her revision of traditional Victorian poetics in which women figure as object in, or muse to, men's poetry. Thain describes how several of Naden's poems offer a close and critical analysis of this ideological division and how through her "renegotiation of traditional poetics" Naden enables the woman writer to "find her identity as subject and poet."[14] Naden's verse wittily dramatizes aspects of her beleaguered position in academic and creative production. Her focus on gender is at its most insightful when she combines it with a wry, humorous take on evolution, effectively expressed in colloquial rhythms that sometimes disarmingly present radical notions.

In the volume *A Modern Apostle*, Naden's poems are grouped under thematic titles; two such groups in particular, "Evolutional Erotics" and "The Lady Doctor," set an emancipated womanhood in the context of evolutionary science. Poems such as "Scientific Wooing" and "The Lady Doctor" evaluate the role of professional, scientific knowledge in both men and women's lives, presenting this as a difficult choice for women between marriage or career, love or learning. Rather than just advising women to make a moral choice between "busy toil" and "fond swain" and dedicate themselves to the public good or to family life, this split has its most complex expression in consideration of the difference education makes in women's identity and outlook and how it determines their selection in love.[15] "The New Orthodoxy" is a letter written by a discerning "sweet girl graduate," Amy, at Girton College. Amy discovers that her lover, Fred, at Oxford, now fails to embrace the scientific creed that they both formerly held. This causes her to hesitate about their marriage, comically underlining the modern factors in female sexual selection. "Advanced" women want men who share their deeply held political and intellectual convictions. An assertive Amy expresses her dismay to Fred that

> . . . having read in vain
> Huxley, Tyndall, Clifford, Bain,
> All the scientific train—
> You're a hardened sceptic!

> (*CPW,* 313)

Taking control of their courtship, Amy promises to continue to be Fred's betrothed on the condition that his belief in Darwinist science remains strong. This lively poem not only highlights how education is integral to a modern female self-identity but also, in particular, presents the assumption that evolutionary science can be a liberatory discourse to a spirited New Woman of autonomy, integrity, and agency. Many of Naden's poems in these groups participate in the new attempt by women poets to redefine middle-class feminine experience and the dilemmas that its ambitions created for such women.

Constance Naden's death, on Christmas Eve 1889, became an occasion for debate over female poetic genius and its relation to the body. In January 1890, the *British Medical Journal* carried a report from the Birmingham and Midland Counties Branch of the British Medical Association of an operation on a woman to remove dermoid cysts of her ovaries in London on 12 December

1889.[16] It stated that Mr. Lawson Tait exhibited the tumors removed from a patient, whom we can infer was Constance Naden.[17]

Posthumous remembrances of the poet in the publication of her collected works were inflected with the tropes of this psycho-physiological economy. Lady Burton remembered the thirty-one-year-old Naden as quintessentially feminine: "a soft, fair girl who, perhaps, would not have attracted much attention from a society of butterflies," yet—as if burdened with an intellect disproportionate to an infantile, female body—she was held to be "born to great things, but her brain was too big for her frail frame, and she died in Mayfair from illness contracted in India (as one might say) little more than a child, leaving the world a flower the less." Other commentators drew on common constructs of "genius" as a quintessentially masculine quality, even when it was displayed by a woman, describing her prose as "combining the woman's delicate intuition with the more masculine power of firm logic."[18] But these constructions had their most forceful expression in Herbert Spencer's commentary.

Herbert Spencer wrote to Robert Lewins, Naden's mentor, on the occasion of her death. His letter gives a reading of her sick body as the evidence of the economy of bodily energies, the wages of grappling after the "demonic influences" of genius. Singling her out as an almost unique Victorian female intellect, Spencer wrote of Naden that "[v]ery generally receptivity and originality are not associated but in her they appear to have been equally great. I can tell you of no woman save George Eliot in whom there has been this union of high philosophical capacity with extensive acquisition." Spencer argued elsewhere that comparisons made between the minds of men and women must distinguish between receptive faculty and originative faculty. "The two are scarcely commensurable; and the receptivity may, and frequently does, exist in high degree where there is but a low degree of originality or entire absence of it."[19] But with reference to Eliot he added, "While I say this, however, I cannot let pass the occasion for remarking that in her case, as in other cases, the mental powers so highly developed in a women are in some measure abnormal and involve a physiological cost which feminine organisation will not bear without injury more or less profound."[20]

If giving birth to ideas would jeopardize a woman's maternal generative powers, rendering her sterile, the implication is that in Naden's case a legitimate form of female authorship might have been the creation of a child. Jane Hume Clapperton quoted Spencer as saying, "Unquestionably her subtle intelligence would have done much in furtherance of rational thought, and her death has entailed a serious loss."[21] This intellectual power of Naden's is precisely what would have been such a forceful dynamic "in furtherance" of the woman's movement had she lived longer, and her feminism is what caused Spencer to temper his praise with misogynist feeling.

Spencer's misogyny was not met without resistance at a site where Naden's identity as a New Woman had been produced: the women's political press. Such feminist papers during the 1880s and '90s provided a public arena in which female and feminist communities and relationships were explored and expressed. It was characterized by feminists' investigations into, and contestations of, one another's ethical and cultural values about the most pertinent and controversial issues for women. The energy of women's commitment to these causes created a field for topical discussion that was an alternative to the ones formed not only by the male mainstream press, such as the *New Review* or *Saturday Review*, but also to other progressive periodicals. Additionally, they were a crucial ground on which to contest and combat the negative images of the New Woman that were constructed in the mainstream press.[22]

In an 1893 review of William Hughes's memoir of the poet, *Constance Naden, A Memoir* (1890), Naden's collection of essays, *Induction and Deduction* (1890), was earnestly recommended to readers of the feminist journal *Shafts* (1892—1900).[23] And in the *Women's Penny Paper* (1888–91), the socialist feminist Jane Hume Clapperton—author of *Scientific Meliorism and the Evolution of Happiness* (1885)—was instrumental in bringing Naden's work to the attention of its women readers. Along with a photographic portrait of Naden, her brand of Spencerian evolutionary thought in *Induction and Deduction* was, through Clapperton's series, introduced to a wider female audience. In her study of Naden's evolutionary ethics, Clapperton notes that although "Mr Spencer had spoken of family ties as pre-eminently favourable to the cultivation of sympathetic feeling,"[24] Naden had demonstrated the insufficiency of his account of the genesis of moral constraints in his *Data of Ethics* (1879), arguing that "these ties frequently help to narrow and specialise the sympathies setting bounds beyond which they cannot easily pass. This is often injurious to deep natures causing them to pour into some narrow channel an intensity of emotion which might have fertilised broad regions of life."[25] It is an objection with which the paper's readers would have been in agreement: middle-class women's limitation to work within the home meant that their feelings were focused on husband and children rather than the wider community, entailing their failure to fulfill their capacities for social, intellectual work and other greater public offices.

Defamation of Naden's name was fiercely contested in this arena. This began with a letter to the editor of the *Women's Penny Paper* in July 1890 from Naden's companion, Madeleine M. Daniell. The pair had traveled together extensively, and it is from such intimacy that Daniell writes. Against the academic weight of Spencer's discourse, Daniell writes from the countercultural space of "romantic friendship," which, in its promotion of women's networks, the *Women's Penny Paper* fostered and gave voice to. Daniell's communication carefully negotiates the cultural capital that Herbert Spencer's praise of Naden conferred on her posthumous reputation but seeks to defend Naden publicly against the connection that Spencer drew between her death and her intelligence.

Identifying herself as a friend of Miss Naden, Daniell carefully notes her and other friends' "gratitude for Spencer's favourable remarks made to Lewins in his valuable letter."[26] But despite her genuflections, she emphatically states, "Miss Naden's lamented death was not caused by her exceptional mental development. Her health up to eighteen months before her death was exceptionally good, and the disease which terminated fatally was one common alike to the dull and to the gifted."[27] Daniell disclaims any pathological associations about the female genius as a fevered, unbalanced artist. She suggests that Naden's intellectual energy, achievement, and patterns of working were in fact attributable to the "strength and healthiness of her brain,"[28] and she stresses the healthy pattern of working that Naden undertook: "She generally wrote for some hours every day, mostly on philosophy, and rose from work as cool and fresh as when she sat down."[29] Although Daniell allows that such intelligence may be "abnormal," she counters that fatal illness is not a "necessary consequence" in either sex. As well as remarking upon the good health of prominent women's rights campaigners "Augusta Ramsay (Mrs Montague Butler), Miss Fawcett and Miss Alford,"[30] Daniell capitalizes on the comparison, made by Spencer, of Naden with George Eliot, citing Eliot's age at her death—sixty-one—as a testimony to the lack of ill effect from intellectualism. Daniell attributes the headaches from which Eliot suffered—no worse than "a vast number of women who scarcely ever open a book"[31]—to the disparity between social expectations of gender and Eliot's marked, intellectual achievement and pleasure taken therein, and lastly to the poor understanding of health and sanitation of the period. Daniell's choice to publish such a letter in this feminist paper, I think, registers the importance of this cultural arena for struggle over women writers' lives and their posthumous reputations in relation to debates about the possibilities and limits of female intellectuality.

In a letter entitled "For Herbert Spencer to Answer" in the *Women's Penny Paper,* another reader posed a challenge. With less personal investment than Daniell in defending Naden's identity, she remarks sarcastically upon Spencer's ungenerous comments about Naden, which had been published in the paper:

> It is very hard on Mr Herbert Spencer and his theories, that Nature should have made the strange mistake of endowing women with brains, especially in such abnormal quantities as she has seen fit to confer on Miss Naden, and numbers of others who the world is beginning to hear. I should like to ask Mr Spencer what ought women to do, to whom Nature has been so unkind as to bestow them mental gifts rare in both sexes? And, when it is accompanied by superabundant physical health, is it still a freak of Nature's and to be deplored?[32]

The diffusion of women's poetry was not, then, confined to the restricted publication of volumes read by those who could afford the typically expensively bound volumes; their work could be read, the impact of their beliefs and status as poets be debated in the feminist press. Naden herself was, of course, painfully aware of the position of the female poet and philosopher; a reading of one of Naden's poems, "Poet and Botanist," will demonstrate her interrogatory resistance with regard to the relationship among death, knowledge and science, and art and nature.

This sonnet is a metacommentary on the role of the scientist-poet. Naden compares the role of each figure in relation to nature, questioning the legitimacy of methods of obtaining and presenting knowledge.[33] The sonnet suggests that our intervention in, knowledge of, and representation of nature is always subjective or incomplete; the bees are the only "innocent thieves" of its treasury. The supposedly objective botanist who seeks "the record of the bud" cannot tell the whole "truth" of nature by opening the bud before it has blossomed (*CPW,* 333). In a metaphor of male surgery operating on a female body "with his cruel knife and microscope" to "[r]eveal the embryo life, too early freed," the botanist's violent intervention prevents the plant from reaching its full cycle of growth, suggesting that there is no unmediated access to nature;

both findings are incomplete representations. The poet's treatment of nature can also be cruel: representing the flower to serve his own aims, he violates it: "crushing the tender leaves to work a spell," he "bids it tell / His thoughts, and render up its deepest hue / To tint his verse." Naden's suggestion that the language of nature is not transparent also highlights the way in which the female body and nature are treated as analogous in the contemporary culture of the text. Both are considered sites of alterity in the process of becoming objects of male knowledge through a subjection to a violence that controls as it "kills." Naden knew that masquerading within the systems of the biologist were patriarchal values veiled in scientific garb.

The death of another female poet in the same year, 1889, became the focus for a debate on the detrimental influence of education for women and more generally as a symptom of the stresses of modernity. Levy committed suicide, dying on 10 September 1889 by asphyxia from breathing in gas emitted by burning charcoal in a sealed room.

The link between female creativity and suicide that featured in Victorian culture throughout the century bound poetic femininity together with suffering.[34] The prevailing myth in the nineteenth century of Sappho's literary fame and subsequent suicide was re-embodied in the beautiful, acclaimed, but suicidal poetess of Madame De Staël's *Corinne, or: Italy* (1807), a French novel popular in Britain during the first half of the century. The reputation of the successful poet and literary society figure "L.E.L." (Letitia Elizabeth Landon, 1802–38) was informed by De Staël's novel and helped to increase her marketability, as Linda Shires has suggested.[35] L.E.L.'s strange, early death—thought to be suicide with prussic acid—contributed to a genealogy of female poet suicides (of which Levy's death would become part), that extends into the twentieth century to encompass Charlotte Mew's suicide in 1928 and Sylvia Plath's in 1963.

Linda Hunt Beckman argues that Levy's *A Minor Poet and Other Verse* (1884) is "groundbreaking—different from the work of nearly all other Victorian women poets—in that many of its poems . . . show people grappling with life in a world that lacks justice and meaning."[36] Levy's engagement with contemporary scientific debate and thinkers,[37] including the increasing reaction to the ideological implications of evolutionary meliorism, is apparent in the philosophical pessimism of her writing. The suicidal poet of "A Minor Poet"[38]— whose sex is not named—tells how a friend, on discovering the poet's attempt at suicide, gives the poet

> . . . a lecture all compact
> Of neatest, newest phrases, freshly culled
> From works of newest culture.

These modern cultural censures express belief in the "common good"; for

> "The world's great harmonies"; "must be content
> With knowing God works all things for the best,
> And nature never stumbles." Then again
> "The common good," and still "the common, good."

The friend's emphasis on "the common good" antagonizes the speaker; moralistic and religious explanations are rejected by the "minor poet," who wishes to voice his individually and socially determined motives and agency in the suicidal act. Levy's treatment of the subject in her poetry can be compared to fin-de-siècle explanations of the causes of suicide. To enable a better understanding of the specific discourse of the relationship between women's education and death that was spun around the event of the poet's suicide, I look briefly at the connections that were being made between suicide and modernity in pessimistic forecasts for society's degeneration.

For some of her contemporaries, Levy's "racial" and gender identity—her Jewishness and her femininity as an educated female poet—would offer grounds for an explanation of the degeneracy of her suicide. In an essay on Levy's feminism and semitic discourse, Emma Francis has described how the existing set of ideas about Jewish mental "degeneracy" drew upon the explanations of urban habitation and racial interbreeding that were being offered by anthropologists and psychiatric theorists in the 1880s.[39] Francis cites Sander Gilman's observation that with the development of statistical "racial sciences" beginning in the mid-nineteenth century, the long-held cultural assumption that Jews were prone to nervous illness became reinforced, and "[b]y the 1880s the linkage of the Jew with psychopathology was a given in anthropological circles."[40] Levy explored these ideas in essays published in the *Jewish Chronicle* in 1886, in which she discussed various issues related to Anglo-Jewish identities and, Francis argues, at points subscribed to the explanations of anthropological theorists. In the last essay of the series, "Jewish Children," Levy suggested that "[m]ental precocity . . . may nearly always be accepted as the sign of a highly developed nervous organisation. And the Jewish child, descendant of many city-bred ancestors . . . is apt to be a very complicated little bundle of nerves indeed."[41] She describes an essentially urban Jew prone to mental and nervous diseases because of the stresses of city living and exacerbated by generations of inheritance; the experience of the Jewish male protagonist of her short story "Cohen of Trinity" (1889), who fails to assimilate into gentile Cambridge society and commits suicide, also seems to participate in this thinking.

John Stokes's examination of literary and other cultural representations of suicide in the 1890s finds that the perceived increase in rates of suicide was understood and represented by many in the press as a response to the stresses of modernity and, in part, its shifting gender roles. By 1895, when Thomas Hardy published *Jude the Obscure*, this perception was well established. The act of the prematurely aged Little Father Time's killing of his siblings and himself "because we are too menny [*sic*]" is in part a response to the strain to which his parents, Jude and Sue, succumbed as a result of their social ostracism. Stokes cites the prevalence of the belief that the suicide rate was proportionate to the increase in rising levels of education—significantly, a belief based on the notion of an intellectual and philosophically informed pessimism rather than a direct correlation between learning and physical or mental damage. A leading study (Henry Morselli's *Suicide: An Essay on Comparative Moral Statistics* [1879], translated into English in 1881) could only suggest that "[s]uicide is an effect of the struggle for existence and of human selection, which works according to the laws of evolution among civilised people"[42]—a generalized conclusion that echoed modern Darwinian narratives, without any hard scientific analysis. Like other social scientific studies of the time, its method was to take the suicidal individual as an index of degeneration and frame that individual's action as evidence of his or her unfitness to live. In Levy's poem "The Minor Poet," the moralistic philosophical reprimands made by the speaker against her friend's thoughts of suicide, and her glib reassurance that all is well in the world—"God works all things for the best, / And nature never stumbles"—are held to be inadequate by the "minor poet." A belief in divine order or, indeed, evolutionary meliorism—"nature never stumbles"—is not available to the suicidal figure.

Edmund Kerchever Chambers's *Westminster Review* article "Poetry and Pessimism" of 1892 is sympathetic to Levy and her poetry.[43] He finds in her work a pessimism characteristic of the post-Darwinian age and indicative of the problems of social evolution at this period: "[F]ifty years of individualism, of free thought, and unrestricted competition, have bitten their mark deep into our civilisation. The suffering which inevitably accompanies the struggle for existence is no less, but greater, for organisms upon a high level of self-consciousness."[44] The trajectory of Levy's melancholy, which culminates in her suicide, is read as an evolutionary outcome from the modern socioeconomic environment of laissez-faire capitalism, destructive to the too highly evolved sensibilities of humanity—in particular, to intellectuals with their individual characteristics of artistic temperament. Chambers reads melancholy in Levy's photographic portrait and notes that it is "scarcely fantastic to suggest that Leonardo's ironically named *La Gioconda*, an alien to our great-grandmothers, is curiously at home among the women of our own generation."[45] A Renaissance scholar, Chambers gives a nod in his analysis toward Walter Pater's treatment of *La Gioconda* in his infamous aestheticist work *The Renaissance: Studies in Art and Poetry* (1869; 1873). In the Mona Lisa, Pater finds a dark, erotic, and gothic beauty in a composite soul "with all its maladies,"[46] a species apart from the healthy and wholesome Victorian maiden, and an aesthetic that notoriously celebrated paganism and Hellenism and was to become a keynote of the decadence movement.

Any association of Levy's melancholic prose with aestheticism is clearly repudiated by Ellen Darwin, a friend of Levy's. In an article in the *Cambridge Review* in 1890, she stated, "I do not think that anyone could confuse [Levy's] poetry with the conventional poetry of cultivated weariness and despair. Her tone indeed is always sad . . . but it is not sad because she feels that the world is empty."[47] Others of the New Woman movement were anxious to disassociate the identity of New Woman literary production from the "impurity" of the French-influenced and sexually charged work of the decadents. In her reading, Darwin warily situates Levy's passionate and tragic poetry in a different field from the morbid and stylized pessimism of the decadents in order to stress its authentic relationship to Levy's lived experience.

Misinformation and conjecture about Levy's life and health circulated after her death. In a notice of Levy's death on 21 September 1889, *The Lady's Pictorial* drew upon a dichotomy of mental strength with its counterpart in physical weakness to describe her death: "With mental power to attack the problems of the age, she lacked in a pitiable degree the bodily vigour to sustain her in [her] fight. . . . [A]ll that was clear to her few friends was that her health was rapidly growing worse. . . . [W]ith failing sight and growing deafness, Miss Levy suffered . . . intensely."[48] Clementina Black—feminist campaigner, journalist, and close friend of Levy's—wrote to the *Athenaeum* to counter reports made against Levy in respect of her suicide, including the remarks that she had been shunned in the Jewish community for her novel *Reuben Sachs* (1888). The novel had been criticized and satirized for its negative portrayals of the Jewish community—including vulgarity and tribalism—in the *Jewish World* and *Jewish Standard*, although not by the *Jewish Chronicle*.[49] Black explains that "[i]t is not true that she ever left her father's house other than on visits to friends or holiday journeys; nor that she suffered from failing eyesight. . . . She did suffer for several years from slight deafness and from fits of extreme depression, the result not of unhappy circumstances or of unkind treatment, but, as those believe who knew her best, her lack of physical robustness and the exhaustion produced by strenuous brain work."[50] Biographical evidence suggests that Levy suffered from extreme depression, at a time when clinical depression was not well understood; her letters speak of "the blues," of being "profoundly miserable," and of "the great devil who lyeth ever in wait in the recesses of [her] heart."[51] Bouts of such misery were compounded by her growing deafness, which alienated her from those around her. Black chose, in the context of the conservative *Athenaeum*, to defend Levy as properly feminine in never leaving the patriarchal home. This claim—which clearly contradicts the accounts by Levy and others describing her full and active social and intellectual life and network both inside and outside the family—colors her with a womanliness, signaling her intellectual identity as one fostered outside the damaging, public arena. Beckman suggests that Black, although herself a suffragist and trade union activist and sociable in London literary and political circles, needed to portray Levy as bound to the domestic sphere as "damage control" to preserve Levy's literary reputation and mitigate her family's suffering.[52] It is also apparent that despite her feminism, Black drew on the myth of the young woman having a bodily frailty unequal to the labors required of intellectual and artistic achievement, a myth that had surrounded the death of Naden. Black chose to depict Levy's literary identity in this culturally recognizable formula despite its being dangerously appropriable by misogynists to cite in their battle against women's higher education.

In the backlash to the New Woman's entry into higher education and the professions, the law of the conservation of energy was pressed into service in medico-scientific discourses to punish the female who—like Constance Naden's Girton Girl, Amy—overreached herself in a project for self-development that might delay or even exclude marriage altogether, with the threat of sterility, illness, and even death. The effects of strenuous "brain work" on the feminine mind and physique, which Spencer had so eloquently theorized, was a favorite hobbyhorse of the journalist, popular scientific writer, and novelist Grant Allen; for him, Levy's suicide made her a fit target for abuse of the higher education of women, and he demeaned her status as a poet in the light of the nature of her death.

Grant Allen befriended Levy when she had become celebrated. The Allens feature in several visits during the first fortnight of May 1889. According to her diary, Levy spent the summer of that year in a cottage in Dorking, where she "spent some time with the novelist Grant Allen and his family at their cottage nearby." Levy's diary records that after dinner the Allens and their guests "[d]iscussed the Woman Question," noting that "GA thinks marriage not permanent."[53]

Despite his friendly acquaintance with Levy, Allen's essay "The Girl of the Future" of the following year was hardly flattering. By 1888—in a *volte-face*—Allen had come to endorse the ethics of selective reproduction proposed by the leading proponent of eugenics, Karl Pearson, a socialist and professor of applied mathematics at University College London. In an essay of 1888 entitled "Woman and Labour," Pearson found that the answer to the Woman Problem lay not in the "equality of opportunity" demanded by the women's movement but in "special protection, in the socialisation of the State."[54] Women would be supported by the state to undertake their true vocation: motherhood. And in "The Woman's Question," Pearson explained that under socialism, women (already conditioned to subjection to men) would learn not to chafe against their subjection to "the restraints demanded by social welfare," as it would be for the good of "race" progress and imperial supremacy.[55] Allen pursued these values and ideas in "The Girl of the Future." From a position responding to the growing public interest in, and anxiety about, ensuring "racial" progress through national fitness, Allen examined the relationship of the marriage problem to an imperial race, finding proper citizenship for women not in their higher education and the vote but in traditional domestic roles: "[T]he race that keeps up the efficiency of its nursing mothers will win in the long run, though none of its girls can read a line of Lucian."[56]

The radical and popular New Woman novelists "Miss Olive Schreiner and Mrs Mona Caird" are singled out for criticism in the first paragraph, as "women who lightly meddle with these high matters": they are viewed as dilettantes in the matter of the "Sex Problem" because of their concern for women's rights within marriage, rather than the "efficiency of the children to be begotten."[57] The South African Schreiner had been a friend of Levy's and had dealt with the disappointments of women's lives and a doomed "free love union" in her novel *The Story of an African Farm* (1883). Caird's radical cultural relativism was powerfully voiced in her *Westminster Review* article "Marriage," in which she attacked the institution and had precipitated an energetic debate on the subject "Is Marriage A Failure?" in the pages of the *Daily Telegraph* in 1888; one of her novels, *The Daughters of Danaus* (1894), was to explore the career of a woman genius thwarted by family expectations and demands. But when addressing Levy's identity as a New Woman in this article, Allen situated her not, like Caird or Schreiner, as a critic of marriage (which her work certainly expressed, for example, with satirical boldness in "A Ballad of Religion and Marriage") but through reference to her education. He explicitly linked Levy's death to the effects of a university education and the woman's movement that had inaugurated it, rather than to her own particular feminist agenda.

Levy, the first Jewish woman to enter Newnham College, Cambridge, had attended from 1879 until 1881; while undertaking some general studies, she also specialized in languages. She completed her second year without taking her final exams; thus, she left the university some eight years before her suicide. In Allen's article, facetious metaphors link Levy's suicide firmly to her university education: "A few hundred pallid little Amy Levys sacrificed on the way are as nothing before the face of our fashionable Juggernaut. Newnham has slain its thousands, and Girton its tens of thousands; the dark places of the earth are full of cruelty."[58] In this article, the Cambridge colleges are portrayed as crushing the life and vitality out of girls by cramming them with maths and Greek, which, according to Allen, are inappropriate subjects for women, whose primary "instruction" should be in motherhood and childbearing, making them subject to male control of their bodies. They should be filled with babies, not facts. He bemoans the way in which universities are "stuffing girls with Sophocles . . . till they are as flat as pancakes and as dry as broomsticks,"[59] analogies that warn of the sterility and sexlessness to befall the (female) classics scholar. The crude but clear triangulated connection made between female education, sexual sterility, and death is a disturbing one.

The feminist papers reacted angrily. One article in the *Women's Penny Paper* responds to "The Girl of the Future" by objecting to the way in which Allen undermined the woman's movement and its figureheads (including Levy) by using science—which should be its ally—to criticize it:

The growth of Positive Science and the Elevation of Women are modern movements which have made great progress. Recently, however these movements have been represented as antagonistic to each other. Grant Allen in the name of Science, attacks the woman movement in two articles —"Plain Words on the Woman Question" and "The Girl of the Future." ...The ghost of poor Amy Levy is invoked with great effect till one recalls such names as Keats or "poor Chatterton," for neither of whom Girton can be held responsible. One suspects that the *scientific imagination,* rather than "scientific research" inspires the lament that Girton has killed her thousands but Newnham her tens of thousands![60]

Among a number of elegies,[61] Allen made an even more personal attack on Levy in his poem "For Amy Levy's Urn,"[62] which was republished in his only poetry collection, *The Lower Slopes.* (Reproduced in full below.) He summons the dead woman to life, only to lay opprobrium upon her ambitions and achievements:

> This bitter age that pits our maids with men
> Wore out her woman's heart before its time:
> Too wan and pale,
> She strove to scale
> The icy peaks of unimagined rhyme
> There, worlds broke sunless on her frighted ken;
> The mountain air struck chill on her frail breath:
> Fainting she fell, all weary with her climb
> And kissed the soft, sweet lips of pitying death.[63]

In "[t]his bitter age" in which women were claiming access to education, the job market, and the franchise, the competition could not be on equal terms; Allen describes the pitting of "maids with men," a phrase that makes women diminutive and childlike. Allen continued to revere Herbert Spencer long after his theories in *First Principles* (1862) had been thoroughly disputed; the metaphors employed here collapse distinctions between intellectual and physical weakness and paucity, putting into play the energy conservation discourses of the Spencerian physiological divisions of labor. "[H]er woman's heart" takes on the biological dimensions of a gendered physiology, rather than emotional or spiritual ones, if Levy's identity is constructed in accordance with Spencer's model. "Fainting" and "weary," she is imagined as bodily frail, paying a physical toll for mental effort: intellectual energy expenditure is fatal to women's weaker constitutions.

In this elegy, poetry is imagined as an inhospitable terrain, not one where women will achieve intellectual enlightenment: "worlds broke sunless." The mountain motif echoes the Mount Helicon of the book's title, identifying Levy as a kindred minor poet skirting the lower slopes of poetic inspiration; yet the mountain also traditionally epitomizes the male sublime. Such imagery suggests that Levy is unable to approach the supreme sublime in her artistic production and its heights of cultural and symbolic capital. The embrace with death is a compassionate image but also suggestive of acquiescence and passivity rather than a heroic or noble image of resistance. In this poem, Allen adopts the position of custodian of poetic form in attacking Levy in her own form to defend his art and his interest, that of securing poetry for male writers and readers.

Allen's criticism may accord with popular conceptions of a "healthy" and normative mode in poetry for female poets. Critics trace a shift from the treatment of social concerns in political poetics earlier in the century toward the development of an emotional register of affective poetry by women.[64] Circumscribed within the modes of expressive and affective poetry that produced appropriately feminine registers of personal feeling and sentiment, women's writing was criticized when it departed from these modes.[65] As Isobel Armstrong has argued, women poets were caught in a double bind: they were expected to stay in the "proper" province of affect yet were simultaneously damned for it because affect was an inferior mode that could not match the symbolic prestige of "serious" poetry. Levy's poetry breaks with the expressive tradition that Armstrong identifies in Victorian women's poetry, based in the assumption that poets should express emotions rather than repress them, toward a characteristic release, and overflow, of feeling.[66] To achieve such release in poetry was considered healthy, Armstrong argues, but hidden feeling that resisted expression could have pathological consequences. Thus, the metaphors of an expressive aesthetic are given "both a negative or pathological and a positive or 'healthy' signification, a hysterical and a wholesome aspect, often implicitly gendered respectively as 'feminine' and 'masculine.'"[67]

Grant Allen's rebuttal, then, is built on a poetic orthodoxy of earlier models of femininity and creativity that suggests that Levy ought to have reserved her breath for the affective female poetry of sentiment and emotion and not attempted the philosophical, as in "A Minor Poet," discussed above. A failure to achieve poetic expression within the affective aesthetic, in which the trope of the breath is integral to the "airs" or songs of the poet, could be figured as the last "frail breath" of a pathologized femininity.

The effect of Allen's elegy is a violent one: it is ultimately to incorporate Levy into a male poetics. If, as Elizabeth Bronfen argues, the cultural representation of a dead woman, as a quintessential site of alterity, functions for psychic processes as a means of reassuring the (male) observer by projecting anxieties onto this "other,"[68] then in the case of Allen, visiting the dead female body through the elegy is a means of lending stability and weight to his own—and, by extension, male—literary and cultural identity. Her body would always already be reworked into the topos of degeneration. Levy's body is "read" through other texts about degeneration and female weakness; that is, patriarchy still rewrites her body into the cultural order. She falls victim to existing cultural conventions and discourses and is replaced by the respective texts of other writers who "kill" the body-text again with their own narratives about femininity. Levy's act of suicide thus both repeats and resists the discursive formations from which it is produced and against which it speaks.

By examining the discourses of biology, sex, and gender surrounding the deaths of Levy and Naden—two very different, young women poets who died in the same year, 1889—we can see that the appropriation of cultural power by these poets had its antithesis in the ways in which the orthodox male scientific establishment sought to undermine New Women for their feminism, just as they claimed an active role in the discussion and dissemination of scientific theories and their implications. For Constance Naden in particular, women's engagement with the implications of evolutionary science, an explicitly modern idiom, was necessary for forging new feminine identities. Naden's poems appropriate and subvert the established cultural dictates; they convey the impact of scientific progress in women's lives and in women's choices as they moved into masculine spheres. Amy Levy's poetry, in contrast, provides a far more rich and complex discussion of femininity and sexual politics. Her writing engages with numerous contemporary scientific ideas, perhaps most significantly and problematically, for today's feminist critic, those about race, degeneracy, and her own Jewish identity, which are perilously entangled with contemporary antisemitic anthropological accounts of Jewishness. The poetry of Naden, Levy, and other women had a broader impact through its reception and dissemination in the feminist press, and the women's papers clearly formed a significant site for the consolidation of the female poet as a New Woman identity, as well as the social, intellectual, and romantic networks in which these women moved. In this arena, both Levy and Naden were defended in discussions that recognized and confirmed their importance as figures for the debate about women's relation to power.

Knowledge—its object and acquisition (particularly scientific knowledge in this culture)—has, George Levine notes, long been equated with death in a cultural configuration in which death is the wages of knowledge.[69] But the discursive formations of this relationship produced by theorists of modern science had a peculiarly gendered aspect regarding the morality of knowledge for women. Critics saw women's participation in high culture as directly damaging both their maternal functions and their mental health. Yet women's protests were not rendered ineffective simply because such protests were turned against them through the supposedly incontrovertible evidence of their bodies. Rather, these poems continued to "speak" after the death of the writer, generating a base of support in their circulation and debate.

Notes

1. See Christine Battersby, *Gender and Genius: Towards a Feminist Aesthetic* (London: Women's Press, 1989).

2. For further discussion, see Cynthia Eagle Russett, *Sexual Science: The Victorian Construction of Womanhood* (Cambridge, MA: Harvard University Press, 1991), 104–29.

3. Herbert Spencer, "A Theory of Population Deduced from the General Law of Animal Fertility," *Westminster Review* 57, no. 263 (1852): 468–501, quotation on 499.

4. Herbert Spencer, "Psychology of the Sexes," *Popular Science Monthly* (1873): 30–38, quotation on 32.

5. Ibid., 32.

6. Ibid., 38.

7. Ibid., 36.

8. Henry Maudsley, "Sex in Mind and in Education," *Fortnightly Review* 21 (1874): 466–83.

9. Henry H. Ellis, *My Confessional: Questions of Our Day* (London: John Lane, 1934), 172.

10. Ibid.

11. H. Havelock Ellis, *Man and Woman* (1894), 371, quoted in Flavia Alaya, "Victorian Science and the 'Genius' of Woman," *Journal of the History of Ideas* 34 (1977): 261–80 (quotation on 274).

12. Ellis quoted in Alaya, "Victorian Science," 274.

13. See Josephine M. Guy, "Self-Plagiarism, Creativity and Craftsmanship in Oscar Wilde," *English Literature in Transition* 41, no. 1 (1998): 6–23.

14. Marion Thain, "Love's Mirror: Constance Naden and Reflections on a Feminist Poetics," *English Literature in Transition* 41, no. 1 (1998): 25–41, quotations on 27.

15. Constance Naden, *The Complete Poetical Works of Constance Naden* (London: Bickers and Son, 1894), 85. Subsequent references to this edition are given parenthetically in the text as *CPW*.

16. The report stated that "the operation had been delayed almost beyond hope of recovery. It was as difficult as anything of the kind could be, but Mr Tait was glad to say the patient was making an admirable recovery." "Reports of Societies," *British Medical Journal* 1, no. 1515 (11 January 1890): 76–81, quotation on 80.

17. James R. Moore has recorded that Tait, who had a highly successful record in ovariotomy, was Naden's surgeon in London. See James R. Moore, "The Erotics of Evolution: Naden and Reflection on a Feminist Poetics," in *One Culture: Essays in Science and Literature,* ed. George Levine, 225–57 (Madison: University of Wisconsin Press, 1987).

18. Quotations in this paragraph are from C. Lloyd Morgan, dean of University College Bristol, *The Complete Poetical Works of Constance Naden* (1894), 8.

19. Spencer, "Psychology of the Sexes," 31.

20. Cited by Phillip E. Smith and Susan Harris in "Brief Articles and Notes: Constance Naden: Late Victorian Feminist Poet and Philosopher," *Victorian Poetry* 15 (1977): 367–70.

21. Jane Hume Clapperton, *"Induction and Deduction," Women's Penny Paper* (2 August 1890), 488.

22. See Michelle Elizabeth Tusan, "Inventing the New Woman: Print Culture and Identity Politics during the Fin de Siècle," *Victorian Periodicals Review* 31, no. 2 (Summer 1998): 169–82.

23. Review of Hughes's *Constance Naden, A Memoir, Shafts* (March 1893), 12.

24. Clapperton, *"Induction and Deduction."*

25. Ibid.

26. Madeleine M. Daniell, letter, *Women's Penny Paper,* 5 July 1890, 440.

27. Ibid.

28. Ibid.

29. Ibid.

30. Ibid.

31. Ibid.

32. "For Herbert Spencer to Answer," *Women's Penny Paper,* 26 July 1890, 475.

33. Women were better represented as practitioners in botany than in other sciences during the nineteenth century. Botany was deemed more suitable for women than were other biological disciplines, such as medicine, because it did not involve visceral contact with the human body; plant life did not offer the threat of forbidden sexual knowledge entailed in human anatomical studies.

34. Angela Leighton argues that there were inherent contradictions in this cultural ideal; the suicide ultimately denied the self and was structured as a response to male criticism or rejection but was also, she suggests, a narrative of triumphant self-expression and a dialogue between women. Angela Leighton, *Victorian Women Poets: Writing against the Heart* (Brighton: Harvester Wheatsheaf, 1992).

35. Linda Shires, "Victorian Women's Poetry," *Victorian Literature and Culture* 27, no. 2 (1999): 601–9, esp. 608.

36. Linda Hunt Beckman, *Amy Levy: Her Life and Letters* (Athens: Ohio University Press, 2000), 102.

37. Christine Pullen writes at length about Levy's relationship with a discussion club and its re-formation by Karl Pearson as the Men and Women's Club, which Levy was not invited to attend. Pullen, "Amy Levy: Her Life, Her Poetry and the Era of the New Woman," PhD diss., Kingston University, 2000. Judith Walkowitz suggests that part of the reason for the disbanding of the club was attributable to Pearson's frustrations with the level of debate on scientific matters among women who were not university educated. Walkowitz, *City of Dreadful Delight: Narratives of Sexual Danger in Late-Victorian London* (London: Virago, 1992), 164.

38. Amy Levy, *A Minor Poet and Other Verse* (1884), reproduced in *Victorian Women Poets: An Anthology*, ed. Angela Leighton and Margaret Reynolds (Oxford: Blackwell, 1995), 598.

39. See Emma Francis, "Amy Levy: Contradictions?—Feminism and Semitic Discourse," in *Women's Poetry, Late Romantic to Late Victorian: Gender and Genre, 1830–1900*, ed. Isobel Armstrong and Virginia Blain (London: Macmillan, 1999), 183–204.

40. Ibid., 188.

41. Amy Levy, "Jewish Children," *Jewish Chronicle*, 5 November 1886, 8.

42. Henry Morselli, *Suicide: An Essay on Comparative Moral Statistics* (London: Kegan Paul, 1881), 354; see also John Stokes, *In the Nineties* (Hemel Hempstead, UK: Harvester Wheatsheaf, 1989).

43. Edmund Kerchever Chambers, "Poetry and Pessimism," *Westminster Review* 138 (1892): 366–76.

44. Ibid., 367.

45. Ibid., 368.

46. Walter Pater, *The Renaissance: Studies in Art and Poetry* (1873; 2nd ed., 1877; Oxford: Oxford University Press, 1988), 80.

47. Ellen Darwin, "The Poems of AL," *Cambridge Review*, 23 January 1890, 158.

48. Obituary, *Lady's Pictorial*, 21 September 1889, 358.

49. See *Jewish Chronicle*, 25 January 1889, 11; *Jewish Chronicle*, 3 May 1889, 12; "The Deterioration of the Jewess," *Jewish World*, 22 February 1889, 5. See also Marshallik [Israel Zangwill], Morour and Charouseth, *Jewish Standard*, 1 March 1889, 9–10.

50. Clementina Black, obituary, *Athenaeum* no. 3232 (5 October 1889): 457.

51. Amy Levy, letters cited in Beckman, *Amy Levy*, 218, 238, 245.

52. Beckman, *Amy Levy*, 3.

53. Ibid., 177.

54. Karl Pearson, "Woman and Labour," *Fortnightly Review* (1888): 561–77, quotation on 569.

55. "She has learnt self-control in the past by subjecting her will to his, so in the future she may be able to submit her liberty to the restraints demanded by social welfare, and to submit to the conditions imposed by race-permanence." Karl Pearson, "The Woman's Question," in Pearson, *The Ethic of Freethought* (London: Adam and Charles Black, 1888), 394.

56. Grant Allen, "The Girl of the Future," *Universal Review* 7 (May 1890): 49–64.

57. Ibid., 49.

58. Ibid., 56.

59. Ibid., 57.

60. "Science and Woman," *Women's Penny Paper*, 30 August 1890, 530.

61. See, for example, Dollie Maitland Radford's husband, Ernest Radford, "An Inscription for an Urn," *Pall Mall Gazette*, 24 September 1889, 2; Vernon Lee's half brother, Eugene Lee Hamilton, "Fumes of Charcoal," in *Sonnets of the Wingless Hours* (London: Elliott Stock, 1894). See Melvyn New, ed., *The Complete Novels and Selected Writings of Amy Levy* (Gainesville: University Press of Florida, 1993), 554–55.

62. Cremation was an unusual choice for a Jewish burial at this time, as a report of Levy's death in the *New York Times* would suggest: "At her own request she was cremated in Woking, being the second of her religion thus treated at this great crematory. A small oak chest containing her ashes was then buried in a Jewish cemetery." *New York Times*, 22 September 1889, 1. Christine Pullen suggests that Levy was the first Jewish woman to be cremated in the United Kingdom. See Pullen, "Amy Levy," 182.

63. Grant Allen, *The Lower Slopes: Reminiscences of Excursions Round the Base of Helicon, Undertaken for the Most Part in Early Manhood* (London: Elkin Matthews and John Lane at Bodley Head, 1894), 21.

64. Isobel Armstrong argues that "by the time of *Aurora Leigh*, 1856, factory and slave poems had ceased to do the work of politics and did the work of the heart instead." See Armstrong, "'Msrepresentation': Codes of Affect and Politics in Nineteenth-Century Women's Poetry," in *Women's Poetry: Late Romantic to Late Victorian*, ed. Isobel Armstrong and Virginia Blain (Basingstoke: Macmillan, 1999), 3–32, esp. 7.

65. For example, see Lynda M. Ely's discussion of the career of A. Mary F. Robinson in Ely, "'Not a Song to Sell': Re-Presenting 'Mary F. Robinson,'" *Victorian Poetry* (2000): 94–108. Ely contextualizes the conditions of literary production for contemporary poet Mary Robinson, implicating her in "the dilemma of many other women writers of the Victorian period: her poetry is caught up in and relegated to the 'chords of emotion' mentioned by Ladislaw, trapped in the precincts of 'feeling' or sentimentalism, and thus never makes the transformation to 'knowledge' key to the production of serious (read male–authored) poetry" (99).

66. See Isobel Armstrong, "Women's Poetry—An Expressive Tradition?" in *Victorian Women Poets: A Critical Reader*, ed. Angela Leighton (Oxford: Blackwell, 1996), 245–76.

67. Ibid., 266.

68. Elizabeth Bronfen, *Over Her Dead Body: Death, Femininity and the Aesthetic* (Manchester: Manchester University Press, 1992).

69. See George Levine, "Objectivity and Death," *Victorian Literature and Culture* 20, no. 1 (1992): 273–91.

Afterword

———

Meri-Jane Rochelson

I FIRST came across Amy Levy while doing research on Israel Zangwill for a master's essay in 1976. Intrigued by this writer whose ordinary Jewish name might have belonged to one of my high school classmates, I searched the University of Chicago stacks for a copy of *Reuben Sachs* or a collection of her poems. Finding nothing, I was at first a bit surprised, then perturbed, and then resigned. At Chicago, one hardly ever used interlibrary loan: if it was not in the Regenstein Library, then it was not worth looking at. Amy Levy must have been, sadly, a minor writer, not very good even if she had influenced Zangwill. In 1976, Elaine Showalter still had not published *A Literature of Their Own;* Sandra Gilbert and Susan Gubar were still working on *The Madwoman in the Attic.* "Jewish literary criticism" more often than not was engaged in examining representations of Jews in the works of mainstream (mostly male) British and American writers. When, in the middle 1980s, I finally ordered a copy of *Reuben Sachs* from the interlibrary loan office at the university where I teach, what arrived was a photocopy of the novel that had been donated to Emory University by Linda Gertner Zatlin; no doubt it was the copy from which she had worked in producing her formative survey *The Nineteenth-Century Anglo-Jewish Novel*, published in 1981. The work of recovery that began with these studies and others—which led to important editions of Levy's work by Melvyn New (1993) and Susan David Bernstein (2006), the fine biography by Linda Hunt Beckman (2000), numerous articles on Levy's prose and poetry, and the collection of essays at hand—startles us with the recognition of what would have been lost had this revision and expansion of literary history not taken place.

Only four decades ago, the British literature considered worth reading and, perhaps more importantly, considered worth teaching was conceptualized as coming from a male, Christian tradition; the experience worth examining through fiction, poetry, and drama was the experience of Christian men with longstanding roots in the United Kingdom—or, as in the ambiguous cases of Henry James, T. S. Eliot, and Joseph Conrad, of Christian men who could effectively simulate such roots. The situation in America was not much different, with the exception that twentieth-century Jewish literature by men had gained recognition in the works of Philip Roth, Saul Bellow, Bernard Malamud, and Joseph Heller. Only recently have nineteenth-century poets and fiction writers such as Emma Lazarus, Mary Antin, and Anzia Yezierska been given their due (along with Abraham Cahan, whose stories of turn-of-the-century Jewish immigrant culture had for years been neglected) and the significance of Jewishness recognized in the work of such contemporary women authors as Erica Jong, Rebecca Goldstein, Allegra Goodman, and Dara Horn and, in Britain, Elaine Feinstein, Eva Figes, and Ruth Prawer Jhabvala, among many others writing in English in the twentieth century and today. But this recognition is a relatively new development. Amy Levy, as woman and Jew, was doubly marginalized in British literary studies until the late twentieth century, when scholars who saw the significance of marginal writers, particularly in the long-overlooked late Victorian era, ensured that her work was discussed, analyzed, and reintroduced to readers. Just pulling two books off my shelf, I find eleven of Levy's poems and one of her essays reprinted in *The Broadview Anthology of Victorian Poetry and Poetic Theory* (1999) and her poetry considered in two essays in

The Cambridge Companion to Victorian Poetry (2000). Today Amy Levy, the outsider, is part of the mainstream.

The present volume draws on the fact that Levy's work is now available to a wide range of readers and considered integral to Victorian studies, even as it acknowledges the ways in which her centrality resides in her marginal position. Particularly compelling is the way we are invited to view Levy as not peripheral but representative of young women intellectuals and writers of her day. That is not to say that her story is either commonplace or simplistically paradigmatic; indeed, what one discovers in these essays is a figure who was Jewish and wrote about Jewish life and letters but did not see herself as a spokesperson for the Jews, a woman whose education at Newnham and love of the urban scene gave her much in common with other independent women of her day but whose writings—in part because of her Jewishness and in part simply through her individual uniqueness—reveal a distinctive voice and a distinctive take on issues of feminism, fame, and racial and ethnic marginality. By situating Levy among New Woman writers, lesbian writers, London poets, socialist authors, and Jewish humorists, today's critics illuminate Levy's writing and her place in literary history by implicitly validating categories that were once considered marginal if considered at all; at the same time, by examining her work (as in this volume) in the contexts of Platonic philosophy, Christianity, and historical re-creations of classical Greek narratives, they affirm her writing's connection to the most established literary reference points and, at the same time, its transcendence of conventional expectations. Our current understanding of depression allows us to slash and discard the veil of the "tragic poetess" as, appropriately, Levy's suicide becomes a frustrating and dismaying endpoint rather than a lens through which to view her work. Her essays, stories, novels, and poems display her as a woman of wit and strong conviction, whose sensitivity to human and specifically female tragedy derived from shrewd observation of life, society, and history and was not unmixed with a sense of humor, perhaps that same bittersweet "Jewish humour" which she praised in an article for the *Jewish Chronicle* in 1886.

Similarly, once we assume Levy's presence in an expanded canon, we can begin to examine her influence on other writers and literary genres, as well as the ways in which previous literary traditions helped develop her work and were expanded by it. In this volume, Naomi Hetherington examines *Reuben Sachs* as a significant influence on Israel Zangwill's *Children of the Ghetto*, a novel of late-nineteenth-century Jewish life that received a much warmer welcome than its predecessor and, indeed, gained iconic status in contrast to the opprobrium that greeted Levy's novel, which his in numerous ways rewrites. Nadia Valman in turn demonstrates how *Reuben Sachs* rewrites, from a feminist Jewish perspective, the conventional plots of nineteenth-century conversion novels aimed at Jewish women readers and how it was then itself rewritten in the conversionist fiction of Violet Guttenberg. Alex Goody's discussion of Levy's late poetry alongside the early-twentieth-century fiction of African American writer Nella Larsen underscores the productive insights to be gained by exploring representations of Jewish difference in relation to other expressions of ethnic marginality, at the turn of the century and in general. And as T. D. Olverson explicates signs of such marginality in Levy's "Xantippe" and "Medea," we find powerful rereadings of Levy's texts in the contexts of classical literature and myth and their interpretive history.

Yet Levy is also ripe for study in relation to established canons of British literature. Karen Weisman has looked at "Xantippe" and "A Minor Poet" as forms of the elegy in a self-reflexive age, encountering in them a rhetoric of "self-cancelling." The essays in the *Cambridge Companion* examine the same poems in their more obvious mode of dramatic monologue, but Cornelia D. J. Pearsall also finds that the Minor Poet's "self-awareness" is exactly what is "to culminate in self-annihilation" (83), and Karen Alkalay-Gut positions Levy's monologues in a fin-de-siècle poetry of disillusionment and paradox. Linda Hunt Beckman, too, has recently considered Levy's connections to aestheticism, recalling the influence of Robert Browning and Tennyson in Levy's work while also suggesting its important connections to the poetry of the French symbolists. I apologize to each of these scholars for my reductive summaries of what are in fact complex and compelling arguments. But while I cite them, in part, to flesh out a discussion of recent criticism, I also intend their approaches to suggest further questions. To what extent was Levy part of aesthetic circles? Did she have any contact with Ada Leverson—another Jewish woman connected with Oscar Wilde, in her case personally as well as professionally? Both Pearsall and Alkalay-Gut examine Levy's poetry in connection with Dante Gabriel Rossetti's "Jenny." Cynthia Scheinberg's important work on Levy's "Magdalen" some years ago began an important discussion of Levy and the fallen woman. Levy's 1888 story "At Prato" suggests ways in which this character type was particularly compelling to Levy, and it deserves further attention. The many kinds of women with whom Levy was connected, the overlapping circles with which she was associated: to what extent did they interconnect? Susan David Bernstein is at work on a study of nineteenth-century women

writers and the British Museum Reading Room that might serve as a prototype for future investigations that foreground not only Levy's life but also the
lives of other intellectual women. Once we see Levy's suicide as an endpoint
and not a starting point, once we decide not to view her life through its
shadow, the questions we might ask become historically as well as biographi-
cally compelling.

In the current volume, Lyssa Randolph's account of published responses
after Levy's suicide illustrates how popular scientific ideas about women's work
and health shaped not only the subsequent reputations of women writers but
also the fears and concerns of nineteenth-century intellectual women such as
Levy and Constance Naden. Elizabeth Evans demonstrates how *The Romance of
a Shop* illuminates Levy's concerns with single women in the city; Evans connects the photographers' studio, central to the plot, to issues of spectacle and
spectatorship in the late-Victorian metropolis. As Emma Francis examines
Levy's writings in comparison to the more political work of Clementina Black,
she reminds us, too, that late-Victorian women's intellectual circles were as significant to the life of the metropolis as was the Rhymers' Club. All these essays
invite further study of how such circles and the women in them were discussed
and written about in their time. Worth examining, as well, are the ways in which
Levy's Jewishness was observed by others. Susan David Bernstein's chapter on
the uses of vulgarity in Levy's fiction and Gail Cunningham's account of "exclusion" and "unfitness" as themes and motifs in Levy's stories explore ways in
which Levy's writing reflects and negotiates her position both inside and outside the Jewish and larger British communities during a pivotal point in Anglo-
Jewish experience. With massive immigration of foreign Jews to the East End
of London and, in the West End, an apparently frenetic rush by more established Jews toward upward mobility and various degrees of assimilation, Anglo-
Jewish society virtually re-created itself in the 1880s and '90s. Future scholarship
will continue to illuminate Levy's life and work in relation to this multivalent
communal ferment. Given Levy's own position as a religiously nonobservant
but self-identified Jew—a position that increasingly characterized Jewish intellectuals and professionals in the nineteenth and twentieth centuries—studies
of Levy's life and work will contribute, too, to the growing body of research
examining cultural or secular Judaism, a new and important area of Jewish
studies.

One final question cannot be answered, yet it is worth recording: Had Amy
Levy lived beyond her twenty-eight years, what directions might her writing
have pursued? Would *Reuben Sachs* have remained her final word on the Jewish

community of her day? Would she have developed her satire in additional directions, or would she have examined contemporary Jewish life through alternative modes of representation? Might she have found a Xantippe in Jewish history to give voice to through dramatic monologue? Would her satire have spread to the decadents themselves, much as Ada Leverson's did? Would *The Romance of a Shop* have become a mere starting point to novelistic considerations of the New Woman, and with what forms of both romance and realism would Levy have continued to experiment?

Today, we must view Levy's oeuvre as both complete and unfinished. But as this volume makes clear, we must view it somehow if we are to understand the complexity and multiplicity of late-nineteenth-century British literary culture. Even more of Levy's work needs to be made available to today's readers. Reprinting the original editions of her poetry, for example, will allow individual poems to be read in the contexts that Levy created for them. A collection of essays such as this, unimaginable thirty years ago, urges us as readers and critics to seek out other, still neglected, poets, novelists, and playwrights. Focusing on Amy Levy, the collection at hand acknowledges the essential interplay between the individual writer and the literary culture. It foregrounds the human dimension in literary production and reception and at the same time reveals the multifacetedness of one author's life and writing. Amy Levy's poetry, fiction, and essays now form part of what we perceive as Victorian and late-Victorian culture, even though they were nearly inaccessible only thirty years ago. I eagerly await the discoveries of the next generation of scholars, for whom the phrase "a minor poet" will connote, more than anything else, the title of a significant collection of poetry by the well-known writer Amy Levy.

selected bibliography

This bibliography includes works by and about Amy Levy and a selection of critical materials that provide contexts for her work and life.

Writings by Amy Levy (in order of publication)

Novels

The Romance of a Shop. London: T. Fisher Unwin, 1888.
Reuben Sachs: A Sketch. London: Macmillan and Co., 1888. 2nd ed., 1889.
Miss Meredith. London: Hodder and Stoughton, 1889 (serialized in *British Weekly,* April–June 1889).

Short Stories

"Mrs Pierrepoint: A Sketch in Two Parts." *Temple Bar* 59 (June 1880): 226–36.
"Euphemia: A Sketch." *Victoria Magazine* 36 (August–September 1880): 129–41, 199–203.
"Between Two Stools." *Temple Bar* 69 (1883): 337–50.
"The Diary of a Plain Girl." *London Society* 44 (September 1883): 295–304.
"Sokratics in the Strand." *Cambridge Review,* 6 February 1884, 163–64.
"Olga's Valentine." *London Society* 45 (February 1884): 152–57.
"In Holiday Humour." *London Society* 46 (August 1884): 177–84.
"In Retreat." *London Society* 46 (September 1884): 332–35.
"Easter-Tide at Tunbridge Wells." *London Society* 47 (May 1885): 481–83.
"Revenge." *London Society* 47 (April 1885): 389–99.
"Another Morning in Florence." *London Society* 49 (April 1886): 386–90.
"Out of the World." *London Society* 49 (January 1886): 53–56.
"At Prato." *Time* 19 (July 1888): 68–74.
"Griselda." *Temple Bar* 84 (September 1888): 65–96.
"The Recent Telepathic Occurrence at the British Museum." *Woman's World* 1 (1888): 31–32.
"Addenbrooke." *Belgravia* 68 (March 1889): 24–34.
"Cohen of Trinity." *Gentleman's Magazine* 266 (May 1889): 417–24.
"A Slip of the Pen." *Temple Bar* 86 (1889): 371–77.
"Eldorado at Islington." *Woman's World* 2 (1889): 488–89.
"Wise in Her Generation." *Woman's World* 3 (1890): 20–23.

Poetry

"The Ballad of Ida Grey: A Story of Woman's Sacrifice," part 1. *Pelican* 2 (April 1875): 20.
"The Shepherd" (from Goethe). *Cambridge Review,* 9 June 1880, 158.
"Newnham College." *Alexandra,* 4 March 1881, n.p.
Xantippe and Other Verse. Cambridge: E. Johnson and Co., 1881.
"From Grillparzer's Sappho." *Cambridge Review,* 1 February 1882, 141.
"From Heine." Translation of Heine, "Mein Herz, mein Herz ist traurig." *Cambridge Review,* 26 April 1882, 270.
"A Ballad of Last Seeing." *Cambridge Review,* 1 May 1883, 337.
A Minor Poet and Other Verse. London: T. Fisher Unwin, 1884. 2nd ed., 1891.
Translations of poems by Jehudah Halevi and Heinrich Heine, in *Jewish Portraits,* edited by Katie Magnus, 10–11, 16–17, 46. London: Routledge, 1888.
"Rondel (dedicated to Mrs. Fenwick-Miller)." *Pall Mall Gazette,* 24 February 1888, 13.
A London Plane-Tree and Other Verse. London: T. Fisher Unwin, 1889.
"A Ballad of Religion and Marriage." Privately printed and circulated by Clement Shorter, [1915], n.p.

Essays

"Junior Prize Review: 'Aurora Leigh.'" *Kind Words* (October 1875).
"James Thomson: A Minor Poet." *Cambridge Review,* 21 February 1883, 240–41; 28 February 1883, 257–58.
"The New School of American Fiction." *Temple Bar* 70 (March 1884): 383–89.
"The Ghetto at Florence." *Jewish Chronicle,* 26 March 1886, 9.
"The Jew in Fiction." *Jewish Chronicle,* 4 June 1886, 13.
"Jewish Humour." *Jewish Chronicle,* 20 August 1886, 9–10.
"Middle-Class Jewish Women of To-Day." *Jewish Chronicle,* 17 September 1886, 7.
"Jewish Children." *Jewish Chronicle,* 5 November 1886, 8.
"The Poetry of Christina Rossetti." *Woman's World* 1 (1888): 178–80.
"Women and Club Life." *Woman's World* 1 (1888): 364–67.
"Readers at the British Museum." *Atalanta: Every Girl's Magazine,* April 1889, 449–54.

Reprint and Critical Editions

Armstrong, Isobel, and Joseph Bristow, eds., with Cath Sharrock. *Nineteenth-Century Women Poets: An Oxford Anthology.* Oxford: Clarendon Press, 1996.
Bernstein, Susan David, ed. *Reuben Sachs.* Peterborough, ON: Broadview Press, 2006.
———, ed. *The Romance of a Shop.* Peterborough, ON: Broadview Press, 2006.
Donoghue, Emma, ed. *What Sappho Would Have Said: Four Centuries of Love Poems Between Women.* London: Hamish Hamilton, 1997.
Hennegan, Alison, ed. *The Lesbian Pillow Book.* London: Fourth Estate, 2000.
Leighton, Angela, and Margaret Reynolds, eds. *Victorian Women Poets: An Anthology.* Oxford: Blackwell, 1995.
New, Melvyn, ed. *The Complete Novels and Selected Writings of Amy Levy, 1861–1889.* Gainesville: University Press of Florida, 1993.

Online Sources

Amy Levy's poetry is accessible online at the Victorian Women's Writers Project (http://
www.indiana.edu/~letrs/vwwp/vwwplib.pl?#levy)

Unpublished Sources

Amy Levy's unpublished papers are in the Beth-Zion Abrahams collection of Amy Levy
material, private collection, UK.

Contemporary Writers on Amy Levy
(in order of publication)

"A Newnham Student's Poems." *Literary World*, 5 August 1881, 90–91.
"Critical Jews." *Jewish Chronicle*, 25 January 1889, 11.
Review of *Reuben Sachs. Athenaeum*, 26 January 1889, 114.
Review of *Reuben Sachs. Academy* 876 (16 February 1889): 103.
"New Novels." *Academy* 876 (16 February 1889): 109.
"The Deterioration of the Jewess." *Jewish World*, 22 February 1889, 5.
Marshallik [Israel Zangwill]. Morour and Charouseth [regular column]. *Jewish Standard*, 1
    March 1889, 9; 8 March 1889, 9; 9 October 1889, 14.
"Mainly about People." *Star*, 1 June 1889, 1.
"New Books." *Jewish Chronicle*, 2 August 1889, 12.
"Today's Tittle Tattle." *Pall Mall Gazette*, 16 September 1889, 6.
Obituary. *Lady's Pictorial*, 21 September 1889, 358.
Obituary. *New York Times*, 22 September 1889, 1.
Retrospect of the Year. *Jewish Standard*, 25 September 1889, 9.
Ernest Radford. "An Inscription for an Urn." *Pall Mall Gazette*, 24 September 1889, 2.
Clementina Black. Obituary. *Athenaeum*, 5 October 1889, 457.
Oscar Wilde. "Amy Levy." *Woman's World* 3 (November 1889): 51–52.
Grant Allen. "Plain Words on the Woman Question." *Fortnightly Review* 46 (1889): 448–58.
Ellen Darwin, "The Poems of Amy Levy." *Cambridge Review*, 23 January 1890, 158.
Grant Allen. "The Girl of the Future." *Universal Review* 25 (7 May 1890): 49–64.
Harry Quilter. "Amy Levy: A Reminiscence and a Criticism." *Universal Review* 24 (1890):
    492–507. Reprinted in Quilter, *Preferences in Art, Life and Literature*, 135–49. London:
    Swan Sonnenschein and Co, 1892.
Thomas Bailey Aldrich. "Broken Music." [1891]. Reprinted in New, *Complete Novels and
    Selected Writings of Amy Levy*, 53–54.
Israel Zangwill. *Children of the Ghetto: A Study of a Peculiar People*. London: W. Heinemann,
    1892.
Edward Kerchever Chambers. "Poetry and Pessimism." *Westminster Review* 138 (1892): 366–76.
Eugene Lee Hamilton. "Fumes of Charcoal I and II." In Hamilton, *Sonnets of the Wingless
    Hours*, 110–11. London: Elliott Stock, 1894. Reprinted in New, *Complete Novels and Se-
    lected Writings of Amy Levy*, 54–55.

Grant Allen. "For Amy Levy's Urn." In Allen, *The Lower Slopes: Reminiscences of excursions round the base of Helicon, undertaken for the most part in early manhood*, 21. London: Elkin Matthews and John Lane at Bodley Head, 1894.

Israel Zangwill. "A Ghetto Night at the Maccabaeans: Dinner to Mr. Samuel Gordon." *Jewish Chronicle*, 25 January 1901, 19.

Warwick James Price. "Three Forgotten Poetesses." *The Forum* 48 (1912): 367–68.

Further Reading

On Amy Levy

Abrahams, Beth-Zion. "Amy Levy and the 'JC.'" *Jewish Chronicle*, 17 November 1961, 13. (See also Lask, Beth-Zion).

Armstrong, Isobel. *Victorian Poetry: Poetry, Poetics and Politics*. London: Routledge, 1993.

Beckman, Linda Hunt, *Amy Levy: Her Life and Letters*. Athens: Ohio University Press, 2000.

———. "Amy Levy: Urban Poetry, Poetic Innovation, and the Fin-de-Siècle Woman Poet." In *The Fin-de-Siècle Poem: English Literary Culture and the 1890s*, edited by Joseph Bristow, 207–30. Athens: Ohio University Press, 2005.

———. "Leaving 'The Tribal Duckpond': Amy Levy, Jewish Self-Hatred and Jewish Identity." *Victorian Literature and Culture* 27, no. 1 (1999): 185–201.

Bernstein, Susan David. Introduction to *Reuben Sachs*, edited by Susan David Bernstein, 11–43. Peterborough, ON: Broadview Press, 2006,.

Bernstein, Susan David. Introduction to *The Romance of a Shop*, edited by Susan David Bernstein, 11–41. Peterborough, ON: Broadview Press, 2006.

Bristow, Joseph. "'All Out of Tune in This World's Instrument': The 'Minor' Poetry of Amy Levy." *Journal of Victorian Culture* 4 (1999): 76–103.

Cheyette, Bryan. "From Apology to Revolt: Benjamin Farjeon, Amy Levy and the Post-emancipation Anglo-Jewish novel, 1880–1900." *Transactions of the Jewish Historical Society of England* 24 (1982–86): 253–65.

———. "The Other Self: Anglo-Jewish Fiction and the Representation of Jews in England 1875–1905." In *The Making of Modern Anglo-Jewry*, edited by David Cesarani, 97–111. London: Basil Blackwell, 1990.

Cheyette, Bryan, and Nadia Valman, eds. *The Image of the Jew in Liberal European Culture 1789–1914*. London: Vallentine Mitchell, 2004.

Endelman, Todd M. *The Jews of Britain, 1656 to 2000*. Berkeley: University of California Press, 2002.

———. *Radical Assimilation in English Jewish History, 1656–1945*. Bloomington: Indiana University Press, 1990.

Feinstein, Elaine. "Amy Levy." In Feinstein, *Collected Poems and Translations*, 156. Manchester: Carcarnet, 2002.

Francis, Emma. "Amy Levy: Contradictions?—Feminism and Semitic Discourse." In *Women's Poetry, Late Romantic to Late Victorian: Gender and Genre, 1830–1900*, edited by Isobel Armstrong and Virginia Blain, 183–204. London: Macmillan, 1999.

———. "Socialist Feminism and Sexual Instinct: Amy Levy and Eleanor Marx." In *Eleanor Marx (1855–1898): Life, Work, Contacts,* edited by John Stokes, 113–27. Aldershot, UK: Ashgate, 2000.

Galchinsky, Michael. *The Origin of the Modern Jewish Woman Writer.* Detroit: Wayne State University Press, 1996.

Goody, Alex. "Murder in Mile End: Amy Levy, Jewishness and the City." *Victorian Literature and Culture* 34, no. 2 (2006): 461–79.

Hetherington, Naomi. "New Woman, 'New Boots': Amy Levy as Child Journalist." In *The Child Writer from Austen to Woolf,* edited by Christine Alexander and Juliet McMaster, 254–68. Cambridge: Cambridge University Press, 2005.

Hughes, Linda K. "A Club of Their Own: The 'Literary Ladies,' New Women Writers, and Fin-de-Siècle Authorship." *Victorian Literature and Culture* 35, no. 1 (2007): 233–60.

Hunt, Linda [later Beckman]. "Amy Levy and the 'Jewish Novel': Representing Jewish Life in the Victorian Period." *Studies in the Novel,* 26, no. 3 (1994): 235–53. (See also Beckman, Linda Hunt)

Jusová, Iveta. *The New Woman and the Empire.* Columbus: Ohio State University Press, 2005.

Laird, Holly. "The Death of the Author by Suicide: Fin-de-Siècle Poets and the Construction of Identity." In *The Fin-de-Siècle Poem: English Literary Culture and the 1890s,* edited by Joseph Bristow, 69–100. Athens: Ohio University Press, 2005.

Lask, Beth-Zion. "Amy Levy." *Transactions of the Jewish Historical Society of England* 11 (1928): 168–89.

Leighton, Angela. "'Because men made the laws': The Fallen Woman and the Woman Poet." *Victorian Poetry* 27 (1989): 109–27.

Levy, Sharona A. "Amy Levy: The Woman and Her Writings." Unpublished PhD diss., Oxford University, 1989.

McDonagh, Josephine. *Child Murder and British Culture, 1720–1900.* Cambridge: Cambridge University Press, 2003.

Nord, Deborah Epstein. "'Neither Pairs nor Odd': Female Community in Late Nineteenth-Century London." *Signs: Journal of Women in Culture and Society* 15 (1990): 733–53; reprinted in Nord, *Walking the Victorian Streets: Women, Representation and the City,* chap. 6. Ithaca, NY: Cornell University Press, 1995.

Olverson, T. D. *Women Writers and the Dark Side of Late-Victorian Hellenism.* Houndmills, UK: Palgrave Macmillan, 2010.

Parsons, Deborah L. *Streetwalking the Metropolis: Women, the City and Modernity.* Oxford: Oxford University Press 2000.

Pullen, Christine. *Amy Levy: Her Life, Her Poetry and the Era of the New Woman.* Unpublished PhD diss., Kingston University, 2000.

Rochelson, Meri-Jane. Introduction to *Children of the Ghetto: A Study of a Peculiar People* (1892), by Israel Zangwill. Detroit: Wayne State University Press, 1998.

———. "Jews, Gender, and Genre in Late-Victorian England: Amy Levy's *Reuben Sachs.*" *Women's Studies* 25 (1996): 311–28.

Scheinberg, Cynthia. "Canonizing the Jew: Amy Levy's Challenge to Victorian Poetic Identity." *Victorian Studies* 39, no. 2 (1996): 173–200.

———. "Recasting 'Sympathy and Judgment': Amy Levy, Women Poets, and the Victorian Dramatic Monologue." *Victorian Poetry* 35, no. 2 (1997): 173–91.

———. *Women's Poetry and Religion in Victorian England: Jewish Identity and Christian Culture*. Cambridge: Cambridge University Press, 2002.

Vadillo, Ana I. Parejo. "New Woman Poets and the Culture of the *Salon* at the *Fin de Siècle*." *Women: A Cultural Review* 10, no. 1 (1999): 22–34.

———. *Women Poets and Urban Aestheticism: Passengers of Modernity*. Basingstoke, UK: Palgrave Macmillan, 2005.

Valman, Nadia. "'Barbarous and Medieval': Jewish Marriage in Fin de Siècle English Fiction." In *The Image of the Jew in European Liberal Culture, 1789–1914*, edited by Bryan Cheyette and Nadia Valman, 111–29. London: Vallentine Mitchell, 2004.

———. *The Jewess in Nineteenth-Century British Literary Culture*. Cambridge: Cambridge University Press, 2007.

———. "Semitism and Criticism: Victorian Anglo-Jewish Literary History." *Victorian Literature and Culture* 27, no. 1 (1999): 235–48.

Wagenknecht, Edward. *Daughters of the Covenant: Portraits of Six Jewish Women*, 56–93. Amherst: University of Massachusetts Press, 1983.

Weisman, Karen. "Playing with Figures: Amy Levy and the Forms of Cancellation." *Criticism* 43 (2001): 59–79.

Zatlin, Linda Gertner. *The Nineteenth-Century Anglo-Jewish Novel*. Twayne's English Authors Series. Boston, MA: Twayne, 1981.

Historical and Cultural Contexts

Alaya, Flavia. "Victorian Science and the 'Genius' of Woman." *Journal of the History of Ideas* 34 (1977): 261–80.

Ardis, Ann. *New Women, New Novels: Feminism and Early Modernism*. New Brunswick, NJ: Rutgers University Press, 1990.

Battersby, Christine. *Gender and Genius: Towards a Feminists Aesthetic*. London: Women's Press, 1989.

Bar-Yosef, Eitan, and Nadia Valman, eds. *'The Jew' in Late-Victorian and Edwardian Culture: Between the East End and East Africa*. Basingstoke: Palgrave, 2009.

Blain, Virginia. "Sexual Politics of the (Victorian) Closet; or No Sex Please—We're Poets." In *Women's Poetry, Late Romantic to Late Victorian: Gender and Genre, 1830–1900*, edited by Isobel Armstrong and Virginia Blain, 135–63. London: Macmillan, 1999.

Bland, Lucy. *Banishing the Beast: English Feminism and Sexual Morality, 1885–1914*. London: Penguin, 1995.

Bluestone, Natalie. *Women and the Ideal Society: Plato's Republic and Modern Myths of Gender*. Oxford: Berg, 1987.

Breay, Claire. "Women and the Classical Tripos, 1869–1914." In *Classics in Nineteenth and Twentieth Century Cambridge: Curriculum, Culture and Community*, edited by Christopher Stray, 48–70. Cambridge: Cambridge Philological Society, 1991.

Castle, Terry. *The Apparitional Lesbian: Female Homosexuality and Modern Culture*. New York: Columbia University Press, 1995.

Cesarani, David, ed. *The Making of Modern Anglo-Jewry*. Oxford: Basil Blackwell, 1990.

Cheyette, Bryan. *Constructions of "the Jew" in English Literature and Society: Racial Representations, 1875–1945*. Cambridge: Cambridge University Press, 1993.

Clauss, James J., and Sarah Iles Johnston, eds. *Medea: Essays on Medea in Myth, Literature, Philosophy, and Art.* Princeton: Princeton University Press, 1997.

Cohen, Deborah, "Who Was Who? Race and Jews in Turn-of-the-Century Britain." *Journal of British Studies* 41 (October 2002): 235–83.

Dowling, Linda. *Hellenism and Homosexuality in Victorian Oxford.* London: Cornell University Press, 1994.

Dyhouse, Carol. *No Distinction of Sex: Women in British Universities, 1870–1939.* London: UCL Press, 1996.

Efron, John M. "Scientific Racism and the Mystique of Sephardi Racial Supremacy." *Leo Baeck Institute Year Book* 38 (1993): 75–96.

Evans, Elizabeth F. "'Counter-Jumpers' and 'Queens of the Street': The Shop Girl of Gissing and His Contemporaries." In *Gissing and the City: Cultural Crisis and the Making of Books in Late-Victorian England,* edited by John Spiers, 109–17. London: Palgrave Macmillan, 2005.

Faderman, Lillian, *Surpassing the Love of Men: Romantic Friendship and Love between Women from the Renaissance to the Present.* London: Women's Press, 1985.

Feldman, David. *Englishmen and Jews: Social Relations and Political Culture, 1840–1914.* New Haven, CT: Yale University Press, 1994.

Freedman, Jonathan. *The Temple of Culture: Assimilation and Anti-Semitism in Literary Anglo-America.* New York: Oxford University Press, 2000.

Galchinsky, Michael. "'Permanently Blacked': Julia Frankau's Jewish Race." *Victorian Literature and Culture* 27, no. 1 (1999): 171–83.

Gilman, Sander L. *Jewish Self-Hatred: Anti-Semitism and the Hidden Language of the Jews.* Baltimore: Johns Hopkins University Press, 1986.

———. *The Jew's Body.* London: Routledge, 1991.

Glage, Liselotte. *Clementina Black: A Study in Social History and Literature.* Heidelberg: Carl Winter Universitätsverlag, 1981.

Hall, Edith, and Fiona Macintosh. *Greek Tragedy and the British Theatre, 1660–1914.* Oxford: Oxford University Press, 2005.

Hall, Edith, Fiona Macintosh, and Oliver Taplin, eds. *Medea in Performance, 1500–2000.* Oxford: Oxford University Press, 2000.

Hapgood, Lynne. "'The Reconceiving of Christianity': Secularisation, Realism and the Religious Novel, 1888–1900." *Literature and Theology* 10 (1996): 329–50.

Hardwick, Lorna. "Women, Translation and Empowerment." In *Women, Scholarship and Criticism: Gender and Knowledge, 1790–1900,* edited by Joan Bellamy, Anne Laurence, and Gill Perry, 180–203. Manchester: Manchester University Press, 2000.

Heilmann, Ann. *New Woman Strategies: Sarah Grand, Olive Schreiner, Mona Caird.* Manchester: Manchester University Press, 2004.

Hickok, Kathleen. *Representations of Women: Nineteenth-Century British Women's Poetry.* Westport, CT: Greenwood Press, 1984.

Holcombe, Lee. *Victorian Ladies at Work: Middle-Class Working Women in England and Wales, 1850–1914.* Hamden, CT: Archon Books, 1973.

Hurst, Isobel. *Victorian Women Writers and the Classics.* Oxford: Oxford University Press, 2006.

Jenkyns, Richard. *The Victorians and Ancient Greece.* Oxford: Basil Blackwell, 1980.

Katz, David S. *The Jews in the History of England.* Oxford: Clarendon Press, 1994.

selected bibliography

Kershen, Anne J., and Jonathan A. Romain. *Tradition and Change: A History of Reform Judaism in Britain, 1840–1995*. London: Vallentine Mitchell, 1995.

Langton, Daniel R. *Claude Montefiore: His Life and Thought*. London: Vallentine Mitchell, 2002.

Ledger, Sally. "Gissing, the Shopgirl and the New Woman." *Women: A Cultural Review* 6 (1995): 263–74.

Levine, George. "Objectivity and Death: Victorian Scientific Autobiography." *Victorian Literature and Culture* 20, no. 1 (1992): 273–91.

Levine, Phillippa. *Feminist Lives in Victorian England: Private Roles and Public Commitment*. Bloomington: Indiana University Press, 1990.

Lipman, V. D. *Social History of the Jews in England, 1850–1950*. London: Watts, 1954.

Livesey, Ruth. *Socialism, Sex and the Culture of Aestheticism, 1880–1914*. Oxford: Oxford University Press, 2007.

McWilliams-Tullberg, Rita. *Women at Cambridge: A Men's University—Though of a Mixed Type*. London: Victor Gollancz, 1975.

Mermin, Dorothy. *Godiva's Ride: Women of Letters in England, 1830–1880*. Bloomington: Indiana University Press, 1993.

Nelson, Carolyn Christensen, ed. *A New Woman Reader: Fiction, Articles, and Drama of the 1890s*. Peterborough, ON: Broadview Press, 2001.

Rabinowitz, Nancy Sorkin, and Amy Richlin, eds. *Feminist Theory and the Classics*. London: Routledge, 1993.

Ragussis, Michael. *Figures of Conversion: "The Jewish Question" and English National Identity*. Durham, NC: Duke University Press, 1995.

Rappaport, Erika Diane. *Shopping for Pleasure: Women in the Making of London's West End*. Princeton: Princeton University Press, 2000.

Richardson, Angelique, and Chris Willis, eds. *The New Woman in Fiction and in Fact: Fin-de-Siècle Feminisms*. Basingstoke, UK: Palgrave: 2001.

Russett, Cynthia Eagle. *Sexual Science: The Victorian Construction of Womanhood*. Cambridge, MA: Harvard University Press, 1991.

Sanders, Lise Shapiro. *Consuming Fantasies: Labor, Leisure, and the London Shopgirl, 1880–1920*. Columbus: Ohio State University Press, 2006.

Sebestyen, Amanda. "Passing Figures: Black and Jewish Border Crossers." *Jewish Quarterly* (Summer 1997): 31–35.

Sharot, Stephen. "Reform and Liberal Judaism in London, 1840–1910." *Jewish Social Studies* 41 (1979): 211–28.

Showalter, Elaine. *A Literature of Their Own: British Women Novelists from Brontë to Lessing*. Princeton: Princeton University Press, 1977.

———. *Sexual Anarchy: Gender and Culture at the Fin de Siècle*. London: Bloomsbury, 1991.

Stokes John, ed. *Eleanor Marx (1855–1898): Life, Work, Contacts*. Aldershot, UK: Ashgate, 2000.

———. *In the Nineties*. Hemel Hempstead, UK: Harvester Wheatsheaf, 1989.

Tusan, Michelle Elizabeth. "Inventing the New Woman: Print Culture and Identity Politics During the Fin-de-Siècle." *Victorian Periodicals Review* 31, no. 2 (Summer 1998): 169–82.

Vicinus, Martha. *Independent Women: Work and Community for Single Women, 1850–1920*. Chicago: University of Chicago Press, 1985.

———. *A Widening Sphere: Changing Roles of Victorian Women.* Bloomington: Indiana University Press, 1977.

Walker, Lynne. "Vistas of Pleasure: Women Consumers of Urban Space, 1850–1900." In *Women in the Victorian Art World*, edited by Clarissa Campbell Orr, 70–85. Manchester: Manchester University Press, 1995.

Walkowitz, Judith R. *City of Dreadful Delight: Narratives of Sexual Danger in Late-Victorian London.* London: Virago, 1992.

———. "Going Public: Shopping, Street Harassment, and Streetwalking in Late Victorian London." *Representations* 62 (Spring 1998): 1–30.

index